Critical Essays on Anne Sexton

Critical Essays on
Anne Sexton

Linda Wagner-Martin

G. K. Hall & Co. ● Boston, Massachusetts

For Andrea

Library of Congress Cataloging in Publication Data

Critical essays on Anne Sexton / [compiled by] Linda Wagner-Martin.
     p.   cm. — (Critical essays on American literature)
    Includes index.
    ISBN 0-8161-8891-2 (alk. paper)
    1. Sexton, Anne—Criticism and interpretation.   I. Wagner-Martin,
    Linda.   II. Series.
    PS3537.E915Z64   1989
811'.54—dc19   89-30569
                                                               CIP

This publication is printed on permanent/durable acid-free paper
MANUFACTURED IN THE UNITED STATES OF AMERICA

CRITICAL ESSAYS ON AMERICAN LITERATURE

This series seeks to anthologize the most important criticism on a wide variety of topics and writers in American literature. Our readers will find in various volumes not only a generous selection of reprinted essays and reviews but also original essays, bibliographies, manuscript sections, and other materials brought to public attention for the first time. This volume consists of reviews and essays tracing the critical reputation of Anne Sexton. It presents a balanced historical record of critical reaction to one of the foremost poets in American literature. It contains both a sizable gathering of early reviews and a broad selection of modern scholarship, including essays on Sexton's poems and her life. Among the reviewers are Joyce Carol Oates, Diane Wood Middlebrook, Neil Myers, and Katha Pollitt. Among the authors of reprinted articles are Maxine Kumin, Diana Hume George, Linda Wagner-Martin, Paul A. Lacey, and Greg Johnson. Also included are three original essays by Carol Leventen, Gwen L. Nagel, and Cheryl Vossekuil commissioned specifically for publication here. We are confident that this book will make a permanent and significant contribution to American literary study.

JAMES NAGEL, GENERAL EDITOR

Northeastern University

CONTENTS

CHRONOLOGY OF SEXTON'S BOOKS

POETRY

1960   *To Bedlam & Part Way Back*

1962   *All My Pretty Ones*

1964   *Selected Poems* (English edition)

1967   *Live or Die*

1968   *Poems* (with Thomas Kinsella and Douglas Livingstone, English edition)

1969   *Love Poems*

1972   *Transformations*

1974   *The Book of Folly*

1975   *The Death Notebooks*

1976   *45 Mercy Street*, edited by Linda Gray Sexton

1977   *The Awful Rowing toward God*

1978   *Words for Dr. Y: Uncollected Poems with Three Stories*, edited by Linda Gray Sexton

1981   *The Complete Poems*

1988   *Selected Poems*, edited by Diana Hume George and Diane Middlebrook

CHILDREN'S BOOKS, WITH MAXINE KUMIN

1963   *Eggs of Things*

1964   *More Eggs of Things*

1971   *Joey and the Birthday Present*

1975   *The Wizard's Tears*

OTHER

1977   *Anne Sexton: A Self-Portrait in Letters*, edited by Linda Gray Sexton and Lois Ames

INTRODUCTION

Anne Sexton, Poet

> Poetry is special, is something else. As a poet . . . I want your real idea, unclothed from your feeling for the writer. . . . Poetry has saved my life and I respect it beyond both or any of us.[1]

In her 1958 letter to W. D. Snodgrass, Sexton expresses the theme that was to continue throughout the sixteen years that remained of her life: she had become a poet, and that identity was going to be the most important one in her existence. As Denise Levertov has so accurately pointed out, Sexton's poetry saved her as long as saving was possible.[2] It gave her productive years as a poet, and also as a woman—mother, wife, lover, friend. Through her art, Sexton was brought back into the mainstream of human response and human interaction. Without it, she was voiceless—worse, without a language, her knowledge and understandings frustrated in not having a means of expression. The wonder of Sexton's poetry is that it provided for her a magical language for communication, after an earlier lifetime of de facto isolation.[3]

One of the fascinations about poetry is that, in many ways, it is literally incomprehensible. Its spark-striking magic reaches beyond logic and reason, intellectual skills we like to pretend can be taught, into a fuller, more integral kind of reason, a reason that synthesizes and connects rather than separates into categories. The poet sees life—or some parts of it—whole. Better, the poet "sees" with multifaceted vision, and if his or her reach into language is commensurate, can find image and metaphor to express vision so comprehensive it can be frightening. As readers, caught in the surprising— sometimes astonishing—grip of a poet's accurate vision and language, we can only marvel at its existence. Literature is filled with praise to muses, white goddesses, other manifestations of inspiration: even the poet is not sure how certain visions come to the poem or, the more difficult part of the art, how those visions were caught and translated into language.

Anne Sexton, as poet, is very much in the mainstream of aeons of traditional poets and poetry. She wrote to give language to her visions, and much of the power of her art accrues from her honesty about those visions. Her first important long sequence poem, "The Double Image," voices her personal confusion over what her scrutiny of herself within her family—

daughter to both a mother and a father—meant. It is a paradigmatic expression of centuries of inherent conflict, divided loyalty, the ambivalence of pride and disdain, love and hate. As an expression of such ambivalence, "The Double Image" becomes every reader's poem. Almost immediately upon her becoming a poet, Sexton was tapping into archetypal conflicts—human concerns—that were meaningful to most human lives.

Sexton's ability to strike to the center of a complex problem in image stemmed in part from her lack of formal training in literature. Unlike the academically successful John Berryman, Adrienne Rich, Robert Lowell, Sylvia Plath, and John Holmes, Sexton did not compare her poems with "great" literature. She did not begin writing in 1957, at the suggestion of her therapist, under the shadow of essential texts and key literary figures, nor was she burdened with long years of adamant instruction in what were good subjects for poems (and what were not), or in the kinds of techniques poets used (or didn't attempt). Sexton knew she had a great deal to learn. What she probably didn't see as the advantage it was, was that she had comparatively little to unlearn.[4] She was free to use whatever subject, skill, form, technique she liked, and though she bounced ideas off countless other writers—endlessly, and demanded their best attention for her work—she made her own choices and, usually, went her own way.

A good example of Sexton's strange mixture of self-confidence and artistic dependence is her situation with the Boston poet John Holmes, one of her earliest teachers and mentors. As Diane Middlebrook retells the story, Sexton enrolled in a poetry workshop Holmes taught at the Boston Center for Adult Education. Regularly a faculty member at Tufts University, Holmes enjoyed teaching his nontraditional students in the workshop, and Sexton was keenly excited to find eighteen other people interested in what was fast becoming her art. During that first year of poetry workshops, Sexton worked "demonically," and as Maxine Kumin remembers, "She would willingly push a poem through twenty or more drafts. She had an unparalleled tenacity in those early days." As a result of Sexton's intense productivity, she soon had poems enough for a book, and approached Holmes about the possibility of publishing a collection. While he liked much of her poetry, he was hesitant to have her publish what he called her "clinical" poems, and replied in a letter, "Something about asserting the hospital and psychiatric experience seems to me very selfish. . . . It bothers me that you use poetry this way." His letter closed with the thought that her later life, and later poems, would grow away from her earlier psychic history, and that once she became "another person," her poems would "haunt and hurt" her.[5] In the face of this rejection of both her work and her self (for Holmes's implication was that what Sexton had been, and been through, was all a skin to be shed in the future, rather than some integral part of what she was becoming), Sexton wrote the fine poem "For John, Who Begs Me Not to Enquire Further." This defense of self and art, phrased cogently and in some ways impersonally, was the image of her understanding of herself as writer. The poem opens,

Not that it was beautiful,
but that, in the end, there was
a certain sense of order there;
something worth learning
in that narrow diary of my mind. . . .

Sexton was drawn to see the importance of her own vision, her own "sense of order," and so she became a poet. And in the same powerful poem, she explains her amazing capacity to translate visions into language. "I tapped my own head; / it was glass, an inverted bowl. / It is a small thing / to rage in your own bowl." So the poem as an internal process of knowing true emotion, experiencing it, coming to it through both feeling and language, changes:

At first it was private.
Then it was more than myself;
it was you, or your house
or your kitchen.

The joy as the poet sees herself becoming more than self through her expression is balanced with the risk to the poet of having that expression rejected:

And if you turn away
because there is no lesson here
I will hold my awkward bowl,
with all its cracked stars shining
like a complicated lie,
and fasten a new skin around it
as if I were dressing an orange
or a strange sun.

Even the poet's rejected expression has value. The poet will try again, assuming chameleonlike existences in the guise of new skins, and even if others cannot respond—regardless of how many new skins, new facades, new languages, as Holmes seemed to feel he could not respond to some of Sexton's poems—the poet continues:

Not that it was beautiful,
but that I found some order there.
There ought to be something special
for someone
in this kind of hope. . . .[6]

Anne Sexton wrote her way to a Pulitzer Prize (for *Live or Die* in 1966), to membership in the Royal Society of Literature in London, and to Crawshaw Professor of Literature at Colgate University—among other academic posts.[7] But she also, ironically, wrote her way into a kind of poetic notoriety, based on her outspoken comments, her dramatic readings, her alcoholism, her personal dependency; and into—and quickly out of—the critical establishment. A major irony of Sexton's career as poet is the speed with which she disappeared from the attention of both reviewers and academics. In the early 1960s, Sexton was talked about, reviewed, taught, published and reviewed widely in England, and called a "major" poet after only two collections had appeared. By the late 1960s, she was hardly reviewed any longer, and seldom taught. There were a number of reasons for the critical distaste for her work during the later 1960s and 1970s: she often wrote about nontraditional literary subjects (not only outré subjects like menstruation but equally threatening—that is, sentimental—topics like a mother's love for her daughters). She was often overly personal, which meant readers had to deal with the facts (or created facts) of both her femaleness and her mental instability, and there were few literary precedents for either. And she used such direct expression that there could be no pretending that she was saying anything other than she was. What alternate interpretations can there be for lines like "A woman *is* her mother," "Fat, white-bellied men, / wearing their genitals like old rags," "Since you ask, most days I cannot remember," or the powerful sequence included late in "In Celebration of My Uterus":

> Many women are singing together of this:
> one is in a shoe factory cursing the machine,
> one is at the aquarium tending a seal,
> one is dull at the wheel of her Ford, . . .
> one is dying but remembering a breakfast,
> one is stretching on her mat in Thailand,
> one is wiping the ass of her child. . . .

Initial reaction to Sexton's first book, the 1960 *To Bedlam and Part Way Back,* was enthusiastic, with most critics being struck by the vitality of voice and emotion. Neil Myers praises "how subtly rhetoric fits thought," admiring Sexton's themes and defending her work from any charge of sentimentality. Geoffrey Hartman contrasts Sexton with Denise Levertov and Jean Garrigue, who believe that the poem sets the poet on a voyage of discovery, and use it for exploration. Sexton's strength is that she *knows* the experiences she chooses to write about, and the experience as she presents it is "simple, moving, and universal." Hartman sees her themes as reflecting deep spiritual wounds, and makes comparisons with both Yeats and Lowell. Rather than finding her poems too personal, he considers them universal and truly moral. Hal Smith, who carefully delineates how much *can* be wrong with women's poetry, makes the point of defining Sexton as not a woman poet, but a poet: "from the first line of her book . . . we know that we are in the hands of a poet firmly in control, fully aware of the twin possibilities of shock and delight."[8]

Even James Dickey's review, which is often quoted to show negative response, is generally favorable. He acknowledges the power of Sexton's "harrowing" topics, though he thinks her treatment less successful than it might have been, largely because of her "poetic" language. His suggestion that her narratives might become important short stories echoes one of

Hartman's comments. As fresh as her subject matter on the poetry scene in 1960 was Sexton's sense of narrative.[9]

Reviews of the 1962 *All My Pretty Ones* continued to mention similarities between Sexton's poetry and that of Robert Lowell and W. D. Snodgrass. May Swenson was impressed by Sexton's seemingly effortless diction, her ability to shape the forms of poems to match their import, and her use of humor and fantasy. Thom Gunn finds the book better than *Bedlam* (which he disliked for its self-dramatizing) because Sexton's poetry is more controlled. Gunn's concluding sentence, that Sexton is "at her best when she presents [experience] indirectly or from a distance," is representative of the opinion that her poems were too much like voice, that the experience was not transformed through the art but rather *became* the art in too real a presentation. In contrast to Gunn, Louise Bogan praised both Sexton's books because they showed the poet writing "from the center of feminine experience, with the direct and open feeling that women, always vulnerable, have been shy of expressing in recent years."[10] It is a rare direction—but for today's readers, a most crucial one—in the criticism, and one could wish that Bogan had written more, and more often, about Sexton's work. *All My Pretty Ones* was nominated for a National Book Award.

Sexton's first books were so well-received in England that in 1964 a volume called *Selected Poems* was published there as a Poetry Book Selection, and as it was reviewed, the critical gulf between the British poetry camps was revealed. Christopher Ricks, writing in the *New Statesman*, called the collection "a remarkable volume," marked by wit and cunning, the poems written with a skill that will outlast the current fascination with the confessional. C. B. Cox, writing in the *Spectator*, praised Sexton's remarkably flexible tone, so that her language can encompass swift changes in mood and content. He admires her "wry self-consciousness" and her tendency to deal with religious themes and images.

For Ian Hamilton, however, Sexton is overrated as a poet. He finds her work promising, but fears that she will become another cult figure of "neurotic breakdown, valued not for what she has written but for what her suffering seems to symptomatize." Hamilton prefers her first book, because by the second, he says, mannerisms have lost their freshness and seem habitual. He criticizes the "slick offhandedness" in Sexton's treatments of life's horrors—"prosy cleverness," "hardboiled whimsicality," "inert evocativeness" are other negating phrases.[11]

The important essay of A. R. Jones published in *Critical Quarterly* helped British readers to place Sexton's work in the tradition of dramatic monologue and pointed out the key distinction that writing that seemed autobiographical might well be fictional.[12] Jones's essay did a great deal to counter the almost frenetic tendency to describe much writing of the time as "confessional," and then to discount it as being too revelatory, too personal (and therefore undisciplined and formless, a definite aesthetic criticism at mid-century). Sexton's obvious connections to Robert Lowell, Snodgrass,

Plath, Jarrell, Roethke, and others were soon to destroy the building current of admiration, but in 1964 and 1965 she still felt as if critics were according her serious readings.

Sexton's reputation in the United States peaked with the 1966 publication of *Live or Die*, the collection that used as an epigraph a quotation from Saul Bellow, in which he admonished Sexton to decide, to choose life or death, but to decide, and not poison everything in the process. Being awarded the Pulitzer Prize for Poetry for this collection meant that Sexton could dismiss detractors, if she had enough confidence to do so. Even in the most positive reviews, however, comparisons with Robert Lowell and Sylvia Plath (increasingly since the latter's suicide in 1963) were attempting to force Sexton into the confessional camp. Joel Conarroe's review in *Shenandoah* begins with that comparison, but concludes that Sexton's poetry of the interior voyage—handled as it is here with honesty and toughness—creates "a fierce, terrible, beautiful book, well deserving its Pulitzer award."[13]

Generally favorable criticism may have been influenced in part by Ralph Mills's serious attention to Sexton in his *Contemporary American Poetry*.[14] Richard Fein credited Sexton with broad thematic range and pointed out her humor as a saving quality; praise was the tone of reviews by Philip Legler, Thomas McDonnell, James Tulip writing in *Poetry Australia*, and even the difficult-to-please Hayden Carruth. Most of the critics of *Live or Die* seem reconciled to the fact that Sexton was a woman poet, and McDonnell speaks directly to the issue: "Anne Sexton is one of the few women writing poetry in the United States today of whom it is possible to say that her womanness is totally at one with her poems. . . . if a woman alone, in the physiological sense, could have written a poem like "Menstruation at Forty," then also a woman alone, in the fullest possible sense, could have written so exquisite a poem as "Little Girl, My String Bean, My Lovely Woman.""[15] McDonnell also speaks to the deeply religious tone in many of Sexton's poems.

If *Live or Die* was a kind of apex for Sexton's reputation, then the 1969 *Love Poems* was the beginning of the descent. Most critics were harsh about the poet-persona's supposed affair—if it were true, they didn't like it; if it were not true (and why, after all, was a "confessional poet" writing un-truths?), they objected on aesthetic grounds. Mona Van Duyn found the book full of macabre humor, as the back cover reported that Sexton was living with her husband and two daughters, after the reader had just been led through the poems about a devastating love affair. Van Duyn states, "*Love Poems* is not sentimental, not trivial, it is simply not believable. The poems have little to do with believable love, having none of love's privacy and therefore too frequently repelling the reader."[16] She compared Sexton's writing to that of Norman Mailer, in self-indulgence and self-absorption. Finally, after the highly critical review, Van Duyn concluded that Sexton writes consistently good poems, though the reader need select among them.

The tactic used by Joyce Carol Oates is to compare the later and what she sees as less scrupulously controlled poems with the strong early ones; whereas Daniel Hughes finds *Love Poems* stronger than the earlier books because it "depends less on shock tactics" and allows Sexton's lyric gift to show. For William Dickey, writing in the *Hudson Review*, it was another of Sexton's self-indulgent collections.

One can almost chart the impact on Sexton's work of negative reviews, and her search for a new kind of poem may have been prompted by the criticism of *Love Poems*. Sexton's poetry was the topic of keen attention from Richard Howard (*Alone with America*), who concentrated chiefly on her skillful craft, from M. L. Rosenthal in *The New Poets*, from Robert Boyers in *Salmagundi*, and from Beverly Fields writing for *Poets in Progress*, edited by Edward Hungerford.[17] But the gist of much of this attention was either to place Sexton in the by now firmly established confessional group, or to continue to question her right to be in any serious poetry classification—and its net effect was demoralization. As she wrote to Tillie Olsen in 1966, "My work, at present, is [in] a dreadful slump . . . when one's poems are damned for being tragic and confessional constantly from both sides of the Atlantic—reviews are bad for us—we should be blinded before we read such public praise or damnation."[18]

She attended to writing her play, *Mercy Street*, and to living in New York while it was produced and ran, with Marian Seldes in the leading role. She attempted prose, and wrote poems that were unlike anything she had tried before. The macabre versions of the Brothers Grimm fairy tales that were to comprise Sexton's 1972 book, *Transformations*, were as much a surprise to her as to her readers—but she liked them, and when Houghton Mifflin tried to discourage her from publishing them, she saw clearly that her choice was to go elsewhere, not to repress the poems. As she wrote to Paul Brooks in 1970, acknowledging that the poems were different for her,

> I look at my work in stages, and each new book is a kind of growth and reaching outward and as always backward. Perhaps the critics will be unhappy with this book and some of my readers maybe will not like it either. I feel I will gain new readers and critics who have always disliked my work and too true, the critics are not always kind to me may come around. . . . I would like my readers to see this side of me, and it is not in every case the lighter side. Some of the poems are grim. In fact I don't know how to typify them except to agree that I have made them very contemporary. It would further be a lie to say that they weren't about me, because they are just as much about me as my other poetry.[19]

Sexton's own assessment is prophetic, because most reviewers said nearly the same kinds of things about the long parodies of the tales. For Louis Martz, *Transformations* was a return to the fresh inventiveness of Sexton's early books, free of what he saw as the bathos of *Love Poems*. For William Pitt Root, the collection was a kind of wry extension of Sexton's usual voice, but the poems themselves were more explicit social criticism than readers expected from her. For Paul Zweig, however, Sexton's adaptations only spoil the stories, and her use of what he calls "mod" language distorts the value of the original tales. He calls *Transformations* a step toward "the death of story telling." Unlike the response of most critics, who even in her earlier work found strong narrative patterns and techniques, Zweig's criticism was typical of reviewers who were determined not to like whatever Anne Sexton published. In contrast to this kind of hypercritical reaction, other poets such as Muriel Rukeyser praised most of what Sexton attempted, saying accurately about *Love Poems, Transformations,* and *The Book of Folly,* "The issue in most of Anne Sexton's poems has been survival, piece by piece of the body, step by step of poetic experience, and even more the life entire, sprung from our matrix of parental madness."[20]

As Rukeyser saw it, Sexton's concerns were age-old archetypal, particularly female, themes. In *Transformations,* the poet had been able to deal with a great many of the larger humanist and feminist issues, those that provided scaffolding for her own more specific narrative poems. The ethos of "Cinderella," for example, lies at the heart of Sexton's countless laments about women trapped in the conventional, traditional female roles. As a result of, in effect, having challenged many social assumptions she had been reared to accept, Sexton's other late poems changed. As Arthur Oberg pointed out in his review of her 1972 *The Book of Folly,* she "shares Galway Kinnell's wish to move beyond the way, or ways, of the world, to a visionary humor that can reject the world's foolish fools for the unworldly wise fools to whose rank the poet has always made some claim. Although Anne Sexton has been intensely aware of herself as woman and a woman poet, there is a new militancy here that I have never detected in her previous work."[21]

What Oberg sees as passing beyond the petty to more essential concerns, Helen Vendler sees as a shift in voice, the first consistent expression of Sexton's lurking acerbic tone, definitely not little-girl "nice." As Vendler points out, "What is occurring in such writing is not so much the shattering of taboos as the expression of an extremity of nonparticipatory vision. . . . [A] satirist feels under no obligation to extend sympathy. Sexton feels a slashing glee in her perfect vignettes . . . , these fiendish cartoons." Whatever the description, Sexton's *Transformations* were clearly a surprise to critics who had already consigned her work to an unenviable predictability. As Charles Gullans had said in an earlier review, the materials of Sexton's poetry are so familiar to the reader that, even before reading, the reader's reaction is "painful, embarrassing, and irritating." Gullans goes on to deny that Sexton writes poems at all. She instead produces what he calls "documents of modern psychiatry," which should never have been published at all. Christopher Lehmann-Haupt builds on this attitude as he reviews *Transformations* positively, stressing that the negative responses to Sexton's art resulted from seeing her poetry as "personal yelps rather than universal cries." Lehmann-Haupt thinks readers will be able to read *Transformations* more intelligibly because "by using the artificial as the raw material of *Transformations* and working her way backwards to the immediacy of her personal vision, she draws her readers in more willingly, and thereby makes them more vulnerable to her sudden plunges into personal nightmare."[22]

Much criticism of Sexton's work was in a stock-taking period. Robert Phillips treats her "confessional" poetry as at least partly fictional (in *The Confessional Poets*), while Paul A. Lacey claims that Sexton's chief motivation is the making of ritual, and that her best poems are "built around rites of communion, prayer, and gift-giving (*The Inner War*). Karl Malkoff's sensible reading of Sexton is also helpful (in the *Crowell Handbook of Contemporary American Poetry*), as is criticism by J. D. McClatchy, who is later to edit the first collection of criticism on Sexton's work.[23]

The puzzlement that greeted *The Book of Folly* in 1972 seemed only to intensify with the publication of *The Death Notebooks* early in 1974. That collection was followed in October of 1974 by Sexton's suicide from carbon monoxide poisoning. A few months later, her collection *The Awful Rowing toward God*—which she had herself prepared for publication—appeared. Response to both collections was strongly influenced by the poet's death, and marked a turn in the tenor of all subsequent criticism. As Carol Duane pointed out in her survey of Sexton criticism, "If the recurrent critical problem of the 1960s was the persistent tendency to evaluate Sexton's poems as signs of process toward mental stability, toward an affirmative objectivity, then the corollary—to link her most recent work to her death—tended to dominate the criticism of the mid-1970s. Moreover, critics who had taken special delight in Sexton's careful crafting of her early poems were faced with a special challenge in these later volumes, which were frequently seen as evidencing poetic as well as psychic disintegration."[24] Although Steven Gould Axelrod said of these poems that Sexton was writing as well as she ever had, he too was bothered by her "jottings" and "notes," and Ben Howard, in *Poetry*, questions why the eloquence of Sexton's early work has disintegrated into such a "limited idiom."[25]

Muriel Rukeyser terms the late poems a second kind of poetry, growing out of the early confessions, enriched by their presence, but vastly different. Erica Jong also, writing a memoir of Sexton soon after her death, sees continuity within the work especially in terms of archetypal myth—not only feminine myth, but myths that expand the human consciousness. Such an approach has been fruitful for many recent critics, among them Diana Hume George whose 1986 book, *Oedipus Anne*, is the first book-length analysis of Sexton's work to appear. Such concerns have also motivated the criticism of Alicia Ostriker, Estella Lauter, Suzanne Juhasz, and Sarah Schuyler.[26]

It was at the point of her death, with the publication of two collections in 1974 and others to follow, quickly, posthumously (*45 Mercy Street*, 1976; *Anne Sexton: A Self-Portrait in Letters*, 1977; *Words for Dr. Y: Uncollected Poems with Three Stories*, 1978) that Sexton's work began receiving summary—rather, hasty—consideration. Because the poet grouped her poetry into categories, designing groups for one collection or another, Sexton's book publication was not necessarily the chronology of her poems individually. Knowing what poem had preceded another, what operating principles were at work, was therefore difficult. Only Maxine Kumin, who worked intimately with Sexton for the fifteen years that their households were connected by private telephone lines, had an accurate sense of the time of composition for Sexton's work. Even with this difficulty in dating, critics could see the immense differences between poems in the posthumously published books and most of the earlier work.

Troubled by what they saw as flaccidity, imprecision in craft, and the pervasive religious subject matter, most critics chose to emphasize disintegration of technique rather than trying to delineate important new directions. One exception to that tendency was William J. McGill's "Anne Sexton and God," an essay in which Sexton's intense desire for God is compared with the intensity in religious literature of all ages. For Sandra M. Gilbert, *The Death Notebooks* crystallized the meditative, haunting concern the poet expressed early for death and its transcendence. "If irony and shrewdness have always characterized Anne Sexton's work, the largeness of her metaphysical ambition is what is newly notable about *The Death Notebooks*," contends Gilbert as she compares Sexton's poems with those of the eighteenth-century poet, Christopher Smart, absorbing a poetic tradition that gives her accrued meaning. For Robert Mazzocco, however, Sexton's themes seem arch, and her treatment inappropriate. He points to the poems titled "psalms", which he calls deliberately horrific (for what purpose)?, and questions Sexton's concept of her own readership. Where is the line between art and trickery? Kate Green points out that there is no excess of feeling, not excess in "the personal nature of the poems but in the images themselves, which seem, at times, to spill out of control."[27]

One of the most disparaging reviews of this group of books comes from Patricia Meyer Spacks, who finds *45 Mercy Street* a collection of poems "hardened into mannerism." Other comments in this review are that Sexton's poems are sentimental, "grotesquely uncontrolled," the work of a "victim of an era in which it has become easy to dramatize self-indulgence, stylish to invent unexpected imagery regardless of its relevance, fashionable to be a woman and as a woman to display one's misery."[28] Because Spacks is an influential critic, and a feminist, her view carried a great deal of significance, but it echoed the long line of critical opinion that was uneasy about Sexton's blend of the personal and the aesthetic. This trend in criticism of Sexton's late work continued, with Robert Pinsky calling *Words for Dr. Y* "mechanical" and its apparent "nakedness . . . another form of evasion." Pinsky described Sexton's poetic method as consistent throughout her work: "locating the emotion and lobbing the artillery of images at it persistently." He faulted her work too because it evinced no range or "intellectual scope."[29]

This is not a new kind of judgment, certainly. What did begin to occur in the usually troubled reviews of Sexton's late work was a different kind of assessment. Just as Sandra Gilbert came to see Sexton's mocking humor as appropriate in even her death poems and the obviously serious psalm-sequence ("poetry that anyone would flirt with almost any disasters to write"), so Rosemary Johnson points up the unpredictability of what she calls the "oil-and-water mix of the absolutely commonplace and the singular, of the quite literal curdled by the incredible" in Sexton's later work. Johnson also saw, accurately, that these poems contain a fuller realization of Sexton as female, as though after writing *Transformations* and seeing her themes in light of archetypal and sociological patterns, Sexton saw how being female was a crucial condition to her life as artist. In Johnson's words,

> Although Anne Sexton toys, for effect one feels, with notions of lack of gender, androgyny, hermaphroditicism, and the like, the obvious needs to be said: . . . the poet's perceptions and her sensibility are female, stem from her womanhood. . . . The description she dashes off to Erica Jong of herself as "The woman of the poems, the woman of the kitchen, the woman of the private (but published) hungers" fits. Indeed a lot of conflicting directions pull her apart. . . .[30]

From Nancy Yanes Hoffman as well came the recognition that Sexton had finally found both her audience and her voice, as she writes "of women growing older but not wiser" and of "choices made and choices lost." Hoffman then reads *The Awful Rowing toward God* as a metaphor for the woman who decides to go it alone, to cast off her dependency—"husband, lovers, psychiatrists, children, all of whom let her down. . . . She is depending upon the self, and that too, at the last, lets her down. . . . What Sexton was searching for was not only transformation of her self, but transcendence, both obsessions which arose out of the conviction of her own worthlessness. Her desire was to be joined to another in love. Each time that love was disappointed, she was left with her own insufficient resources—left, finally, rowing toward God, that ultimate transcendence of self which seemed to be the only love of which she could be certain because it was love imagined. But love imagined sustains only so long as the imagination works and reality does not impinge too agonizingly."[31] Even Sexton's psychological state seemed to grow from the various difficulties women experienced as they matured.

Margaret Atwood, too, reviewing the Sexton letters, writes emphatically, "Anne Sexton was one of the most important American poets of her generation." For her, too, much of the mystery of the discrepancy between Sexton's letters—which are full of animation, enthusiasm, and life—and her poems, speaking consistently of death, lies in Sexton's position in the world as woman. In that, that difficulty to come to full voice, Atwood compares Sexton with Plath, both gifted writers caught in a labyrinth of frustrations and barricades to expression.[32]

Among the most insightful comments available on Sexton's writing and her personal reliance on her poetry are those of Maxine Kumin in her fore-word ("How It Was, Maxine Kumin on Anne Sexton") to Sexton's 1981 *The Complete Poems*. In that essay Kumin pointed out how diametrically opposed the divided critical camps had been: "The intimate details divulged in Sexton's poetry enchanted or repelled with equal passion." Helpfully tracing key events in Sexton's life, including her two postpartum depressions that began her life of mental torment, Kumin points out that Sexton consistently relied on male authority figures. She even came to poetry—and stayed with it—because of the advice of, first, her male psychiatrist and, second, a Catholic priest. Kumin says, "I am convinced that poetry kept Anne alive for the eighteen years of her creative endeavors. When everything else soured; when a succession of therapists deserted her for whatever good, poor, or personal reasons; when intimates lost interest or could not fulfill all the roles they were asked to play; when a series of catastrophes and physical illnesses assaulted her, the making of poems remained her own constant. To use her own metaphor, 'out of used furniture she made a tree.' "

Kumin also spoke authoritatively in this preface about Sexton's later work, and since most critics were so bewildered about it, her remarks are useful. Kumin saw Sexton's turn to Jesus as an extension of her fascination with the fable as form, an interest she had initially found writing *Transformations*. When she applied that form to the Jesus figure, who still suffered knowingly in order to endure, the result was "The Jesus Papers." Kumin identifies Sexton's themes as being "Jesus, Mary, angels as good as the good fairy, and a personal, fatherly God to love and forgive her. . . . Always Sexton explored relentlessly the eternal themes that obsess her: love, loss, madness, the nature of the father–daughter compact, and death—the Death Baby we carry with us from the moment of birth."

Kumin describes Sexton's sense of freedom after *Transformations* was so well-received, her increased daring in her poetry and her consistent use of the parody name, Ms. Dog (*God* in reverse, with a feminist nod in *Ms.* to the women's movement). God was increasingly the subject of her poems, and she wrote even a quantity of imperfect poems as a way to try to reach what might be said about transcendent experiences. Kumin reminds readers of the humor, the joy, the affirmation Sexton brought to her work—for it was her work—and to trying to live so that her art would continue to provide meaning. As she concludes, "Women poets in particular owe a debt to Anne Sexton, who broke new ground, shattered taboos, and endured a barrage of attacks along the way because of the flamboyance of her subject matter, which, twenty years later, seems far less daring. . . . Today, the remonstrances seem almost quaint."[33]

Perhaps because of this excellent introduction, *The Complete Poems* of Anne Sexton was usually relatively well-reviewed—if it was reviewed at all. Unfortunately, its publication came during the same year that Sylvia Plath's long-awaited *Collected Poems* was issued, and the longer wait, the greater anticipation, brought the Plath volume into much greater prominence. When in the spring of 1982 Plath's collection won the Pulitzer Prize for Poetry, that award seemed the final quietus to the efforts by the Sexton estate to garner for Sexton what could just as rightfully have been hers. Among the most interesting reviews of the Sexton volume were James M. Rawley's assessment in the *National Review*. Calling *The Complete Poems* "an indispensable book" and Sexton "one of her generation's best poets," Rawley wonders why there had been such uproar about her work (was it objectionable, perhaps, for its sense of humor?). Part of his favorable review is a somewhat caustic assessment of her unhappy reception from critics: "The critics . . . blamed her for the facile melodrama of her lines, but said she had promise. Later, amid similar caviling, they would say she had failed to live up to her gifts. Meanwhile, prizes and praise rained on her, though prudery kept many from liking poems with titles like 'In Celebration of My Uterus'. . . ."[34]

As if to illustrate Rawley's points, Alan Williamson's review of Sexton (paired with Plath's *Collected Poems*) finds little to redeem. After censuring Sexton for her untragic tone in what could have been tragic poems, Williamson asserts, "But it is much easier, at this point, to bury Sexton than to praise her." While he still admires her first two books, he sees only bad writing after that time ("What can explain so rapid a poetic decline in an initially serious and scrupulous writer?"). Williamson seems quick to jump to his answer—in part, "Mental instability and alcoholism"—though he does equate Sexton with a Dylan Thomas kind of syndrome. He saves his most vituperative comments for Maxine Kumin's introduction, where—he says—she "lashes out in all directions." Perhaps his tolerance was at low ebb, though he clearly found Plath's poems admirable and convincing—and the similarities between Plath and Sexton are common knowledge. But this review shows the critical world at its most typical—finding reasons for disliking poetry because of its "quality," though giving no proof of qualitative criteria.[35]

Katha Pollitt's *Nation* review, though also praising Sexton's first three books and lamenting the quality of some of her later poems, places Sexton, her poems, and the reviewer's own response into credible context. For Pollitt, Sexton's importance as a *woman* poet is indisputable—subject matter, manner of expression, voice all had to contend with a male-dominated art world. Her *range* is also indisputable, and her willingness to make the attempt, rather than to play it safe. The same acknowledgment of Sexton's power, even if there are some mistakes, occurs in Diane Wood Middlebrook's somewhat later review (in *Parnassus*, 1985). For Middlebrook, however, the unevenness of Sexton's poems was an understandable result of her poetic method—that of "milking the unconscious." This tactic often produced a

> loosely-structured poetry dense with simile, freaked with improbable associations. In a poem addressed to James Wright, Sexton herself acknowledged she knew the effect offended certain tastes: "There is too much good and no one left over / to eat up all the weird abundance" ("The Black Art"). Weird: uncanny, magical, unconventional. While some of Sexton's most admired poems work, like little machines, on well-oiled armatures of rhythm or rhyme (such as "All My Pretty Ones," "The Starry Night," "Wanting to Die"), others equally powerful depend on manic or despairing

or ecstatic cascades of association ("The Furies," "O Ye Tongues") that flow like an open spigot. The gems, or closed forms, tend to be early; the looser style, later. In this collection, the reader can watch Sexton evolve her second style as a way of exploring a changing relation to her subject matter.

Middlebrook is, of course, the authorized Sexton biographer, so she brings a great deal of information and understanding to her reading of *The Complete Poems*. As she points out, "The witch-persona of Sexton's poetry is the voice Sexton invented to tell the story of her changing relationship to a severe, incurable, but apparently undiagnosable malady. . . . Sexton's *Complete Poems* yields most when read as if it contained a narrative: an account of a woman cursed with a desire to die. Why is she different from other women? Where did the curse come from? A story line with a beginning, middle, and end takes shape . . . as Sexton systematically exhausts a set of culturally acceptable explanations for the condition of her kind. These are, first, a psychiatric explanation; later, a sociological explanation; and finally a spiritual explanation."[36]

Luckily, published criticism on the oeuvre of Sexton's writing has begun to catch up with the large reading public that exists—more criticism has been published in the last three or four years, and is projected for the next several years, than appeared in the past ten. It seems important to recognize that the kind of stock-taking that needed to occur was directed at not only Sexton's place in the literary establishment, but at the place generally of poetry by women, and of so-called confessional poetry. For that reason, I have chosen to end this book with an important 1987 essay by British critic Laurence Lerner, assessing what confessional poetry—American confessional poetry as centered in the highly controversial poems of Anne Sexton—really is, and what its influence has been on the world of contemporary poetry. Sexton was, thoroughly and admittedly, an integral part of her culture. Complete with her mental instability and her worries about where she fit into the social structure, Sexton expressed much of the mid-century attitudes about women writers, women as professionals, women as independent beings. Critical reactions to her expressions were as typical as her writings were themselves.

This collection attempts, in some ways, to reflect Middlebrook's classifications of Sexton's work; essays included here deal with craft and text, particularly the essays written particularly for this book, which focus on single poems or groups of poems. They deal with psychiatric motivations, explanations, and the relationships between poet and poem, poet and culture, poet and self. Several also deal with sociology: Sexton as woman writer, as expressive writer, and as defensive writer; and they deal in more recent times with Sexton as spiritual writer. This may be the most difficult approach of all, because twentieth-century art of all kinds has been so thoroughly and antagonistically divorced from formal religion for much of its eighty-nine years.

One wonders, assessing the criticism of Sexton's work, if some more moderating tone, some more balanced perspective, might have saved the poet from the bitterness she evidently experienced as her career continued, and the savage criticism grew more and more frequent. One wishes Sexton could have seen the range of expert and wise readings collected here, because it seems clear—judging from her late poems—that part of her image of herself as failure was based on the critical reception her books received. Much of *The Awful Rowing toward God* reflects the poet's sensitivity to the response, just as much of her admitted fear of readings stems from her knowledge that many people who came to her readings were detractors rather than admirers. She wrote in "The Play";

> I am the only actor.
> It is difficult for one woman
> to act out a whole play.
> The play is my life,
> my solo act. . . . The curtain falls.
> The audience rushes out. . . .

And, even more poignantly, in "The Dead Heart," the poem in which the poet observes the small inert fact, she wrote:

> What it has cost me you can't imagine,
> shrinks, priests, lovers, children, husbands,
> friends and all the lot. . . .

Its demise occurred, however, as the last stanza recounts:

> How did it die?
> I called it EVIL.
> I said to it, your poems stink like vomit.
> I didn't stay to hear the last sentence.
> It died on the word EVIL.
> I did it with my tongue.
> The tongue, the Chinese say,
> is like a sharp knife:
> it kills
> without drawing blood.[37]

Once Sexton had put her whole identity into becoming a poet, surely the printed and verbal response to her art was of great importance to her, given her personal dependencies and the acculturation she had learned as an American woman at mid-century.

LINDA WAGNER-MARTIN

University of North Carolina, Chapel Hill

Notes

1. *Anne Sexton: A Self-Portrait in Letters*, ed. Linda Gray Sexton and Lois Ames (Boston: Houghton Mifflin, 1977), 42; dated "circa November 15, 1958."

2. Denise Levertov, "Anne Sexton: Light Up the Cave," *Ramparts* 13 (January 1975): 61–63.

3. Sexton's letters are filled with references to having no language, or to finding people with whom she has language (see Sexton and Ames, *Letters*, 244–46).

4. See Linda Wagner-Martin, *Sylvia Plath, A Biography* (New York: Simon & Schuster, 1987), for information about Plath's long process of self-discovery, and for some indication of Sexton's importance to Plath's late poems; see also Diane Wood Middlebrook, " 'I Tapped My Own Head': The Apprenticeship of Anne Sexton" in *Coming to Light*, ed. Diane Wood Middlebrook and Marilyn Yalom (Ann Arbor: University of Michigan Press, 1985), 199.

5. Middlebrook, "I Tapped My Own Head," 195–213.

6. Anne Sexton, *The Complete Poems* (Boston: Houghton Mifflin, 1981), 34–35. Poems cited are also from this edition and will not be referenced.

7. Sexton's awards and various kinds of recognition are one mark of the distinctiveness of her writing, because I know of no other contemporary poet who received this quantity of attention. She began writing poetry when she was twenty-eight and published during the first year in *Audience*, *Beloit Poetry Journal*, the *Hudson Review*, *Harper's*, and soon after that, in the *New Yorker*, *Accent*, *Epoch*, the *Yale Review*, *Antioch Review*, *Voices*, and other little magazines. As soon as she had put a collection together, Houghton Mifflin accepted it, and that company remained her publisher throughout her career. During the 1960s, she held the Robert Frost fellowship at Bread Loaf and was for two years a fellow at the Radcliffe (now Bunting) Institute. She won the *Audience* poetry prize, *Poetry's* Levinson Prize, the traveling fellowship from the American Academy of Arts and Letters, the Congress for Cultural Freedom travel grant, a Ford Foundation grant for a year's residency with a professional theater, the Shelley Memorial Award, and in 1967 the Pulitzer Prize for Poetry. In 1969 she received a Guggenheim fellowship and honorary doctorates from Tufts University, Regis College, and Fairfield University. She held a teaching post at Boston University, and became a member of Phi Beta Kappa.

8. Neil Myers, "The Hungry Sheep Look Up," *Minnesota Review* 1 (October 1960): 99–104; Geoffrey Hartman, "Les Belles Dames Sans Merci," *Kenyon Review* 22 (Autumn 1960): 696–700; and Hal Smith, "Notes, Reviews and Speculations," *Epoch* 10 (Fall 1960): 253–55.

9. James Dickey, "Five First Books," *Poetry* 97 (February 1961): 316–20.

10. May Swenson, "Poetry of Three Women," *Nation*, 23 February 1963, 164–66; Thom Gunn, "Poems and Books of Poems," *Yale Review* 53 (October 1963): 140–41; Louise Bogan, "Verse," *New Yorker*, 27 April 1963, 175.

11. Christopher Ricks, "Beyond Gentility," *New Statesman* 68 (27 November 1964): 842; C. B. Cox, "New Beasts for Old," the *Spectator* 219 (28 July 1967): 106; see also John Fairfax in *Poetry Review* 55 (Winter 1964): 249–51; Ian Hamilton, "Poetry," *London Magazine* 4 (March 1965): 87–88.

12. A. R. Jones, "Necessity and Freedom," *Critical Quarterly* 7 (Spring 1965): 14–17, 24–30.

13. Joel O. Conarroe, "Review of *Live or Die*," *Shenandoah* 18 (Summer 1967): 84–85.

14. Ralph J. Mills, Jr., *Contemporary American Poetry* (New York: Random House, 1965), 218–34.

15. Richard J. Fein, "The Demon of Anne Sexton," *English Record* 18 (October 1967): 16–21; Philip Legler, "O Yellow Eye," *Poetry* 110 (May 1967): 125–27; Thomas P. McDonnell, "Light in a Dark Journey," *America*, 13 May 1967, 729–31; James Tulip, "Three Women Poets,"

Poetry Australia 21 (December 1967): 37–39; Hayden Carruth, "In Spite of Artifice," *Hudson Review* 19 (Winter 1966–67): 698.

16. Mona Van Duyn, "Seven Women" *Poetry* 115 (March 1970): 430–32; Joyce Carol Oates, "The Rise and Fall of a Poet: *The Complete Poems* of Anne Sexton," *New York Times Book Review*, 18 October 1981, 3, 37; Daniel Hughes, "American Poetry 1969: From B to Z," *Massachusetts Review* 11 (Autumn 1970): 668–71; William Dickey, "A Place in the Country," *Hudson Review* 22 (Summer 1969): 347–52.

17. Richard Howard, "Anne Sexton: 'Some Tribal Female Who Is Known but Forbidden,' " *Alone with America: Essays on the Art of Poetry in the United States Since 1950* (New York: Atheneum, 1969), 442–50; M. L. Rosenthal, "Other Confessional Poets," *The New Poets: American and British Poetry Since World War II* (New York: Oxford University Press, 1967), 131–38; Robert Boyers, "*Live or Die:* The Achievement of Anne Sexton," *Salmagundi*, no. 2 (Spring 1967): 61–71; Beverly Fields, "The Poetry of Anne Sexton," *Poets in Progress*, ed. Edward Hungerford (Evanston, Ill.: Northwestern University Press, 1967), 251–85.

18. Sexton's *Letters*, 278.

19. Ibid., 362.

20. Louis L. Martz, "Review of *Transformations*," the *Yale Review* 61 (1972): 414–16; William Pitt Root, "*Transformations*," *Poetry* 123 (October 1973): 48–51; Paul Zweig, "Making and Unmaking," *Partisan Review* 40 (1973): 277–79; Muriel Rukeyser, "Glitter and Wounds, Several Wildernesses," *Parnassus* 2 (Fall/Winter 1973): 215–21.

21. Arthur Oberg, "The One Flea Which Is Laughing," *Shenandoah* 25 (Fall 1973)): 87–89.

22. Helen Vendler, "Malevolent Flippancy," *New Republic* 185 (11 November 1981): 33–36; Charles Gullans, "Poetry and Subject Matter: From Hart Crane to Turner Cassity," the *Southern Review* 7 (Spring 1970): 497–98; Christopher Lehmann-Haupt, "Grimms' Fairy Tales Retold," *New York Times*, 27 September 1971, 31.

23. Robert Phillips, "Anne Sexton: The Blooming Mouth and the Bleeding Rose," *The Confessional Poets* (Carbondale: Southern Illinois University Press, 1973), 73–91; Paul A. Lacey, "The Sacrament of Confession," in *The Inner War* (Philadelphia: Fortress Press, 1972), 8–31; Karl Malkoff, "Confessional Poetry" and "Anne Sexton," *Crowell Handbook of Contemporary American Poetry* (New York: Thomas Y. Crowell, 1973); and J. D. McClatchy, "Anne Sexton: Somehow to Endure," *Centennial Review* 19 (Spring 1975): 1–36, and expanded in *Anne Sexton: The Artist and Her Critics* (Bloomington: Indiana University Press, 1978).

24. Carol Duane on Sexton in "Three Contemporary Women Poets: Marianne Moore, Anne Sexton, and Sylvia Plath"; Cindy Hoffman, Carol Duane, Katharen Soule, and Linda Wagner, in *American Women Writers*, ed. M. Thomas Inge, Jackson R. Bryer, Maurice Duke (Westport, Conn.: Greenwood Press, 1982), 392.

25. Steven Gould Axelrod, "Anne Sexton's Rowing Toward God," *Modern Poetry Studies* 6 (Autumn 1975): 187–89; Ben Howard, "Shattered Glass," *Poetry* 127 (February 1976): 286–92.

26. Muriel Rukeyser, "Glitter and Wounds, Several Wildernesses," *Parnassus* 2 (Fall-Winter 1973): 215–21; Erica Jong, "Remembering Anne Sexton," *New York Times Book Review*, 27 October 1974, 63; Diana Hume George, *Oedipus Anne, The Poetry of Anne Sexton* (Urbana: University of Illinois Press, 1986); Alicia Ostriker, "That Story: The Changes of Anne Sexton" in *Writing Like a Woman* (Ann Arbor: University of Michigan Press, 1983), 59–86; Estella Lauter, *Women as Mythmakers, Poetry and Visual Art by Twentieth-Century Women* (Bloomington: Indiana University Press, 1984); Suzanne Juhasz, " 'The Excitable Gift': The Poetry of Anne Sexton" in *Naked and Fiery Forms: Modern American Poetry by Women, a New Tradition* (New York: Harper & Row, 1976), and "Seeking the Exit or the Home: Poetry and Salvation in the Career of Anne Sexton," in *Shakespeare's Sisters: Feminist Essays on Women Poets*, ed. Sandra M. Gilbert and Susan Gubar (Bloomington: Indiana University Press, 1979), 261–68; Sarah Schuyler, "Their Ambivalent Adventures with a Mother: Freud, Milton, Sexton," *Literature and Psychology* 32 (1986): 11–17.

27. William J. McGill, "Anne Sexton and God," *Commonweal,* 13 May 1977, 304–6; Sandra M. Gilbert, "Jubilate Anne," *Nation,* 14 September 1974, 214–16; Robert Mazzocco, "Matters of Life and Death," *New York Review of Books,* 3 April 1975, 22–23; Kate Green, "Inventory of Loss," *Moons and Lion Tailes* 2 (1976): 87–90.

28. Patricia Meyer Spacks, "*45 Mercy Street,*" *New York Times Book Review,* 30 May 1976, 6.

29. Robert Pinsky, "A Characteristic Figure," *New York Times Book Review,* 26 November 1976, 7.

30. Rosemary Johnson, "The Woman of Private (But Published) Hungers," *Parnassus* 8 (Fall / Winter 1979): 92–107.

31. Nancy Yanes Hoffman, "A Special Language," *Southwest Review* 64 (Summer 1979): 209–14.

32. Margaret Atwood, "Anne Sexton: A Self-Portrait in Letters," *New York Times Book Review,* 6 November 1977, 15.

33. Maxine Kumin, "Foreword" to Anne Sexton, *The Complete Poems* (Boston: Houghton Mifflin, 1981), xix–xxxv.

34. James M. Rawley, "Part Way Back," the *National Review* 33 (11 December 1981): 1491.

35. Alan Williamson, "Confession and Tragedy," *Poetry* 142 (June 1983): 170–78.

36. Katha Pollitt, "That Awful Rowing," the *Nation* 233 (21 November 1981): 533–37; Diane Wood Middlebrook, "Poet of Weird Abundance," *Parnassus* 12–13 (1985): 293–315.

37. "The Play" and "The Dead Heart," in Sexton, the *Complete Poems,* 440–1, 439–40.

Reviews

The Hungry Sheep Look Up
Neil Myers*

Anne Sexton, like Robert Lowell, clearly derives from the romantic tradition of the despairing poet. Unlike Starbuck and like Lowell, she writes to explore experience rather than to make poems of it. One thinks of Sexton and Lowell not in terms of verbal facility, ironic texture, and other technical sports, but in terms of sheer affective power, and of their inward pain.

It is startling to read a contemporary poem as one reads *La Belle Dame* or *Sir Patrick Spens*, mainly to see what happens. Explication of such poetry just isn't as interesting as the original poem, whatever one is going to do with it afterwards—fill a review (as I will), kill a 9:30 class, cop that promotion, etc. Explicating Lowell and Sexton is like explicating Thoreau or D. H. Lawrence; it helps, but the explicator seems to end only fooling himself:

> For all the way I've come
> I'll have to go again. Instead, I must convert
> to love as reasonable
> as Latin, as solid as earthenware:
> an equilibrium
> I never knew. And Lent will keep its hurt
> for some one else. Christ knows enough
> staunch guys who hitched on him in trouble
> thinking his sticks were badges to wear.

The problem here is not how subtly rhetoric fits thought—it obviously does—so much as whether the result is true. In terms of the entire book, it is.

Sexton's power comes first from her sense of situation. Although she echoes Stevens and Auden, she also breaks from the symbolist-prophetic pattern of most contemporary poetry. She tells stories. Her book is full of undistinguished, unmythological people, in tensely dramatic situations which can be exploited only by an equally intense inward sympathy: a lonely empty-headed old woman, a speechless unwed mother, the author's own agonizing journey "part way back" from insanity and her complex relation to her dying

*Reprinted with permission of the author from *Minnesota Review* 1 (October 1960): 99–104.

mother and her unfamiliar child. Sexton's best work has qualities of the modern short story: the brutal tale like a forced confession, "better unsaid, grim or flat or predatory"; the compressed dramatic pattern of *hybris*, catastrophe, and recognition; the primitive irony of actual experience rather than the witty irony of meditation on it; the intense inward awareness of the teller; the concentration on a narrow circle of concrete persons and events; the forced brevity of narrative and lack of transition; the refusal to easily generalize. When truth bursts from the tight surface of such poems with the violence of sudden discovery, it seems the result of actual struggle.

"A Story for Rose on the Midnight Flight to Boston" is an extraordinary example of this power. The poker-faced frame describes the still unresolved flight, unknown characters, and a "story" about them:

> Riding my warm cabin home, I remember Betsy's
> laughter; she laughed as you did, Rose, at the first
> story.

Catastrophe always hangs behind the prosaic surface of such poetry; it emerges without the slightest change of tone, and without transition. We move from reminiscence of a "humdrum / school for proper girls" to terrified comedy:

> The next April the plane
> bucked me like a horse, my elevators turned
> and fear blew down my throat, that last profane
> gauge of a stomach coming up.

When the basic "story" appears it "explains" the tension of the "warm cabin" just as psychoanalytic confession "explains" a normally inexplicable symptom. We are looking at drama, violent and astonishing, not at ironic symbolic illustration:

> Half a mile down the lights of the in-between cities
> turn up their eyes at me. And I remember Betsy's
> story; the April nights of the civilian air crash
> and her sudden name misspelled in the evening paper,
> the interior of shock and the paper gone in the trash
> ten years now. She used the return ticket I gave her.
> This was the rude kill of her; two planes cracking
> in mid-air over Washington, like blind birds.
> and the picking up afterwards, the morticians tracking
> bodies in the Potomac and piecing them like boards
> to make a leg or a face. There is only her miniature
> photograph left, too long ago now for fear to remember.
> Special tonight because I made her into a story
> that I grew to know and savor.

Despite the jolly airline ads, *this* is the world of flight, this absurd union of dull calm and implicit disaster. In the poem's honest, colorless language "things," not generalizations, appall. One usually associates such plain reportorial power with journalism, not with poetry. But in such poetry, we do not "read" so much as experience.

Where Lowell is Corinthian, Sexton is Senecan. Her diction is clinical, elemental, and humble. She talks about "innocence," "symptoms," "guilt," "suicide," her child who must "love her self's self where it lies"; the writer herself, "who was never quite sure about being a girl, needed another / life, another image to remind." Her observations are intensely simple: "I needed you"; "But I lie"; "You kissed your grandmother / and she cried." The perfect soberness, the repose behind such speech makes both pretense unnecessary and grace inevitable, in the form of a return to health and a power in the telling of it. Her work suggests that the real sicknesses of life are at once irresistibly hard and simple, and that the refusal to face them creates the kind of sloppy obscurity that muddles most contemporary poetry. She gives the impression of facing everything. Her situation, "the antiseptic tunnel / where the moving dead still talk / of pushing their bones against the thrust / of cure," forces her to; self-pity and verbal irony seem irrelevant to it. She has passed through the standard romantic experience of despair, of spiritual and psychological death, beyond the condition of the neurotic who is too busy being ironic to be simple, to survive as a responsible creator, and as a major poet. She is perfectly outright in word and deed, and there seems little distinction between the two. When she left Bedlam, she carried a book:

> I checked out for the last time
> on the first of May;
> graduate of the mental cases,
> with my analyst's okay,
> my complete book of rhymes,
> my typewriter and my suitcases.

Even more than Lowell, Anne Sexton is on *that* side, rather than *this*, of sentimentality. Sentimentality means rottenness of subject matter; whoever is dominated by fear of it lives in a world of rotten subjects. Such fear has informed our literature since 1920, and is a major cause of its present conservatism. Obviously gifted contemporaries—W. D. Snodgrass and Donald Hall are good examples—seem trained to turn from wit only back to their original saccharine narcissicism. But the real choice is not to be either sentimental or ironic; it is to deny the proposition itself. Escape lies only in commitment, in, as Martin Buber would say, saying "Thou" to experience. Lowell and Sexton are too concerned with their subjects to worry about censoring their feelings, about laboring over trivial masking turns of phrase, about how silly or shameful or "out" their gyrations may appear. They conquer sentimentality by accepting feeling at the core, without any restraints except those demanded by sanity. If the alternative is madness, thinking—and writing—honestly becomes essential therapy. The real writer does not intend to prophesy, to be humanistic, socialistic, pastoral-tragical, light, heavy, dark, or medium. Fame may be the spur—it always is—but he writes for his health alone. Lowell and Sexton are uniquely powerful not because they are uniquely gifted—their major gifts are vicious cases of our universal neurosis and a tradition of Yankee honesty—but because they write as Jeremiah had to prophesy, "like a fire shut up within my bones," literally to avoid madness.

Thus many of these poems smack of the asylum. The excessively wooden surface and the tension below; the gnarled, surrealistic jumble of symbols; the hints of a strange history of human relationships; the sense of confession; the wild, driving power and desolation, can be found in most therapeutic poetry. What distinguishes Sexton's work from most of the genre is that she has survived. The sense of willed, unrelenting struggle dominates almost every poem here. Behind it is the quality which impels and is the end of the struggle, a rich awareness of precisely what Lawrence calls "tenderness," of love made real by consciousness of its necessity, in this book by consciousness of death. Death saturates the book; not only psychological death, like "glass, an inverted bowl" over the author's head, but time, the decay of Yankee families and houses, of abandoned old women, a brother, of Elizabeth:

> You lay in the crate of your last death,
> But were not you, not finally you.
> They have stuffed her cheeks, I said;
> This clay hand, this mask of Elizabeth
> Are not true. From within the satin
> And the suede of this inhuman bed,
> Something cried, *let me go let me go*.
>
> They gave me your ash and bony shells,
> Rattling like gourds in the cardboard urn,
> Rattling like stones that their oven had blest.
> I waited you in the cathedral of spells
> And I waited you in the country of the living,
> Still with the urn crooned to my breast,
> When something cried, *let me go let me go*.

Against such an intractable vision is a sense of love so hard and intense that it is almost tactile, always described in consciousness of inward strife, of limitations and ugliness, always earned by struggle. Love is needed here; it is not an indulgence—the love of a brother who

> gave in like a small wave, a sudden
> hole in his belly and the years all gone
> where the Pacific noon chipped its light out,

of an old woman—

> visiting the pulp of her kiss, bending to repeat
> each favor, trying to comb out her mossy wig
> and forcing love to the last—

or, in one of the most astonishing poems of this or any other contemporary book, the love of a speechless mother for a child she cannot keep and wants desperately:

> Yours is the only face I recognize.
> Bone at my bone, you drink my answers in.
> Six times a day I prize
> your need, the animals of your lips, your skin
> growing warm and plump. I see your eyes
> lifting their tents. They are blue stones, they begin
> to outgrow their moss. You blink in surprise
> as I wonder what you can see, my funny kin,
> as you trouble my silence. I am a shelter of lies.
> Should I learn to speak again, or hopeless in
> such sanity will I touch some face I recognize?

One thinks of Sexton in terms of the specifics of her love as well as of her pain. The culmination of the book comes at the end, not only when she refuses to take Lowell's course of conversion, but when she describes her delight in her daughter. The contrast of this passage with the darkness which, throughout the book, has prevented it, gives it startling power:

> I remember we named you Joyce
> so we could call you Joy.
> You came like an awkward guest
> that first time, all wrapped and moist
> and strange at my heavy breast.
> I needed you. I didn't want a boy,
> only a girl, a small milky mouse
> of a girl, already loved, already loud in the house
> of herself. We named you Joy.
> I, who was never quite sure
> about being a girl, needed another
> life, another image to remind me.
> And this was my worse guilt; you could not cure
> nor soothe it. I made you to find me.

In the series of poems in part 2, love and death move together like a ballet, against the author's slow recovery of consciousness and responsibility. There is nothing in our literature like these last poems.

When Sexton's techniques are missing, as in *Venus and the Ark*, she produces direct, dull social satire. When they don't fully work, as in *The Kite*, *Where I Live* and *The Expatriates*, the result is cryptic and uninteresting. When they do work, as they do in most of these poems, they create major literature. They vindicate Trilling's judgment that if the artist is sometimes neurotic, art itself is always health. This is one of the few books of mature poetry—of poetry which we can accept with total seriousness, directly relevant to the primitive problems of our basic lives—since the death of Lawrence. It is directly in the tradition of Thoreau; it flowers in the implicit knowledge that our moral problems are individual before they are social, that Hiroshima was just an extension of Bedlam. It assumes, in perfectly concrete terms, that we must painfully forge an inward peace, loving our "self's self where it lies," before we attempt any outward reform. Until individuals commit themselves to the discipline of such a journey "part way back," to inward honesty and responsibility of feeling, society will remain silly and murderous, and literature pompous, trivial, and dull.

A Regime of Revelation   Robert Bagg*

Anne Sexton's book is intelligent, charming, beleaguered, full of the superbly obsessive use of one's life which makes of honesty a fashion, and spoken in rich urgent speech, distraught rather than devastated, more exhilarated than exalted, which is just now enlivening American verse. It is a good book and it raises a lot of questions. It carries the following chip of praise by Robert Lowell on the top of its jacket: ". . . Her poems stick in my mind. I don't see how they can fail to make the great stir they deserve to make." We'll do our best, but enthusiasm is bound to be less spontaneous and more grudging for the third or fourth person to walk overland to the South Pole, tremendous as the achievement is. If I say that Anne Sexton's book might not have been written, or written as well, without Lowell's *Life Studies* and W. D. Snodgrass' *Heart's Needle*, it's less to call her an imitator than to point out that her predecessors have liberated her for a most powerful and exacting style. Unlike the high style of the last decade, used with great distinction by Merrill, Hecht, and Wilbur, it asks a gift wretched beyond emotional resources, verbal élan, superlative intelligence. It demands of the poet neuroses and personal misfortune. And a regime of lyric revelation, written between spells of insanity or despondency, racked by jittery rage at one's scrawny personality and tremendous ancestors, an ease in hospitals, and a knack for getting more emotion to reflect from mistletoe or restyled hair than one had thought they could stand without wilting. Nobody really knows why Lowell, Snodgrass and now Anne Sexton are so good, why they are not put down by sentimentality. The critics are confused, left behind, in inarticulate admiration. We may have to revise our glib notions of sentimentality and self pity. But if we are to believe this poetry is the most effective literature of the moment, must we admit insanity and bitterness is the most honest response to our overnourished, DEW protected age? I'm not carried away by this dilemma, because Anne Sexton's poems come out so firmly right and sane.

Her long poem, "The Double Image," sounds uncomfortably (but necessarily) similar to "Heart's Needle." Although not so good a poem, it manages to put its images to a narrative use, and to fulfill its themes in a way the

*Reprinted with permission from *Audience* 7 (Summer 1960): 121–25.

Snodgrass poem doesn't, and doesn't need to. Mrs. Sexton writes her poem to a daughter she was once separated from, not because of divorce, but because she's too unstable to care for her. Getting her daughter's love back mirrors her return to sanity. The poem is simple, beautiful, well thought out. Two portraits, one of herself she feels her family had done to rub in her guilt, another of her dying mother's reproachful face, become the reliquaries their discarded selves have been exorcized to; her daughter becomes the living image of her health.

I will quote a few stanzas to give an idea of the poem's momentum, and how lively and plainspoken it is. In the first stanzas she seems to be saying insanity is no less natural than the death of leaves, if that's natural.

> I am thirty this November.
> You are still and small, in your fourth year.
> We stand watching the yellow leaves go queer,
> flapping in the winter rain,
> falling flat and washed. And I remember
> mostly the three autumns you did not live here.
> They said I'd never get you back again.
> I tell you what you'll never really know:
> all the medical hypothesis
> that explained my brain will never be as true as these
> struck leaves letting go.
>
> . . . I pretended I was dead
> until the white men pumped the poison out . . .
>
> Part way back from Bedlam
> I came to my mother's house in Gloucester,
> Massachusetts. And this is how I came
> to catch at her; and this is how I lost her.
> I cannot forgive your suicide, my mother said.
> And she never could. She had my portrait
> done instead.
>
> On the first of September she looked at me
> and said I gave her cancer.
> They carved her sweet hills out
> And still I couldn't answer.
>
> I checked out for the last time
> on the first of May . . .
> . . . All that summer I learned life
> back into my own
> seven rooms, visited the swan boats,
> the market, answered the phone,
> served cocktails as a wife
> should, made love among my petticoats

and August tan. . . .
. . . And I had to learn
why I would rather
die than love, how your innocence
would hurt and how I gather
guilt like a young intern
his symptoms, his certain evidence.

. . . I rot on the wall, my own
Dorian Gray.

. . . You scrape your knee. You learn my name,
wobbling up the sidewalk, calling and crying.
You call me *mother* and I remember my mother again,
somewhere in greater Boston, dying.

I remember we named you Joyce
so we could call you Joy.
You came like an awkward guest
that first time, all wrapped and moist
and strange at my heavy breast.
I needed you. I didn't want a boy,
only a girl, already loved, already loud
in the house of herself. We named you Joy.
I, who was never quite sure
about being a girl, needed another
life, another image to remind me.
And this was my worst guilt; you could not cure
nor soothe it. I made you to find me.

There are a dozen other fine poems, none perfect; but no perfection imagined by a critic would do them any good. Her "Lullaby" about a sleeping pill,

My sleeping.pill is white.
It is a splendid pearl;
it floats me out of myself,
my stung skin as alien
as a loose bolt of cloth . . .

as well as her monologue of an unwed mother,

Six times a day I prize
your need, the animals of your lips, your skin
growing warm and plump. I see your eyes
lifting their tents. They are blue stones, they begin
to outgrow their moss. You blink in surprise
and I wonder what you can see, my funny kin . . .

have a fine feminine fancy. The poems of hers which don't come off seem
those with the smallest personal stake in them: poems on Daphne, gulls, a

spaceflight to Venus. She has a nice sense of how experience, which seems so loosely worn at the time, gets us down. Her love poems are of this mood, and so is a masterful piece about a girl's faroff youth in Europe, and her aging, prim and deaf in Boston. From "Some Foreign Letters":

> . . . The Count sweated
> with his coat off as you waded through top snow.
> He held your hand and kissed you. You rattled
> down on the train to catch a steamboat for home;
> or other postmarks: Paris, Verona, Rome.

The imaginative ideas behind Mrs. Sexton's poetry impress me, because they are suggestive without being symbolic. The dangers of symbolism, how it kills personality, were got out in the open the other day by W. D. Snodgrass, who said that trying to feel out the symbols in your poem was like plugging into a trolley grid—the streetcar took you some same old way whether you desired or not. Picking queer, obsessively commonplace, even superficial details, Snodgrass thinks gives a poet a better chance of arriving at fresh and rewarding statements. Anne Sexton seems bent on refreshing these inexplicable needs (see her poem "The Lost Ingredient"); so mistreated are these needs they've grown insensitive to symbols that once satisfied them.

> Today is made of yesterday, each time I steal
> toward rites I do not know, waiting for the lost
> ingredient, as if salt or money or even lust
> would keep us calm and prove us whole at last.

Frost somewhere says a poem's meaning and form should arrive as an American eagle does when you rub a pencil lightly over paper, under which lies a half dollar. Some bridle at this description of art, thinking it too easy, too much like fun. A poem should be shaped, they say, by conclusive melody, a coherent archetypal scheme, by a meaning worn well, or shrugged off. But poets like Anne Sexton who have handsome, high eagles in them; too often feel such cash burning holes in the pocket: it's to her credit she has a light touch and enough economy to afford the wasteful virtues.

Notes, Reviews and Speculations   Hal Smith*

If Anne Sexton's new book arouses less excitement than *To Bedlam and Part Way Back*, and I suspect that for most readers it will, I think I know why: *To Bedlam* was for me an almost shockingly direct experience; the poems sometimes seemed to get up off the page and confront us face to face in the world we continue to call real. Many of the poems in *All My Pretty*

*Reprinted with permission from *Epoch* 12 (Fall 1962): 124–26.

Ones are written no less close to the nerve, bone and muscle of solid, pulsing and frequently disgusting flesh, but we have been initiated; we know, or think we know, what demons are likely to spring at us around the corner and we are prepared for the blow. Our initiated ability to ward off the expected attacker might seem at first to weaken the effect of *All My Pretty Ones;* oddly enough, it points to the real strength of it. Poetry, after all, is not a sledge-hammer; whatever sort of weapon it is, it is a weapon which reminds us constantly that we are alive, a weapon not necessarily "life enhancing," "ennobling," or "beautiful," but one which insists, by all possible resources of subtlety, strength and skill, that we cease to live as clods, that we open up our hearts and brains, even our livers if we must, to respond with everything we have to everything that is. The way a poem works on us may involve much that is painful and distressing, and many of the poems in this book are painful and distressing; living through a hangover headache is painful and distressing, but at least it reminds us that we have heads.

All this by way of prelude. Readers of *To Bedlam* will undoubtedly come to this book, look around for a while, and say "I've been here before." It may take a little time to realize that, though the landscape looks the same, the place is different. In *All My Pretty Ones* almost every poem shows a deepening of inquiry and a technique which has grown subtler and more confidently able to track down more intricate responses. These poems would be recognized even without the author's name on the cover, but things have changed. I feel uncomfortable about the generalization I want to make to describe this change; it's probably only about 75 percent true, but the reader can check it for himself. Anne Sexton's poems are all intensely personal, vividly and deeply felt; but I have the notion that in her first book she was going as far down as she could into the cave of herself to find out exactly what was there, that in this book she is coming back from the exploration, trying to bring with her as much as she can of what she has found. Thus, so many of the poems are addressed, they are "for" or "to" someone, they are filled with the love and pain and tenderness of one who knows that other people exist, that one can even, if one is a poet, talk to them; for example (from "The Fortress"):

> Your feet thump-thump against my back
> And you whisper to yourself. Child,
> what are you wishing? What pact
> are you making?
> What mouse runs between your eyes? What ark
> can I fill for you when the world goes wild?
> The woods are underwater, their weeds are shaking
> in the tide; birches like zebra fish
> flash by in a pack.
> Child, I cannot promise that you will get your wish.

"Love Song for K. Owyne" is a good example of what I mean, and so is "I Remember," a splendidly breathless one-sentence poem which I break into only because I want room for another quotation:

                                    and some nights
we took our gin warm and neat
from old jelly glasses while
the sun blew out of sight
like a red picture hat and
one day I tied my hair back
with a ribbon and you said
that I looked almost like
a puritan lady and what
I remember best is that
the door to your room was
the door to mine.

These two passages illustrate my major point well enough, and they also give an opportunity for some of the minuteness of appreciation which Jane Austen thought was the only kind of criticism worth bothering about. The first passage ought to show at least some of the truth of my feeling that this book might well serve as a kind of postgraduate course in the delicate and perceptive handling of rhyme. Lines 5–9 of the first passage also indicate how very far Miss Sexton has come in her use of the fantastic, the askew, and the surreal. In her first book it seems to me always a little adventitious and forced; here it serves thoroughly and well the vision of the entire poem. ". . . the sun blew out of sight / like a red picture hat" in the second passage is as good an example as any of one of Miss Sexton's poetic mannerisms which has annoyed a good many readers: the frequent use of seemingly irrelevant similes. The reader can find other examples for himself, but I think that the annoyed are probably wrong. Many of the similes are irrelevant, but that is not the point; the point is that the poet is doing everything she possibly can to make the experience come clear, that she is willing to get along without our rather bookish notions of neatness and tidiness (we like to call it "order" when we're being pretentious) so that the experience may be lucidly expressed. The effect is much like Chekhov's famous mannerism of grabbing his auditor by the lapels and saying "Listen!"

Necessity and Freedom   A. R. Jones*

At present, to talk of an *English* poetic tradition at all seems curiously parochial, for in this century the initiative in English poetry has largely been taken by Americans. In spite of the example of Pound and Eliot, it is only in recent years that English critics have awoken to the fact that American poets and critics no longer exist in a state of colonial dependence on the English tradition. The case of Robert Lowell is indicative of the critical parochialism

*Reprinted with permission from *Critical Quarterly* 7 (Spring 1965): 14–17, 24–30.

which dominated the 1950's. In fact, Lowell's reputation was assured as early as 1947 when he was awarded the Pulitzer Prize. With the successive appearance of *Land of Unlikeness, Lord Weary's Castle, The Mills of Kavanaughs, Life Studies, Imitations,* and *For the Union Dead,* six volumes of poetry published over a period of twenty years, American critics had no doubt of his stature. The English attitude towards his work, however, is indicated by the fact that when the English edition of *Life Studies* was published, Part II, a prose interlude, "91 Revere Street," crucial to the volume as a whole, was omitted. This was surely a somewhat casual treatment of a poet whose work was already exercising a decisive influence on the poetry of his younger contemporaries.

Indeed, largely as a direct result of Robert Lowell's example, American poetry is moving towards an acceptance of the dramatic monologue as the predominant poetic mode. But it is a dramatic monologue in which the *persona* is not treated dramatically, as a mask, that is, in the manner of Browning's *Dramatis Personae,* but is projected lyrically, as in Whitman's *Song of Myself* or in Pound's *Pisan Cantos.* In other words, although the poem's style and method is unmistakably dramatic, the *persona* is naked ego involved in a very personal world and with particular, private experiences. This private world into which the reader is drawn has established, in Lowell and his followers, something like a confessional orthodoxy in so far as the *persona* adopts the attitudes of a patient on the analyst's couch, revealing, often in images of violence and fantasy, a sick alienation. The intolerable compulsion to confess is irresistibly tied to a free-floating and neurotic guilt, so that the world into which we as readers are drawn is, in the end, phantasmagoric, intensely personal and painfully private, the world of Kafka, of Joseph K. in fact: a nightmare world of guilt, suffering and sudden confrontations. It is significant, in this respect, that Anne Sexton, perhaps Robert Lowell's most brilliant and powerful follower, quotes as her epigraph from a letter Kafka wrote to Oskar Pollak:

> . . . the books we need are the kind that act upon us like a misfortune, that make us suffer like the death of someone we love more than ourselves, that make us feel as though we were on the verge of suicide, or lost in a forest remote from all human habitation—a book should serve as the axe for the frozen sea within us.

Such an attitude is overtly psychological; the aesthetic experience is tragic, we are to be drawn into a world of despair, of lost, lonely, wandering souls, which is at once terrifying, pitiable and cathartic, the effect of which is to release a deep compassion through the experience of intense suffering. But if the experience of the work is inevitable and necessary suffering, then the release must somehow represent freedom from suffering, at least the freedom to rise above it, for even if freedom is the knowledge of necessity we must know what the necessity is in terms of which we can said to be free. In 1946, Randall Jarrell, commenting on *Lord Weary's Castle* (and this was subsequently endorsed by Lowell himself) remarked that Lowell's poems "understand the world as a sort of conflict of opposites". On the one side there are the forces of "Stasis or inertia of the stubborn self, the obstinate persistence in evil that is damnation. Into this realm of necessity the poems push everything that is closed, turned inward, incestuous, that blinds or binds." On the opposite side are those forces that represent "everything that is free or open, that grows or is willing to change . . . this is the realm of freedom, of the Grace that has replaced the Law, of the perfect Liberator . . ." Lowell's poems normally move from the "closed" to the "open," into liberation; from the "realm of necessity" to the "realm of freedom"; through the knowledge of personal and often painful experience to Grace and a totally different, aesthetic and largely impersonal stasis; indeed in many cases (cf. the poem *In Memory of Arthur Winslow*, for instance) death is the final stasis, the ultimate liberator.

In many ways this opposition of forces barely restates the traditional dualism between the flesh and the spirit or, at least, bearing in mind that Romanticism has been described as "split religion," the Romantic one between the mechanical and the organic. A volume of poems by Robert Lowell or Anne Sexton, or Sylvia Plath's *Ariel*, if these poets can be seen as a group, makes an unmistakeably autobiographical impact. (Indeed, one factor—and perhaps not the least important—that those critics who insist on the poem as an autonomous whole neglect, is the impact of a *volume* of poems, a total impact sometimes greater than the sum of its parts—*The Songs of Innocence* or *Lyrical Ballads* for example—in so far as it is the complete volume which creates a distinct and homogeneous world rather than the individual poem.) Anne Sexton's poems, for example, create largely the world of her *persona*, the "I" of the poems which undergoes a continuing development and is clearly related, intimately and painfully, to the poet's autobiography. Part of the interest of such poems is focussed on the poet's response to unusual experience and unbearable suffering and deprivation. This is different in some degree to the Romantic approach which insists on the excitement of usual, even commonplace, events as experienced by a very unusual sensibility. Moreover, whereas the Romantics would have agreed that their examination of personal experience is intended to release the "frozen sea within us" their poems move, always, towards an intensification of self-awareness through self-revelation. Anne Sexton's poems, however, are often a dialogue with the self in which the self struggles to find "wholeness" rather than "awareness." The world of her poems is certainly a world of enclosed perspectives, at the centre of which is the lyrical *persona* who represents too often an unstable and hysterical response to experience. Whereas the Romantic "I" is the omniscient and often omnipotent centre of poetic consciousness, who confronts experience directly, the *persona* of Anne Sexton is essentially passive, a patient rather than an agent, who suffers *under* experience. Indeed, passive suffering is one of Anne Sexton's main concerns and irresistibly recalls W. B. Yeats's objection to Wilfred Owen's poetry: "passive suffering is not a theme for poetry," a sentiment which would have our agreement, had it *not* been applied to Owen's poetry. Yet Yeats, in another axiom and in a different context, asserts that, "We make out of the quarrel with others rhetoric but out of the quarrel with ourselves poetry"—and Anne Sexton makes her poetry largely out of the quarrel, the tense dialogue with the self; for her, poetry is a way of handling and coming to terms with painful and intensely personal experience. T. S. Eliot's assertion that, "the more perfect the artist, the more completely separate in him will be the man who suffers and the mind which creates" indicates the dualism that is operating in these poems, for in so far as the *persona* represents the "man who suffers," the artist creates the poem within which the suffering is contained and given meaning. If the man is patient and passive under suffering, the creative mind is certainly both agent and active. The creative mind—which is largely released and refined in suffering—knows freedom and achieves Grace, through the act of creation itself. The poet exercises his traditional power in using the beneficent passion of poetry to expel the malignant forces of private suffering. In this sense such poetry, though always directed towards intellectual and moral ends, is therapeutic. The dialogue with the self is, in effect, the dialogue between the man who suffers and the mind which creates, and the separation between them is more or less complete, so much so, in fact, that they constitute something in the nature of two identities, the one struggling to organise into meaningful patterns the overwhelming chaos of the world of suffering inhabited by the other. The poetry that results very closely corresponds to the emotional pattern of tragedy that Maud Bodkin tried to isolate in psychological terms:

> In the gradual fashioning and transforming, through the experience of life, of an idea of self, every individual must in some degree experience the contrast between a personal self—a limited ego, one among many—and a self that is free to range imaginatively through all human achievement. In infancy and in the later years of those who remain childish, a comparatively feeble imaginative activity together with an undisciplined instinct of self-assertion may present a fantasy self—the image of an infantile personality—in conflict with the chastened image which social contact, arousing the instinct of submission, tends to enforce. In the more mature mind that has soberly taken the measure of the personal self as revealed in practical life, there remains the contrast between this and the self-revealed in imaginative thought—wellnigh limitless in sympathy and aspiration. (*Archetypal Patterns in Poetry*, 1, vii.)

This restates, in effect, the opposed forces that Randall Jarrell sees as representing the basic conflict in Robert Lowell's poetry between the realm of necessity and the realm of freedom, the practical, habitual world of suffering man and the imaginative, limitless world of the creative mind. In a poet such as Anne Sexton the contrast between the two selves is so sharp as to be appropriately described, psychologically, as schizophrenic; and if the *persona* is on the analyst's couch re-enacting a private terror, the creative mind is the analyst himself whose insight enables him to give pattern and meaning to what the *persona* sees only as incoherent experience. . . .

Sylvia Plath recorded her debt to Robert Lowell and linked her work to that of Anne Sexton. She acknowledged her excitement at Lowell's "intense breakthrough into very serious, very personal emotional experience," and remarked that these "peculiar private and taboo subjects" had been explored by Anne Sexton, who writes "also about her experiences as a mother; as a mother who's had a nervous breakdown, as an extremely emotional and feeling young woman. And her poems are wonderfully craftsmanlike poems, and yet have a kind of emotional and psychological depth which I think is something perhaps quite new and exciting".

Notice that she relates, almost incidentally, the idea of "breakthrough" with the idea of "breakdown," and that she isolates the dualism between the taboo nature of the subject of the poetry and the "wonderfully craftsmanlike" quality of the poetry itself.

Anne Sexton's recently published *Selected Poems* are drawn from her two volumes of poems, *To Bedlam and Part Way Back* (1960), and *All My Pretty Ones* (1962). On the whole the poems of the second volume are richer in texture, more diversified in subject matter and more composed than the poems of the earlier volume, which are often powerful and raw. At her best there is no doubt of her craftsmanship; her control of diction and rhythm is remarkably assured, and commands immediate attention and respect. Her themes are those of love, motherhood and death, of suffering and break-down, and at their best her poems are both harrowing and compassionate. Like Lowell, her framework of reference is ultimately religious; without being overtly theological, traditional religious values are gently but firmly insisted upon. The world of her poems is intimately personal, and her diffi-culty is to relate morally a world of physical and mental suffering that can only be diagnosed clinically. She sees evil and suffering as the condition of humankind:

> I was born
> doing reference work in sin, and born
> confessing it. This is what poems are:
> with mercy
> for the greedy,
> they are the tongue's wrangle,
> the world's pottage, the rat's star.

She is very conscious of evil and of Original Sin, and if she sees the relation between confession and poetry it is because she believes poetry to be mor-ally directed. In her poetry she transcends imaginatively what she can only otherwise patiently accept as the lot of man. Her best poems are filled with a profound compassion for man as a suffering being and for the human predica-ment, and often the image of the suffering self tends to merge into the figure of the crucified Christ. Thus far from endorsing or exploiting madness or pain her poetry comes to terms with human suffering in order to redeem it. Poetry is not a way of evading the purgatory of human experience but a means of facing and controlling it. In her poem, "For John, Who Begs Me Not to Enquire Further," she claims on behalf of the poet that courage to face experience which Schopenhauer in a letter to Goethe claimed for the philosopher:

> It is the courage to make a clean breast of it in face of every question that makes the philosopher. He must be like Sophocles's Oedipus, who, seeking enlightenment concerning his terrible fate, pursues his indefatigable enquiry, even when he divines that appalling horror awaits him in the answer. But most of us carry in our heart the Jocasta who begs Oedipus for God's sake not to inquire further . . .

Her poetry describes in images of powerful violence the suffering and terror of life, not for the sake of the suffering or the terror, but for the sake of a different order of reality that she finds through them. Thus her poems achieve something of a tragic dignity, and display an attitude of mind that is neither cynical nor despairing, but which is clearly related to the whole powerful tradition of Christian stoicism, to King's "Exequy" and Johnson's "Vanity of Human Wishes."

Her poems are mostly formally organized as dramatic narratives; set in a particular place at a particular time, they tell a story in an almost old-fashioned way, except that whereas the narrative seems to move longitudinally, so to speak, the meaning of the poem moves latitudinally, across and below the narrative line. At its most direct, in a poem such as "Flight," for instance, the narrative structure is extremely simple and describes a woman driving through Boston to the airport and back again through Boston; but the subject of the poem is revealed through the state of mind of the woman, the sudden and desperate need for love and the despair when that need is frustrated. The description of the drive to the airport is full of anticipation and outward-going images:

> There was rose and violet on the river
> as I drove through the mist into the city.
> I was full of letters I hadn't sent you,
> A red coat over my shoulders
> and new white gloves in my lap.

At the airport, the turning point of the poem and of the journey, there is a terrible note of finality:

> All flights were grounded.
> The planes sat and the gulls sat,
> heavy and rigid in a pool of glue.

The return journey is marked by a sense of almost cosmic desolation and the realisation that there is no escape, that flight from the self and the world that self creates is illusory:

> I drove past the eye and ear infirmaries,
> past the office buildings lined up like dentures,
> and along Storrow Drive the street lights
> sucked in all the insects who
> had nowhere else to go.

Although she drives to the airport through "Sumner Tunnel" and away from it along "Storrow Drive," a happy coincidence of naming, the symbolic level of the narrative is not schematised or insisted upon but allowed to emerge naturally and gradually through the narrative.

She has a remarkable sense of particularities, a fine awareness of the detail that will bring the whole scene vividly before the eyes and that, at the same time, will be psychologically telling and exact. This ability to realize complex landscapes of mind in visually concrete terms is one of the main sources of her poetic strength. Curiously enough, this can be seen as clearly in her unsuccessful poems as in her best work. Because her poems, particularly those concerned with mental breakdown, build such intense and violent conflicts, she sometimes escapes conclusions glibly in the way that the last couplet of the Shakespearean sonnet is occasionally used to distract attention from the fact that the tensions the poem creates have not been fully resolved. Thus what ought to have been dramatic is merely theatrical. In the poem "The Abortion," the *persona* driving back from the abortionist rationalises her sense of guilt and loss and concludes by turning upon herself:

> Yes, woman, such logic will lead
> to loss without death. Or say what you meant,
> you coward . . . this baby that I bleed.

However brilliantly horrible the last image may be in itself, the effect of this last stanza is to turn an already sensational subject into sensationalism, to drop from the reality of drama into the over-simplifications of melodrama. In poems such as this, and it must be said that her *Selected Poems* contains a number of them, it is as if the subject has got out of control, become indeed almost hysterical, and that the poet has asserted herself in an arbitary way, forcing the poem to a conclusion.

In her best poems, in a poem such as "The Operation," for example, she uses all her imaginative resources to create a statement of disturbing, even terrifying, beauty. The poem is straightforwardly narrative in structure, beginning with a description of her visit to the doctor's and his diagnosis that she is suffering from hereditary cancer of the womb, which killed her mother the previous year:

> I come to this white office, its sterile sheet,
> its hard tablet, its stirrups, to hold my breath
> while I, who must, allow the glove its oily rape,
> to hear the almost mighty doctor over me equate
> my ills with hers
> and decide to operate.

The description is almost horrifyingly precise, and, apart from the image of the glove, almost clinical. The rhythms fall gently, rather hesitantly, into place and the rhyme is regular but unobtrusive. The second and third sections of the poem describe in similar detail the operation and recovery, re-enacting the patient's feelings in the dramatic and vivid present tense:

> I glide down the halls
> and rise in the iron cage towards science and pitfalls.
>
> The great green people stand
> over me; I roll on the table
> under a terrible sun, following their command
> to curl, head touching knee if I am able.
> Next, I am hung up like a saddle and they begin.
> Pale as an angel I float out over my own skin.

In the operating theatre she is commanded to adopt a foetal position, and her recovery, slow and bewilderingly painful, is like the re-enactment of the birth trauma. The association between the evil of disease and birth is established earlier in the poem in the connection between her own birth and her mother's cancer of the womb:

> It grew in her
> as simply as a child would grow
> as simply as she housed me once, fat and female.
> Always my most gentle house before that embryo
> of evil spread in her shelter and she grew frail.

Although the child is in some senses innocence, there is no doubt that the traditionally religious idea of being born into a world of evil and disease is suggested in these images. In so far as the operation is seen as a re-birth, her ultimate discharge from hospital is a re-emergence into childhood; chivied and cajoled, like a child, she is again ready to participate in the bitter and sorrowful game we call life:

> Time now to pack this humpty-dumpty
> back the frightened way she came
> and run along, Anne, and run along now
> my stomach laced up like a football
> for the game.

The humour is sardonic, the attitude stoical compassion. While the patient faces the violent and painful images of suffering, the creative mind uses the operation to establish a complex and comprehensive image of the continuity of human life, evil and suffering, the jest, the glory and the riddle of the world. The poet meaningfully organizes the incoherent and meaningless world of suffering. However startling or gruesome, it is not the quality of the experience itself or the fact of its confession that hold our attention, but the quality of the imaginative energy.

Although she avoids any ready-made theological conclusions she does endorse the traditional idea of redemption through suffering. In several of her poems she associates suffering with the agony of Christ crucified. Sometimes the association is direct as in the poem "In the Deep Museum":

> My God, my God, what queer corner am I in?
> Didn't I die, blood running down the post,
> lungs gagging for air, die there for the sin
> of anyone, my sour mouth giving up the ghost?

Or, again, in the poem "For God While Sleeping":

> Sleeping in fever, I am unfit
> to know just who you are:
> hung up like a pig on exhibit,
> the delicate wrists,
> the beard drooling blood and vinegar;
> hooked to your own weight,
> jolting toward death under your nameplate.

But in the poem "With Mercy for the Greedy" she examines the crucifixion as both suffering and symbol and relates it directly to her poetry:

> I detest my sins and I try to believe
> in The Cross, I touch its tender hips, its dark jawed face,
> its solid neck, its brown sleep.
>
> True. There is
> a beautiful Jesus.
> He is frozen to his bones like a chunk of beef.
> How desperately he wanted to pull his arms in!
> How desperately I touch his vertical and horizontal axes!
> But I can't. Need is not quite belief.

She rejects the consolations of a "beautiful Jesus," for, however much she would like to believe such an idea, it runs counter to her experience of sin and suffering. The Christ in which she believes is the suffering Christ of the crucifix, whose pain she recreates so physically in the line "How desperately he wanted to pull his arms in!" But the crucifix is not only an image of tortured suffering: it is also a symbol of unselfish love and redemption. Thus the cross is at one and the same time an image of intense agony which can be realized personally, and a geometric symbol of the intersection of the timeless eternity of God and the world of man which is changeless and impersonal. Similarly, the man who suffers in a world of suffering and evil can be transcended by the mind that creates in the unchanging, timeless world of art. Through the world of poetic imagination, man can move from the realm of necessity into the realm of freedom.

Robert Lowell, Sylvia Plath and Anne Sexton are all extremely traditional poets. Not, of course, in the sense that they see tradition as an unchanging force to which they should submit themselves—in this sense tradition is a dead hand—but in the sense that they see the tradition of poetry as a living and growing force, which must be constantly extended in order to be kept vitally alive. All three poets are self-conscious and accomplished craftsmen, who delight in the poet's traditional role of maker; and all three are incidentally concerned in trying to define a specifically contemporary sensibility. They are, of course, all Americans to whom the tradition means, say, Hart Crane, as much as it means, say, Thomas Hardy. But, above all, these poets are willing to experiment, to take chances and to run risks. Indeed, in America during the last decade a great deal of exciting and experimental poetry was written, quite apart from the poetry of the Beats. By comparison, the poetry written in England during that period seems extraordinarily safe. The most exciting English poets of the period, such as Ted Hughes and Thom Gunn, tend, interestingly enough, to be those poets who are most aware of contemporary American poetry.

O Yellow Eye   Philip Legler*

In her third volume of poetry, Anne Sexton has fashioned a brilliantly unified book. Though thematically related to *All My Pretty Ones* and to her first book, *To Bedlam and Part Way Back, Live or Die* is more passionate in its intensity and more abundant in its desperate concentration on vision. What Mrs. Sexton does so painfully well is announced in *The Sun:* "O yellow eye, / let me be sick with your heat," says the poet, with the fire of seeing and blindness, reality and dream, creation and destruction. Consumed by the "eye"—sometimes praising it, never escaping it—"under the burning magnifying glass," the poems are the "mouth" to tell us "stories."

With *To Bedlam* Mrs. Sexton was accused by those who said she couldn't write about madness. She did!—the madness that is insanity, that is sanity, the madness in us all. In *All My Pretty Ones* she continued to search and to reflect. In *Live or Die* she furthers her journey, but we are helped by her arranging the poems as they were written. With so little space, I will talk briefly about a few of the finest.

Flee on Your Donkey, a work which may not sustain its length, is a major poem for the poet and the reader. For it deals with the speaker's return to a mental institution (a dark night of the soul) and establishes a major concern; it is a terrifying trip in which recognition brings discovery:

> Anne, Anne,
> flee on your donkey,
> flee this sad hotel,

*Reprinted with permission from *Poetry* 110 (May 1967): 125–27.

ride out on some hairy beast,
gallop backward pressing
your buttocks to his withers,
sit to his clumsy gait somehow.
Ride out
any old way you please!
In this place everyone talks to his own mouth.
That's what it means to be crazy.
Those I loved best died of it—
the fool's disease.

Like *Somewhere in Africa*, all of Mrs. Sexton's poems are "from the interior."
Many of the narratives create themselves through images of memory.
In *Those Times . . .* the eye remembers itself as a girl "locked in my room
all day behind a gate, / a prison cell." But after finding that "When I
wanted to visit, / the closet is where I rehearsed my life, / all day among
shoes, / away from the glare of the bulb in the ceiling," the speaker can
say

I did not know the woman I would be
nor that blood would bloom in me
each month like an exotic flower,
nor that children,
two monuments,
would break from between my legs
two cramped girls breathing carelessly,
each asleep in her tiny beauty.

Such knowledge not only discovers and accepts miraculous change; it knows
a poison in each of us: a poem for Sylvia Plath finds that worm a "sleepy
drummer"—leaving the friend saying "and I know at the news of your death,
/ a terrible taste for it, like salt."
Many other poems embrace that salt taste—*Man and Wife, Your Face
on the Dog's Neck, Suicide Note* (see *Flee on Your Donkey*), the grotesque
Cripples and Other Stories—how we mutilate ourselves and others!—*Pain
for a Daughter*, and *The Addict*, in which the speaker tells of the eight pills
she takes nightly:

Actually I'm hung up on it.
But remember I don't make too much noise.
And frankly no one has to lug me out
and I don't stand there in my winding sheet.
I'm a little buttercup in my yellow nightie
eating my eight loaves in a row
and in a certain order as in
the laying on of hands
or the black sacrament.

The poems are rituals, many of them with a lyric quality, such as *Little Girl, My String Bean, My Lovely Woman,* with its childlike and magical moments—

> I say hello
> to such shakes and knockings and high jinks,
> such music, such sprouts,
> such dancing-mad-bears of music,
> such necessary sugar,
> such goings-on!

And some of the writing in *A Little Uncomplicated Hymn:* "I tried at the teeth of sound / to draw up such legions of noise; / I tried at the breakwater / to catch the star off each ship."

Live, the final poem in the book (though it takes again the sun as "purifier"), does not need to appear at the end. All the poems are affirmations of a kind.

This is a crazily sane and beautifully controlled work. It is the Oedipal eye; its poems are honest, terrifying! And the voice is terrifying—the voice of the human being *seeing* the nightmare and the dream that is man. It is a book—to borrow from Mrs. Sexton's *The Black Art*—of "trances and portents!," of "cycles and children and islands." It is a "weird abundance."

Light in a Dark Journey   Thomas P. McDonnell*

Anne Sexton's latest book of poems, *Live or Die,* presents a good opportunity to look at her achievement in three published volumes. It is by now a rather worn observation to say that her poetry is not only personal but clearly the autobiography of the psyche itself. (Poetry has come around again, since the excesses of nineteenth-century romanticism, to recognizing something like the existence of the soul.) It is the kind of poetry frequently written by Robert Lowell, W. D. Snodgrass, and Jon Silkin, and by Sylvia Plath in her last tragic years. And it is a kind of poetry that seems much in favor today, chiefly because it has been so long denied as legitimate matter for poetry by the art-as-dissociation critics.

Anne Sexton's poetry, however, is not a poetry of spasmodic revelation or of occasional incident transformed from similitude to artifact: in its continuing wholeness one perceives the suggestion of a journey. The journey is not a calculated one, marked with clear directions along the way (". . . here are no signs to tell the way"), but a journey in and out of the various dark. The poems are fragments of light that illuminate not so much the general landscape as parts of the immediate terrain—and that only now and then.

*Reprinted with permission from *America* 116 (13 May 1967): 729–31.

In the first poem of her first book, *To Bedlam and Part Way Back*, Anne Sexton said: "Late August, / I speed through the antiseptic tunnel / where the moving dead still talk / of pushing their bones against the thrust / of cure," in that immediate terrain where she is "queen of this summer hotel / or the laughing bee on a stalk / of death." Of course, "bones" has all but become a poetic cliché in modern verse and "thrust" a sociological one. Nevertheless, Anne Sexton very early wrote a kind of poetry in which you were not always sure whether the center was in motion and the periphery still, or the periphery in motion and the center still—with a stillness not of tranquillity but, ineffably, at the point of fear itself.

"Kind Sir," she says in a poem addressed to Thoreau, "lost and of your same kind, / I have turned around twice with my eyes sealed / and the woods were white and my night mind / saw such strange happenings, untold and unreal. / And opening my eyes, I am afraid of course / to look—this inward look that society scorns— / Still, I search in these woods and find nothing worse / than myself, caught between the grapes and the thorns." But not all the early poems—remarkable poems, really—have "this inward look that society scorns," Anne Sexton looks outward, too, "up there" to the gulls "godding the whole blue world"; and she listens ("Oh, la la la") to the music that swims back to her:

> The night I came I danced a circle
> and was not afraid.
> Mister?

Not afraid, but still there is that implication—perhaps supplication—in "Mister?" at the end: thus in and out of the shadows of the still journey again.

What is at once perfectly clear about Anne Sexton's verse is that it so stunningly reveals the poetry of psychic disturbance in all its frightful fluctuations between terror and clarity—and the poetry is in both the terror and the clarity. A young Catholic girl, some years ago, wrote a book of poems called *Songs of a Psychotic*, which was both more naive and more innocent than the knowledgeable but dark world of Anne Sexton. Where the younger poet was indeed all but otherworldly, Anne Sexton is a poet and woman intensely of this world. It was evident, even in *To Bedlam and Part Way Back*, that we were witness to a dimension of poetry unique in English literature, a poetry uniquely ours in this post-Freudian era.

Such poetry exists, surely, in "Her Kind," "Ringing the Bells," "A Story for Rose on the Midnight Flight to Boston," and "For John, Who Begs Me Not to Enquire Further," which is a poetic statement on the book's epigraph by Schopenhauer, and which also introduces Part Two of the *Bedlam* poems. (Anne Sexton's epigraphs to the several volumes, by the way, are extremely pertinent to the revelation of the poems.) Too, in these poems of the first volume, we begin to recognize certain tensions that later inform—though in larger freedoms of organization—the stark yet delicate impact of Anne Sexton's poetry.

In the last poem in *To Bedlam and Part Way Back*, "The Division of Parts," autobiography becomes poetic catharsis on that Good Friday when "In Boston, the devout / work their cold knees / toward that sweet martyrdom / that Christ planned." But "It does not please / my yankee bones to watch / where the dying is done / in its ugly hours." Still, "Such dangerous angels walk through Lent. / Their walls creak *Anne! Convert! Convert!*" At last, though, the poet herself resigns to the non-miraculous grace of reality: "And Lent will keep its hurt / for someone else. Christ knows enough / staunch guys have hitched on him in trouble, / thinking his sticks were badges to wear."

In *All My Pretty Ones*, Anne Sexton reaches into the full power of the autobiographical poem, at once, with "The Truth the Dead Know," on the death by cancer of her mother, at fifty-seven, and of her father by heart attack, at fifty-nine, only three months later. The book's title poem begins: "Father, this year's jinx rides us apart"—a line that comes much too close, perhaps, to the rub-off from Robert Lowell's obvious influence on Anne Sexton. But the whole poem manages to recover itself in the working out of her own authentic idiom. Disconcertingly, though, the poem ends: "Whether you are pretty or not, I outlive you, / bend down my strange face to yours and forgive you." Here, unfortunately, the reader cannot get close enough to the personal anguish of the poet to disabuse himself of the notion that to forgive the dead is the ultimate condescension of the living.

The journey into autobiography continues in "The Operation"—surely one of the remarkable poems of its kind in English—and in "The Abortion" ("*Somebody who should have been born / is gone*"). This is followed by "With Mercy for the Greedy," with the epigraph, "For my friend, Ruth, who urges me to make an appointment for the Sacrament of Confession." The poem itself carries the journey farther: "Concerning your letter in which you ask / me to call a priest and in which you ask / me to wear The Cross that you enclose"; and the reader—at least this reader—says to himself: Oh, no, don't ask this of the poet, don't proselytize at this point of her genuine anguish, which is all confessional, anyway: and who are we to say whether it is sacramental in the formal sense or not, or even in the most understanding empathy of friendship, to press more upon the poet than is actually necessary? But the poet herself answers this best in the last stanza of the poem:

> My friend, my friend, I was born
> doing reference work in sin, and born
> confessing it. This is what poems are:
> with mercy
> for the greedy
> they are the tongue's wrangle,
> the world's pottage, the rat's star.

Poem follows remarkable poem: "For God While Sleeping," "In the Deep Museum," "Water," "Letter Written on a Ferry While Crossing Long

Island Sound," each like a flash of light on the landscape of Anne Sexton's journey in and out of the dark. And not all dark at that, because in "From the Garden" Anne Sexton has written one of the loveliest poems of love that we have in contemporary American poetry, and one of the most beautifully dark ones ("Though I was bony you found me fair") in "Love Song for K. Owyne."

Not so incidentally, by the way, Anne Sexton is a strikingly beautiful woman, as anyone can see from the photo on the back dust jacket of her latest volume, *Live or Die*. The fact is that press agents and movie makers do not know what authentic glamour is, chiefly because they don't know what a woman is; and Anne Sexton is one of the few women writing poetry in the United States today of whom it is possible to say that her womanness is totally at one with her poems—and never more so than when she partially and poetically, in "Consorting With Angels," denies it: "I was tired of being a woman. . . . / I'm no more a woman / than Christ was a man." But if a woman alone, in the physiological sense, could have written a poem like "Menstruation at Forty," then also a woman alone, in the fullest possible sense, could have written so exquisite a poem as "Little Girl, My String Bean, My Lovely Woman."

Now, in *Live or Die*, Anne Sexton is writing in a more powerful and a freer mode of poetic expression than that already, and almost at once, achieved in her two previous volumes. Her poems have a marvelously wrought discipline of free form in, say, "Flee on Your Donkey," as well as the discipline of strict form in "Cripples and Other Stories," notably so here, and in the elegy to a fellow New England poet in seven *a b a b* quatrains with the concluding couplet:

> John Holmes, cut from a single tree,
>   lie heavy in her hold
> and go down that river with the ivory,
>   the copra and the gold.

Sometimes, though rarely (as in "Those Times"), Anne Sexton's confessions become almost too much the poetry of the couch. Still, even here of course, it is a perfectly valid kind of poetry and surely in keeping with the journey backward as well as with the one that probes the present and the future tense: of the woman who "did not know the woman I would be / nor that blood would bloom in me / each month like an exotic flower." Too, the poem "To Lose the Earth" seems to me about as Freudian as a poem can get, even in these days when the couch has become a rack of pain rather than a bed of pleasure. In the poem on Sylvia Plath's suicide, "Sylvia's Death," one can almost read the terrible anguish of people who know not too little of themselves but perhaps too much.

Anne Sexton is a deeply religious poet in the existential sense of that depleted term. For her, the religious experience has nothing whatever to do with the ordinary comforts of piety; it daily involves one's struggle to survive, to somehow come to terms with the terrible mystery of existence and at last to find a measure of salvation in the life one has to live. For example, "For the Year of the Insane" is no idle prayer in poetry but the poetry of prayer itself. In following immediately upon "Protestant Easter," it perfectly reveals the modality from rote to authentic supplication.

The journey in and out of the dark continues in "Crossing the Atlantic," a passage in "steel staterooms where night goes on forever":

> Being inside them is, I think,
> the way one would dig into a planet
> and forget the word *light*.

But the journey always comes home again, from "Walking in Paris" to dialing a telephone number in Boston, and indeed walking again down Marlborough Street. The later poems in *Live or Die*—all dated 1965, and the last two, 1966—are powerful "meditations" of the kind the saints might reveal if they were poets (in the technical sense) as well as humanists caught in the terrors of the modern world; and I think it is folly to pretend that our world is no different, say, from the mystical age of the seventeenth century. These remarkable poems could have been written by no one not thoroughly a child of this century:

> . . . I am not what I expected.
> Not an Eichmann.
> The poison just didn't take.
> So I won't hang around in my
>   hospital shift,
> repeating The Black Mass and all of it.
> I say *Live, Live* because of the sun,
> the dream, the excitable gift.

If the excitable gift is life itself, it is also life transformed by art as personal catharsis. In this age of dehumanization, Anne Sexton's is a necessary kind of poetry to have on the record. We need the poetry of a woman who couldn't drown the eight Dalmatians in the pails of water set aside for them. Anne Sexton is a woman and poet who "kept right on going on, / a sort of human statement," in that long and intricate journey where the dark is neither all nor forever.

Three Women Poets   James Tulip*

In Anne Sexton there is little of that radical privacy that acts both as obstacle and discipline in Sylvia Plath's work. It is a poetry of *effects* that we find here, a rhetorical projection of a personality set off against a world of

*Reprinted with permission from *Poetry Australia* 21 (December 1967): 37–39.

hard factual things. Both elements are forcibly objectified, and we find ourselves in a vivid world of hospitals, asylums, cities, bedrooms, and meeting
there the tense individuality of the poet. But whether there is any real
relation between these elements, a relation where the one might affect and
alter the other and where some larger perception of life might be liberated,
this is the problem.

> Imagine it. A radio playing
> and everyone here was crazy.
> I liked it and danced in a circle.
> Music pours over the sense
> and in a funny way
> music sees more than I.
> I mean it remembers better;
>
> remembers the first night here.
> It was the strangled cold of November;
> even the stars were strapped in the sky
> and that moon too bright
> forking through the bars to stick me
> with a singing in the head.
> I have forgotten all the rest.
>   from "Music swims back to me"

Here, there is a certain interplay and pressure between subject and object
that heightens the verse. Elsewhere, however, Mrs. Sexton's writing sprawls
passively over the page in a readable, journalistic fashion; but nothing new
gets made in the process. The poems too often are simple illustrations of
positions known and knowable prior to the poem's being written. Hence the
middles of many poems are soft and stodgy, and the tone of a long dying fall
dominates her work. In spite, then, of the flamboyant "I" presence and the
poignant situations in Mrs. Sexton's work, her genre is recognizably the
languid New Yorker short story-cum-essay in verse, and its achievement is to
have made sadness chic.

Of the three volumes available, I felt that *All My Pretty Ones* was the
best. A very striking kind of wit, that of the fast cosmopolitan, intellectualized American female, comes across here.

> Over my right shoulder
> I see four nuns
> who sit like a bridge club,
> their faces poked out
> from under their habits,
> as good as good babies who
> have sunk into their carriages.
> Without discrimination
> the wind pulls the skirts
> of their arms.

> Almost undressed,
> I see what remains:
> that holy wrist,
> that ankle,
> that chain.
>> from "Letter written on a ferry
> while crossing Long Island Sound."

and

> Some women marry houses.
> It's another kind of skin; it has a heart,
> a mouth, a liver and bowel movements.
> The walls are permanent and pink.
> See how she sits on her knees all day,
> faithfully washing herself down.
> Men enter by force, drawn back like Jonah
> into their fleshy mothers.
> A woman *is* her mother.
> That's the main thing.
>> "Housewife"

To emphasize the Mary McCarthy in Anne Sexton is, perhaps, to direct the reader away from the more general and serious intentions in her writing. But these intentions, along with the overt confessional manner, seem only to lead to a pretty negative sort of melodrama.

The impact of a recognizably personal voice is not only Mrs. Sexton's strength but the strength generally of contemporary poetry. It will be false, however, to assume that this quality of itself is a guarantee of good poetry; indeed, this point needs further generalising still by way of saying there are no qualities at all that of themselves are good and necessary to poetry. . . .

Review of *Transformations*   Louis L. Martz*

Anne Sexton's first book, in 1960, brought her sudden fame through its eerie, abrupt, confessional mode, and all of her three intervening books have had to struggle, unsuccessfully, against the reader's high expectations. Her poems have become more and more conventional, until the *Love Poems* of 1969 reached even the bathetic ("Notice how he has numbered the blue veins / in my breast. Moreover there are ten freckles"). Approaching her new book *Transformations* with considerable diffidence, the reader may be pleasantly surprised to find that Anne Sexton has recovered something of the quality described in one of her earliest poems:

*Reprinted with permission from the *Yale Review* 61 (1972): 414–16.

I have gone out, a possessed witch,
haunting the black air, braver at night;
dreaming evil, I have done my hitch
over the plain houses, light by light:
lonely thing, twelve-fingered, out of mind.
A woman like that is not a woman, quite.
I have been her kind.

I have found the warm caves in the woods,
filled them with skillets, carvings, shelves,
closets, silks, innumerable goods;
fixed the suppers for the worms and the elves:
whining, rearranging the disaligned.
A woman like that is misunderstood.
I have been her kind.

She has recovered some of that wild and magical air by transforming seventeen tales from the Brothers Grimm into highly personal modern anecdotes, stressing the horror and wonder of that ancient world, but bringing home a universal application. Thus she begins by turning the story of the Gold Key into a prologue:

The speaker in this case
is a middle-aged witch, me—
tangled on my two great arms,
my face in a book
and my mouth wide,
ready to tell you a story or two.
I have come to remind you,
all of you:
Alice, Samuel, Kurt, Eleanor,
Jane, Brian, Maryel,
all of you draw near.

Each tale, "Snow White," "Rapunzel," "Rumpelstiltskin," and the rest, opens with a commentary, sometimes only a short stave, but often running to two or three pages, in which the personal and universal aspects of the story are developed. Thus "Red Riding Hood" becomes a parable of all deceivers:

I built a summer house on Cape Ann.
A simple A-frame and this too was
a deception—nothing haunts a new house.
When I moved in with a bathing suit and tea bags
the ocean rumbled like a train backing up
and at each window secrets came in
like gas. My mother, that departed soul,
sat in my Eames chair and reproached me
for losing her keys to the old cottage.
Even in the electric kitchen there was
the smell of a journey. The ocean

> was seeping through its frontiers
> and laying me out on its wet rails.
> The bed was stale with my childhood
> and I could not move to another city
> where the worthy make a new life.

So the tales become the vehicles for extended associations, until the very last one, "Briar Rose," almost disappears into an enfolding commentary that concludes the volume with these words:

> It's not the prince at all,
> but my father
> drunkenly bent over my bed,
> circling the abyss like a shark,
> my father thick upon me
> like some sleeping jellyfish.
>
> What voyage this, little girl?
> This coming out of prison?
> God help—
> this life after death?

As the first quotation may suggest, the style is based upon the manner in which one might recount a tale to a child, with funny local asides and ingeniously naïve comparisons:

> Once there was a witch's garden
> more beautiful than Eve's
> with carrots growing like little fish,
> with many tomatoes rich as frogs,
> onions as ingrown as hearts,
> the squash singing like a dolphin
> and one patch given over wholly to magic—
> rampion, a kind of salad root,
> a kind of harebell more potent than penicillin,
> growing leaf by leaf, skin by skin,
> as rapt and as fluid as Isadora Duncan.

But of course the asides and comparisons move far beyond the child's comprehension ("The day was as dark as the Führer's headquarters"), and the darker associations are very far from childish:

> The drunken poet
> (a genius by daylight)
> who places long-distance calls
> at three A.M. and then lets you sit
> holding the phone while he vomits
> (he calls it "The Night of the Long Knives")
> getting his kicks out of the death call,
> would understand.

Would understand, that is, something about the inner meaning of the tale of the Twelve Dancing Princesses. The difficulty with this mode of rendition lies in its continuous oscillation between extremes of the childish and the adult. The childish effects too often seem only "cute" ("His head is okay / but the rest of him wasn't Sanforized"), while the adult associations are too often highly congenital. As a whole the book is better on a first reading than on the second.

Transformations   William Pitt Root*

> The speaker in this case
> is a middle-aged witch, me—
> tangled on my two great arms,
> my face in a book
> and my mouth wide,
> ready to tell you a story or two.

The speaker is Anne Sexton and the book is *Transformations*, in which seventeen of the tales collected by the Brothers Grimm are revamped for a sophisticated, perhaps even jaded, contemporary readership. They work well on the page, but probably have even more effect read aloud. Some have, in fact, already been dramatically presented by at least one college thespian group and I'm told they worked very well.

Exactly what is the "work" they are designed for? They are styled to amuse and appall, and they do both. They are taken out of the dark Germanic woods and reinstated in the well-lit but equally dark places at the heart of American consumer culture. When the dwarfs revive Snow White from the Queen's first attack, in which she winds a piece of lace "tight as an Ace bandage" around Snow White's bodice, Snow White is "as full of life as soda pop." In another tale, the twelve dancing princesses "sprang out of their beds / and fussed around like a Miss America Contest." After a night of dancing, each of their shoes is "as worn as an old jockstrap." A night nurse "keeps vigil like a ballistic missile." Godfather Death turns someone over "like a campchair," and on and on. The plots of the tales are retained, the surfaces are studded with contemporary reference, inevitably derogatory reference, and a radical change in tone results.

Here are some of the openings and closures of tales as told in *Transformations:*

> No matter what life you lead
> the virgin is a lovely number:

*Reprinted with permission from *Poetry* 123 (October 1973): 48–51.

cheeks as fragile as cigarette paper,
arms and legs made of Limoges,
lips like Vin Du Rhône,
rolling her china-blue doll eyes
open and shut.
Open to say,
Good Day Mama,
and shut for the thrust
of the unicorn.

SNOW WHITE

A woman
who loves a woman
is forever young.
The mentor
and the student
feed off each other.

RAPUNZEL

Hurry, Godfather death,
Mister tyranny,
each message you give
has a dance to it,
a fish twitch,
a little crotch dance.

.   .   .

His white head hung out like a carpet bag
and his crotch turned blue as a blood blister,
and Godfather death, as it is written,
put a finger on his back
for the big blackout,
the big no.

GODFATHER DEATH

When Hawthorne rewrote Greek myths for children, he removed the gore, the deaths, the tragedies and the sex, rendering that gritty material into an insubstantial stew of false bliss considered suitable for the children of the time. Anne Sexton certainly couldn't be accused of siding too much with the angels in her versions, not at first glance anyway. Whom she sides with, finally, are the live ones, the survivors who stay intact, partaking of a vitality neither moral nor immoral. In the process, she ruthlessly attacks the fairy tales which have sprung from the original Grimm tales and simultaneously attacks the aspects of our culture which have used those fairy tales "to banquet / at behest of usura."

Characters originally given to us in the prospects of courage, wisdom, or simple purity, become in these transformations—"Transform?" asks the poet—the "dumb bunny" (Snow White) or "Regular Bobbsey Twins" (Cinderella and her Prince), and in the place of the other saleable virtues, in the void of their absence, we are given the purposeful disparagement of the poet's voice, a dauntless and offhandedly colloquial voice. The sources for her imagery are few and telling: war ("The day was as dark as the Führer's headquarters."), technology and politics ("He speaks up tiny as an earphone / in Truman's asexual voice"), mental wards and organized religion ("for I have left the three Christs of Ypsilanti / . . . and the church spires have turned to stumps"), and the world of "The suburban matron, / proper in the supermarket, / list in hand so she won't suddenly fly. . . ." Common to each of her citings is an awareness of how pathetically misused, wasted, perverted are the assets with which consumers, all of us, diligently surround ourselves: this is not the logical extension of fairy-tale psychology, it is the actual extension.

Anne Sexton, "middle-aged witch," renders this assessment peripherally for the most part, keeping her eye on the movement of each tale, although one could hardly fail to notice the spice she dashes into it. Above all, the tales do entertain. There are moments when they strain a bit to entertain ("her secret was as safe / as a fly in an outhouse"), but these moments are overwhelmed by the main force of a dark and often direly sympathetic laughter. The voice, primarily witty and knowing, frequently is possessed by a lyricism that is stunning. Here's the conclusion of Briar Rose (Sleeping Beauty) and, incidentally, the conclusion of the book:

> It's not the prince at all,
> but my father
> drunkenly bent over my bed,
> circling the abyss like a shark,
> my father thick upon me
> like some sleeping jellyfish.
>
> What voyage this, little girl?
> This coming out of prison?
> God help—
> this life after death?

Time and again, notes are struck here which remind me of Randall Jarrell's poetry, not in an imitative way, but rather in a way that is inevitable, given the shared concerns of these two poets. He, too, was entranced by these tales, wrote of them, absorbed them and applied them to the "dailiness of life," entering into the being of the sleeping girl, the suburban matrons moving through their limboes, yearning for changes that would change, for real transformations. I believe he would have loved this book and been its best, or second best, reader.

Anne Sexton: Self-Portrait in Poetry and Letters
Joyce Carol Oates*

"My mouth blooms like a cut," the poet announces in a poem called "The Kiss." Her body has undergone a resurrection: her nerves are turned on, like musical instruments. "Where there was silence / the drums, the strings are incurably playing." A mysterious *you* is to account for the miracle. A "genius" of a lover, a composer, a carpenter, a man of many hearts. Does he exist, is he merely human? Mortal? In one incarnation he is the object of an adulterous passion, he is one half "of a pair of scissors / who come together to cut, without towels saying His. Hers" (from "Eighteen Days Without You"). In another incarnation he is distant and unfathomable, moving away, leaving his beloved "private in her breathbed" and placing her, like a phone, back on the hook. He has become God. God and lover have inexplicably fused. Love, which has drawn the poet out of her body, out of her deathly preoccupation with herself, has now failed, and the poet sinks back into the grave of herself. It is a miracle, too, of a kind.

Images of wounds, broken bones, blood, masks. The poems themselves are small angry wounds that bloom, blossom fiercely, like flowers, but, like flowers, have no strength, no permanency. Everything is provisional, no matter how ebullient, how joyful the poet's cry. "Your hand found mine," Sexton declares in "The Touch," and "Life rushed to my fingers like a blood clot." Is the imagery in this instance deliberately macabre, is it ironic—or merely a consequence of the poet's carelessness? No matter: life rushes to her fingers like a blood clot, and we know the role of blood clots in the body's history.

Sexton is the poet of ephemeral, dizzyingly ephemeral emotions. She is the poet of instantaneous moods. They are flicked before us like playing cards: now she is happy, now she is plunged into depression, now she is passionate and fulfilled, now she is empty, abandoned, ready to die. The obsession of her poetry as a whole is with the tragic limitations of this kind of life, the failure of the imagination to be equal to the demands of the soul, specifically the failure of the female to be equal to her exaggerated idea of herself: daughter but also mother, mother but also daughter, wife, beloved, "small jail," the woman who cries out "my sex will be transfixed!"

After the critical success of her first books, *To Bedlam and Part Way Back* and *All My Pretty Ones*, Sexton was frequently criticized for the narrow range and intensity of her preoccupations: always the self, the self as victim, the self as Narcissus, the self as destructive unappeasable bully, more than

*Review of Anne Sexton, *Love Poems*, (Boston: Houghton Mifflin, 1969); *The Awful Rowing Toward God*, (Boston: Houghton Mifflin, 1975); *A Self-Portrait in Letters* (Boston: Houghton Mifflin, 1977). Reprinted with permission of the author from *The Profane Art: Essays & Reviews* (New York: E. P. Dutton, 1983), 165–83.

half in love with sickness and madness and her own "violent heart." Yet *Live or Die* and *Love Poems* attempt a celebration of sorts, however unconvincing it might strike the reader, and in the best poems of these volumes the haranguing voice is exactly right, the ironic, deft, bemused touch never overdone: despite her grim subject matter Sexton has always been a genuinely funny writer when it is her intention to be so. More often the tone is frank, even childlike; the ubiquitous *I* that is sounded throughout all the volumes makes its solemn pronouncements, its vows—"In celebration of the woman I am / and of the soul of the woman I am / and of the central creature and its delight / I sing for you. I dare to live."

Love Poems contains many small measured successes. The poet knows herself "unbalanced" but it is, here, not an issue; she is far more concerned with the bewildering experience of an adulterous love that has had the power to transform her, yet has not the "power" to last. In "For My Lover, Returning to His Wife," language is curt, hard, dry, even sardonic; if there is anger it has been rigorously pared away and the tone now is elegiac. The "victorious" wife is the presence that endures. She is *all there*, while the poet, the mistress, has begun to fade. The wife is "Fireworks in the dull middle of February / and as real as a cast-iron pot." And:

> . . . She is all harmony.
> She sees to oars and oarlocks for the dinghy,
> has placed the wild flowers at the window at breakfast,
> sat by the potter's wheel at midday,
> set forth three children under the moon,
> three cherubs drawn by Michelangelo . . .

"As for me, I am a watercolor," Sexton says. "I wash off." Is she bitter, is she angry, is she merely disappointed? One cannot really judge. One senses her masochistic preoccupation with her own hurt, which blocks a more realistic assessment of the situation; one can see, in a way, through her words to a shadowy guilty self-absorbed lover, whose behavior in the affair is questionable. Her lover has returned to his wife: very well, Sexton seems to think, it is somehow *her* fault, or it is a consequence of the wife's superiority. She does not seem to consider the possibility that the man who has been the object of her excited, almost delirious, passion was never, perhaps, equal to her emotion; nor does she consider—but this, too, is an element in her victim's strategy—that the man might be simply shallow, deceitful, childish, a liar. A victim of love customarily looks to himself or herself for all explanations; it is a form of colossal egotism, but a curiously innocent kind. That her former lover deceived his wife and eventually deceived her—that he is, in short, a liar—did not seem to occur to Sexton, and consequently did not draw forth poems of anger and accusation and disgust that might have more satisfactorily rounded off the experience of *Love Poems*.

The volume is prefaced by a quotation from Yeats which is not, I think, altogether appropriate, but it suggests the thematic concerns Sexton believed she had as she organized the book. One should say to himself, according to Yeats:

> I have lived many lives. I have been a slave and
> a prince. Many a beloved has sat upon my knees
> and I have sat upon the knees of many a beloved.
> Everything that has been shall be again.

(That Yeats was an influence of a sort on Sexton is clear from several of the poems, and one in particular, "Just Once," which echoes Yeats's famous "Vacillation" in which the poet, past his fiftieth birthday, suddenly experiences a mystical sense of harmony in a crowded London street. For twenty minutes, Yeats says, it seemed to him that his body "blazed" and "that I was blessèd and could bless." Sexton's poem is more complex, and sadly, less convincing, except for its predictable conclusion:

> Just once I knew what life was for.
> In Boston, quite suddenly, I understood;
> walked there along the Charles River . . .
>
> . . . .
>
> counted the stars, my little campaigners,
> my scar daisies, and knew that I walked my love
> on the night green side of it and cried
> my heart to the eastbound cars and cried
> my heart to the westbound cars and took
> my truth across a small humped bridge
> and hurried my truth, the charm of it, home
> and hoarded these constants into morning
> only to find them gone.)

Elsewhere, there are echoes of Elizabeth Bishop and Whitman, whose deleterious influence on certain strains of American poetry still continues ("In Celebration of My Uterus" with its long catalog of women imagined by Sexton, implausibly joining in a continent-wide hymn to female sexuality and fertility—

> one is in a shoe factory cursing the machine,
> one is at the aquarium tending a seal,
> one is dull at the wheel of her Ford,
> one is at the toll gate collecting,
> one is tying the cord of a calf in Arizona,
> one is straddling a cello in Russia,
> . . . and one is
> anywhere and some are everywhere and all
> seem to be singing, although some can not
> sing a note.)

The majority of the poems, however, attempt a bitterly reflective acerbity reminiscent of Sylvia Plath in *Ariel*. At times the pulse beat of Plath's discordant music is uncanny—one hears it without consciously recognizing it, and one cannot help but wonder if Sexton was altogether conscious of the influence herself. Perhaps she would have excised it had she known. "The room stinks of urine. / Only the two-headed baby / is antiseptic in her crib" (from "Eighteen Days Without You"). In the disjointed "Loving the Killer" the poet cries "Oh my Nazi, / with your S.S. sky-blue eye— / I am no different from Emily Goering." (Elsewhere there is a helpless acquiescence to a lover with a "Nazi hook.") Perhaps most direct is Sexton's statement in "Barefoot": "The surf's a narcotic, calling out, / *I am, I am, I am*, / all night long." (Compare with Plath's ". . . his blood beating the old tattoo / I am, I am, I am" from "Suicide Off Egg Rock.") "The trouble was not / in the kitchen or the tulips / but only in my head, my head," Sexton says in "The Touch," alluding to Plath's "Tulips"; but her control of her material is almost always looser than Plath's, and when she is not fuzzily "surreal" (she saw Surrealism as being merely "unconscious") she makes the mistake of being too explicit, too summary. And she has fallen into the habit—a lamentable one in Plath as well—of repeating words to fill out lines. Sometimes the repetition is mechanical, at other times it seems faintly desperate, as in "The Touch"; and it is difficult to know what to make of playful apostrophes like "Oh my love, oh my louse" from the long sequence that ends the book, "Eighteen Days Without You."

But the poems are ultimately her own. The echoes persist, but the vehemence, the decision for life, the prankish multiplication of details are solidly Sexton, as well as the conviction (almost too dogmatically sounded) that love has the miraculous power to transform the personality. Or should. Or did, once. When the memory of the love affair is least burdensome it is most effective. Mistress and lover are conspirators, rather like children. Of course they are sometimes—perhaps often—drunk ("No whatever it was we had, / no sky, no month—just booze"), but their most delightful moments are characterized by a marvelous playfulness that translates itself into some of Sexton's best poetry. It is appropriate that the volume ends with the mistress saying to her lover, "Catch me. I'm your disease," and with the imperatives of "December 18th"—

> Swift boomerang, come get!
> I am delicate. You've been gone.
> The losing has hurt me some, yet
> I must bend for you . . .
>
> . . . .
>
> Look, lout! Say yes!
> Draw me like a child. I shall need
> merely two round eyes and a small kiss.

A small o. Two earrings would be nice. Then proceed
to the shoulder. You may pause at this.

....

Draw me good, draw me warm.
Bring me your raw-boned wrist and your
strange, Mr. Bind, strange stubborn horn.
Darling, bring with this an hour of undulations, for
this is the music for which I was born.
Lock in! Be alert, my acrobat
and I will be soft wood and you the nail
and we will make fiery ovens for Jack Sprat
and you will hurl yourself into my tiny jail
and we will take a supper together and that
will be that.

In a characteristically frank memoir of her friend Sylvia Plath, "The Barfly Ought to Sing," published in *Triquarterly* (7, 1970), Anne Sexton made the claim that suicides are special people. "We talked death," she said, "and that was life for us." Unnerving, to imagine these two young and gifted and very attractive women poets exchanging—not news of their poetry, or advice, or even gossip—but details of their suicide attempts! And after Plath's successful attempt some years later, Anne Sexton wrote a poem that belongs with the most despairing and yet the most intelligent and convincing work of what is loosely called the "confessional mode." This poem is "Wanting to Die" and it is included in *Live or Die,* Sexton's third volume. Since her death we may come to think of it as her central poem, the calm, dispassionate, and coolly crafted statement that makes critics' charges of hysteria quite irrelevant:

Since you ask, most days I cannot remember.
I walk in my clothing, unmarked by that voyage.
Then the almost unnameable lust returns.

Even when I have nothing against life.
I know well the grass blades you mention,
the furniture you have placed under the sun.

But suicides have a special language.
Like carpenters they want to know *which tools*.
They never ask *why build*.

Ironically, the thirty-nine poems of Sexton's posthumous volume, *The Awful Rowing Toward God,* do set out reasons, explanations, and occasionally rueful apologies for her emotional predicament; like some of the stronger poems of *The Book of Folly* of 1972, these poems attempt not simply the poetic expression of emotion—that "unstoppered fullness" Robert Lowell praised—but intelligent and sometimes highly critical analysis of the suicidal impulse. In fact, we are mercifully not told *which tools* so much as instructed in the much more valuable *why build*. *The Awful Rowing Toward God* contains poems of superb, unforgettable power, but it would be disingenuous of any reviewer to suppose that the book will be bought and eagerly read for the excellence of its craft. (Many contemporary poets are fine craftsmen, in fact; never have so many people been capable of writing so well, and with so little possibility of being justly recognized.) The book will probably be bought because it is the posthumous volume Anne Sexton had planned and because it describes, with more candor and wit and warmth than Sylvia Plath allowed herself, the stages of the "rowing" toward what Sexton calls "God."

The volume begins with a poem called "Rowing" and ends with "The Rowing Endeth" and the "untamable, eternal, gut driven *ha-ha*" that is the triumph of the union of God and man. Between are poems of sorrow, poems of anger, poems of befuddlement and terror and love, and while some are almost too painful to read ("The Sickness Unto Death," "The Big Heart"), many are as slangy and direct as those "Eighteen Days Without You" that conclude the volume *Love Poems*. In "The Play," for instance, the poet describes herself as the only actor in the play that is her life; she knows her concerns are dismayingly solipsistic, she knows the speeches she gives are "all soliloquies" and that the audience will boo her:

> Despite that I go on to the last lines:
> To be without God is to be a snake
> who wants to swallow an elephant.
> The curtain falls.
> The audience rushes out.
> It was a bad performance.
> That's because I'm the only actor
> and there are few humans whose lives
> will make an interesting play.
> Don't you agree?

There are poets who seem to choose their surreal images with fastidious care, as if seeking physical images to describe what are primarily intellectual or even ideological beliefs; Anne Sexton, however, gives the impression of selecting from a great flood of dreamlike or nightmarish images precisely those which communicate most directly to the reader (and to the poet herself). Her painful honesty is well known. What her unsympathetic critics have charged her with—an overvaluing of her private sorrows to the exclusion of the rest of the world—seems to have been felt by Sexton herself. This sort of knowledge, however, rarely brings with it the ability to *change*. The hearty optimism of a certain kind of American temperament—these days, most obviously illustrated in the plethora of "easy" psychotherapies—is absolutely balked by the fact that some people are unchangeable despite their own deepest wishes; optimists either turn aside from the problem of "evil" (or unhealth), or deny strenuously that it is really a problem. The death-driven personality, whether fated to murder others or itself, is only "neurotic" and can be made more "healthy" by being subjected to the right treatment. And Sexton, then, can be dismissed as "sick" and her poetry dismissed as the outpouring of a pathological imagination, unless one is willing to make the risky claim, which will not be a popular one, that poets like Sexton, Plath, and John Berryman have dealt in excruciating detail with collective (and not merely individual) neuroses of our time.

It is probable that a serious artist exercises relatively little control over the choice of subjects of his or her art. The more fortunate artist is simply one who, for reasons not known, identifies powerfully with a unit larger than the self: Faulkner with his "postage stamp" of earth, Shakespeare with the glorious, astounding variety of human personality, Dostoyevsky with all of Russia. Such artists surely dramatize their own emotions, but they give life to the world outside the self by means of these emotions, and in so doing often draw up into consciousness aspects of the collective human self that would otherwise not be tapped. If this sounds like a mysterious process, it must be admitted that it is mysterious: but most artists understand it intuitively. Anne Sexton yearned for that larger experience, that rush of near-divine certainty, that the self *is* immortal; she knew it existed but she could not reach it. "The place I live in / is a kind of maze / and I keep seeking / the exit or the home" ("The Children"). Trapped within her specific, private self, she seems to have despaired of any remedy short of actual death—

> . . . I have a body
> and I cannot escape from it.
> I would like to fly out of my head,
> but that is out of the question.
> It is written on the tablet of destiny
> that I am stuck here in this human form.
> That being the case
> I would like to call attention to my problem.
>   —"The Poet of Ignorance"

> Only my books anoint me,
> and a few friends,
> those who reach into my veins.
> Maybe I am becoming a hermit,
> opening the door for only
> a few special animals?
> Maybe my skull is too crowded
> and it has no opening through which
> to feed it soup?
> Maybe I have plugged up my sockets
> To keep the gods in?
>   —"The Witch's Life"

It is a dismaying journal, not always poetry, though always hopeful of being "poetic." Critical assessment seems somehow beside the point; surely Sexton knew that these poems were not good, that they rambled, faltered, shouted where once they might have whispered, were boozily explicit where once, in the early volumes at least, they would have been enigmatic. "Frenzy" is aptly titled, and one can picture the poet in a frenzy dashing it off—

> I am not lazy.
> I am on the amphetamine of the soul.
> I am, each day,
> typing out the God
> my typewriter believes in.
> Very quick. Very intense,
> like a wolf at a live heart.

The lover, the faceless giver-of-life, is gone. Even the fairy-tale parents— the evil mother, the inexplicable father—are gone. In their place is Sexton's "God," a child's desperate fantasy, a violent projection that is both stern father and cruel lover, as well as the "body of fate" that cannot be assimilated. Suicides are indeed special people, one senses from reading Sexton, and from reading Plath and Berryman as well: they are children, they have always been children, and no matter how brilliant their minds, they are under the spell, always, of emotions they cannot guess at, and certainly cannot control. As precocious children they delight and terrify us for they strike that chord, in us, which is infantile, and which is certainly *there;* but they go on too long, their self-absorption is finally tedious, the bell jar of their preoccupations will suffocate us—as it did them. Suicide in literature is frequently cleansing: one might speculate that all works of tragedy deal with "suicide" of a kind, as impractical, unworkable, outgrown, inadequate, myopic ideas or states of mind are tested and found lacking. Oedipus's impetuosity brings about his defeat, not his buried "sin"; Lear is frankly silly and unforgivably selfish; Hippolytus's "chastity" is a prig's satisfaction at having no desire. Distance is all: the creator is not absorbed in his subject, though he may give voice to it from the inside. He is dispassionate, contemplative, removed—by the very act of writing he should be removed from the heat, the "frenzy," of inspiration. One knows perfectly well that Dostoyevsky *is* Stavrogin, though he should like to be Bishop Tikhon or Father Zossima; but one knows also that the laborious creation of *The Possessed* and *The Brothers Karamazov* has forced the author into a position of detachment that would have been impossible had the formidable, rather terrifying, challenge not been met.

Sexton, of course, could not meet this challenge, which is aesthetic and philosophical as well as—perhaps more important, in fact—psychological. She did not work to imagine a structure that would contain her own small despairing voice amid many other voices; she did not commit herself to the *labor* of such a creation. For it is a labor. It can be dismayingly difficult: one can be tempted at any point to turn back, to content oneself with the merely personal, the merely local and emotional. "Why not say what happened?" Lowell asks rhetorically, in *Day by Day*, and in general he has been applauded for acquiescing to what, in my opinion, is an imaginative and aesthetic impotence: his demon, rather like Sexton's, was not his inadequacy in his art, but a strange pride in what might be called the artlessness of the life, the old naturalistic fallacy. (Why invert? Why invert content, or even structures? Simply say what happened.)

The fallacy of such an aesthetic is that one cannot always *know* what has happened. One knows emotions, moods, subjective responses, but rarely their causes; the world becomes smaller and smaller as "external" events are greedily assimilated into a life's scenario. Everything is material for poetry precisely because nothing is given a reality of its own, an integrity—or even an existence—apart from the poet's imagination. In Sexton the experience of "God" is simply another experience of terrible, and terrifying, dependency. The self is small, ravenous for certainty, a "God-monger" that seeks an authority, however improbable, however cruel, that might help to explain the self's predicament. There are moments of contentment, even of joy, in this posthumous volume, poems like "Welcome Morning" and "What the Bird with the Human Head Said" ("Abundance is scooped from abundance, / yet abundance remains"), yet more frequently the tone is breezily fatalistic. Sexton's God is masculine: and being masculine he is inevitably outside her—in fact far away, inaccessible in this life. *God* is simply fate, imagined as an agent that might account for the poet's condition. When she rows, finally, to the Island of God, which is to say to her own death, the two of them play cards and He wins "because He holds five aces" ("The Rowing Endeth"). Sexton does not regret His victory, however—

> He starts to laugh,
> the laughter rolling like a hoop out of His mouth
> and into mine,
> and such laughter that He doubles right over me
> laughing a Rejoice-Chorus at our two triumphs.
> Then I laugh, the fishy dock laughs,
> the sea laughs. The Island laughs.
> The Absurd laughs.

There is no longer any attempt, we see, at translating emotion into coherent poetic "image." The chilling *ha-ha* of Sexton's last poem is not, as she thought, blissful and all-forgiving: it is a deliberate betrayal of the art set forth so rigorously, and with such memorable power, in the early books. The almost unnameable lust becomes, finally, a lust to destroy poetry itself.

SELF-PORTRAIT IN LETTERS

"A woman who writes feels too much, / those trances and portents!" Anne Sexton exclaimed in a poem titled "The Black Art" (in *All My Pretty*

Ones, 1961). No one who has read Sexton's poetry can doubt that she felt "too much" or at any rate excessively; what comes as a surprise is the sheer quantity of writing she did. Quite apart from the nine books of poems she completed, and the play *Mercy Street* which was never published during her lifetime, Anne Sexton wrote lengthy letters nearly every day, complete with carbon copies. At the time of her death in October 1974, she left behind some 50,000 pieces of paper and an enormous collection of memorabilia: boxes of items that constitute, according to the editors of this book, a documentary of her life.

Linda Gray Sexton, Anne's elder daughter, and Lois Ames (a professor of Social Welfare at Northeastern University who is writing the authorized biographies of both Sylvia Plath and Anne Sexton) have put together what will strike some readers as a fascinating book, and others as a possibly premature one. The difficulties the editors faced must have been prodigious. For not only were they confronted with a massive, even dispiriting quantity of letters of uneven worth; they were also confronted with the very real problem of sifting through these letters with an eye for what might be construed as an invasion of privacy by Anne's friends, acquaintances, and relatives. (And enemies. Anne's *bête noir* seems to have been James Dickey, who not only savagely reviewed one of her books for the *New York Times* but seems to have been quite ardent in his pursuit of her for a year or two afterward.)

This autobiography in letters is an extraordinarily difficult book to read, and a still more difficult book to review. How, after all, does one presume to review a life. . . ? How can one assess a "self-portrait in letters" in meaningful critical terms? Readers who admire Sexton's poetry will find much to admire in the letters, but they will also find much to cause grief; and they will surely wish that Linda Sexton and Lois Ames had edited the collection even more judiciously. (For there are innumerable letters that must have been written while Sexton was heavily drugged, or in a drunken stupor, and one very much doubts that she would have wished them printed.) Readers who have not admired the poetry will find the letters nearly impossible to read, for they not only dwell upon the poet's relationship to her art in great detail but they set forth, without the often complex strategies of that art, the same feelings—the same raw, ungovernable, inchoate emotions—that fueled it.

"Madness," Sexton said to a disturbed fan who had written to her, in 1965, "is a waste of time. It creates nothing. . . . Nothing grows from it and you, meanwhile, only grow into it like a snail." It is clear from her letters that Anne Sexton resisted her own madness, at least most of the time. She seems always to have dramatized herself—even as a child she had a wild, uncontrollable craving to be noticed—but at the same time a sterner, harsher wisdom cautioned her against succumbing to the self-consuming "energies" of the demonic. What is extraordinary about the letters, and in fact one of their redeeming features, is the tone the poet takes when she addresses correspondents who are recognizably sick. In writing to friends and acquaintances like W. D.

Snodgrass, Maxine Kumin, Lois Ames, and others who are engrossed in their own work and lives, Anne is at times astonishingly effusive; her letters to Snodgrass—"Snodsy"—are almost hysterical, and must have caused him some exasperation and pain. But letters written to emotionally unbalanced acquaintances are remarkably sober. It is as if the carapace of gay, insouciant energy were dropped, and in its place Anne Sexton speaks with the restraint of one of her own psychiatrists. To a monk who seems to have fallen in love with her, or who has at any rate suffered a violent projection of his fantasies onto her, Sexton is quick to point out that the letters she has written to him are not, in an important way, "real." In letters it is possible, she says, to be loving and lovable, more possible to reach out and to take in, "and no one really need live up to them." Having excited in the man emotions she had not anticipated, she draws back, prudently: "Oh dear God. You must listen to me, for I feel I have somehow deceived you into thinking this is really a human relationship. It is a letter relationship. . . ."

Elsewhere, in writing to one "Philip Barlow," a university professor who seems, like the young monk, to have fallen in love with an image of her, Anne is equally sober. "Yes we love each other—but it's a mirror—of sorts—it's the male of the female and the female of the male. In other words, you're me. Also I'm you. . . . This way leads us both into madness." Such a love is "sick" and a lover locked into such an obsession needs professional help. And in writing to the innumerable would-be poets who wanted her advice, and her friendship, Sexton is helpful indeed. She cautions them to discipline themselves; to labor at their craft without impatience; and to study Rilke's *Letters to a Young Poet*, one of her favorite books.

Among the many recipients of Anne's letters over the years are Maxine Kumin (of whom she says in a letter to someone else, "Thank God for Maxine. She is close by always and knows me. No one else who is within literal reach allows me to be real or to think"); Tillie Olsen, whose "Tell Me a Riddle" impressed her greatly; "Dr. Anne Clarke," a California psychiatrist with whom she seems to have identified strongly, and to whom she speaks most openly about her psychological distress and her obsession with suicide (". . . You have a certain power . . . power over what? well, life for instance . . . and death too. I guess I see [suicide] as a way of cheating death"); W. D. Snodgrass, to whom she sent many of her poems after having been his student at the Antioch Writers' Summer Conference in 1958, and whose *Heart's Needle* greatly inspired her; Robert Lowell, whose student she was in a writing seminar at Boston University, and about whom she says in a letter to Snodgrass ("I guess I forgive him for not liking me . . . because he has such a soft dangerous voice. . . . He is a good man; I forgive him for his sicknesses whatever they are. I think I will have to god [*sic*] him again; gods are so necessary and splendid and distant"); Nolan Miller of the *Antioch Review*, which was the first quality magazine to publish her poetry; Carolyn Kizer, then of *Poetry Northwest*, who took the time to criticize Anne's submissions in detail; John Holmes, whom she met in a Boston poetry workshop; Hollis Summers, whom she met at Antioch and who seems to have intrigued her because he did not succumb to her need for intimacy ("I, frankly, do not mind you not being in love with me. Really. No need to be in love with me. But must you be frightened of me?"); Frederick Morgan of *The Hudson Review*, whose early encouragement helped her greatly; Louis Simpson, whose work she admired ("I would write just like you if I could"); Philip Rahv of *The Partisan Review*, who published some of her poems; Anthony Hecht, a close friend in the early 1960s who seems also to have drawn back from Anne's intensity ("I think that I'm cross with you. . . . When you say that I am giving vent to a wild, romantic fantasy of a rather suspect kind. . . . What I meant very simply is that I love you . . . but that I'm not *in love* with you. . . . I don't dislike you for coming back with your feelings on the subject but I am very cross with you for not allowing me some room for a very female emotion that wasn't meant to bother you or tempt you . . ."); Galway Kinnell; Jon Stallworthy; Charles Newman, who invited her to participate in a special issue of *TriQuarterly* devoted to the work of Sylvia Plath; James Dickey ("I do not want or look for a *mad passionate* affair. . . . I would run to the end of town to avoid it. . . . please believe me, I do not want a lover. . . . I want a friend. . . . I cannot promise that I am geared to your kind of self," and, later: "My instincts keep going two ways about you. One says it's O.K., the other says be careful. After I met you, in New York State, I heard nothing but gossip about you. Things rather nasty . . ."); Robert Bly; Ted Hughes; C. K. Williams, one of her favorite new poets, whose first book she encouraged Houghton Mifflin to publish in 1968; George Starbuck; and Stanley Kunitz, to whom she sent *Transformations* in manuscript, in 1970, and whose praise for the experimental work was highly supportive.

The most spontaneous letters are those to her daughters Linda and Joyce (the last letter she wrote before her suicide was a tender note to Linda), and to her husband "Kayo" (Alfred Sexton II). Their marriage seems to have been, for the most part, a good one, yet Anne insisted upon a divorce in 1973, after twenty-four years of marriage; and by October 1974 she was dead.

"I wonder if the artist ever lives his life—he is so busy recreating it," Sexton said in a letter of 1972. "Only as I write do I realize myself. I don't know what that does to 'life.' " One of the difficulties with such a position—whether it is philosophical, or emotional—is that the poet's distrust of his own most powerful instincts works against the highest realization of those instincts. If one believes that artistic re-creation of one's life is in some way antithetical to life, or even peripheral to it, art itself will come to seem destructive. "Yet," says Anne Sexton in one of her last poems, "I am in love with words." Her combative relationship with herself, the near-ceaseless warring between a violent will to live and an even more violent and insidious will to die, allowed her, for a brief, intense period of time, the transcendence of genuine art. The poetry did not cause her death, but postponed it: in that sense Anne Sexton the poet was a triumph, a triumphant event in our literature. Though her later books—*The Death Notebooks, The Awful Rowing Toward God, The Book of Folly*—display a deterioration of vision and control, partly as a consequence of her drug-and-alcohol addiction, there is achievement of the highest quality in *To Bedlam and Part Way Back, All My Pretty Ones*, and *Live Or Die*.

Anne Sexton's letters are, as she knew, too breezy, too disjointed and emotional to compete with her art, and the question of whether she would have wished her letters published will probably be raised. (She *did* keep carbon copies, after all, and evidently, near the end of her life, willed to "re-create" herself through these letters—that is, explain herself, defend herself, attempt to enlist others in her feuds with relatives, friends, and professional acquaintances. One wonders, in fact, whether the poet was not consciously creating an artificial persona.) It might also be pointed out that, in order to avoid injuring people, and in order to avoid lawsuits, the editors have been forced to censor many letters, and to leave out others altogether. Consequently we learn very little about the reasons behind Anne Sexton's sudden desire for a divorce, which her husband contested; we learn nothing at all about a "disastrous love affair" she evidently had during the last years of her life. Though *Anne Sexton: A Self-Portrait in Letters* is a remarkably rich and detailed book, it does read like a novel whose final pages have been ripped out. What might the editors have done? Delay publication for many years? (A tradition that seems to be fast fading in our culture.) That the letters are, in this version, incomplete and possibly misleading cannot be helped; yet to delay publication until all the letters could be published would perhaps be quixotic, since interest in Sexton is high at the present time, and is apt to diminish as the years pass.

In the end one feels that Sexton would be pleased with this book, for it is, after all, *hers*. Her voice is there, on every page; her presence is mesmerizing, indefatigable. And she came not to care very much whether her vision was "artful" or not: she was a witness of her own life, her own destruction, and perhaps there is a communicable wisdom in the very experience of breakdown, emotional and esthetic both. How else might we interpret such poems as "The Play," in *The Awful Rowing Toward God*—

> Suddenly I stop running.
> (This moves the plot along a bit.)
> I give speeches, hundreds,
> all prayers, all soliloquies.
> I say absurd things like:
> eggs must not quarrel with stones
> or keep your broken arm inside your sleeve
> or I am standing upright
> but my shadow is crooked.
> And such and such.
> Many boos. Many boos.

If there is a kind of courage in the final, most brutal exposure of the self, the artist's presentation of himself without the qualifying guise of his art, then Anne Sexton was a highly courageous woman. One cannot read her poetry, or her letters, without being both deeply disturbed and moved.

Anne Sexton's Rowing toward God   Steven Gould Axelrod*

I met Anne Sexton once, the summer before she died in 1974. Wearing a bright yellow dress, she was gracious and incredibly lovely. Unlike other poets I've met, she refused to say unkind things about rival poets. She told me that she hated roses, that her favorite flower was the daisy, which grows wild by the side of Massachusetts roads. In my mind's eye now, in her yellow dress, she looks to me like a daisy—morally innocent, her gaiety a badge of her despair. And yet *The Awful Rowing Toward God* reveals that out of this despair grew faith. Ultimately the struggle toward belief proves the single most important fact about her life, her poetry. Wallace Stevens has written that "it can lie in the temperament of very few of us to write poetry in order to find God," but that is precisely what Anne Sexton did in her more recent books, and perhaps throughout her poetic career. In this last volume, her "awful rowing" reaches its goal.

The poems of *The Awful Rowing Toward God* are written in the free style characteristic of Sexton's later volumes. In contrast to the highly crafted poems of her first books, these poems resemble episodes of consciousness rather than completed, unified objects. Like many another American writer, she shed the coat of form in her drive toward naked truth. These "poems," then, should be seen as psychological jottings and prophetic notes. Frequently her "language fails," Sexton admits; yet in the manner of Whitman, the poems are not to be understood merely as a literary performance. They are acts of the mind in discovery of itself, its world, its God. For Sexton as for the other American prophets, from Whitman and Dickinson to Stevens and Ginsberg, poetry is a "church" and the words "whisper something holy."

The volume may be roughly divided into halves, each with its own special emphasis. The first half focuses on the poet's inner self and its painful frictions with outer environment. This section contains the kind of self-explorations we think of as typical of Sexton's art. The tone is almost unrelievedly anguished. An overwhelming, incredible self-loathing dominates her consciousness, turning every possible happiness sour. The poet thinks herself "a pig in a trenchcoat"—a swine partially disguised as a person. In other images, she describes herself as a witch, as worse than Hitler. She is internally possessed by a "gnawing pestilential rat," by "saws working

*Reprinted with permission from *Modern Poetry Studies* 6 (Autumn 1975): 187–89.

through my heart," by a "beggar" who needs to be cut out with a scissors, by a "plague," by "acid," by a "crab." Images of pain abound, as if only pain can awaken. This is a world where the day drives nails into the heart, where light pokes, where courage is "a small coal / that you kept swallowing," where holy words themselves only "pinch me / into the grave." This intolerable physical pain figures the poet's psychic pain, and has several implications. It suggests her moral horror at the evil in the world—frequently symbolized by the Nazis—and at the kindred evil she carries within her. On a related level of meaning, the pain derives from her separation from or "ignorance" of God. And finally and paradoxically, the pain is the force that drives her to God.

The peripeteia comes in "The Sickness Unto Death," the poem at the exact numerical center of the book. The spiritual condition adumbrated in the preceding poems is here retrospectively summarized:

> I kept saying:
> I've got to have something to hold on to.
> People gave me Bibles, crucifixes,
> a yellow daisy,
> but I could not touch them,
> I who was a house of bowel movement,
> I who was a defaced altar,
> I who wanted to crawl toward God
> could not move nor eat bread.
> So I ate myself.

But then comes a moment of grace: Jesus "put His mouth to mine / and gave me His air."

The second half of *The Awful Rowing* devotes itself almost exclusively to the quest for God. This theme, latent in all of Sexton's poetry and indeed in virtually all "Confessional" poetry, now at last becomes explicit and primary. The non-Christian reader may be initially discomfitted by these God poems, yet Sexton knows that and, indeed, shares the discomfiture: "As I write this sentence I too writhe." She reverses the process of Robert Lowell's "Beyond the Alps"; much against her will she arrives at the city of God. For me, the most compelling of her God poems is "Is It True?," which openly confronts the question of belief. Wanting to "pour gasoline over my evil body / and light it," she turns instead to Christ who forgives her everything. She does not know that Christ is divine, she imagines that he is, she needs to imagine that he is; and this need to imagine is itself a kind of evidence.

> Is it true?
> I can only imagine it is true
> that Jesus comes with his eggful of miracles,
> his awful death, his blackboard of graffiti.

The gift that the poet receives from Christ she shares with her reader in the poems that close the volume. It is the gift of "hope everywhere," of imaginative harmony of self, world and God, of believing oneself loved. In the last poem of the volume, "The Rowing Endeth," she has come, through pain, despite herself, to existential faith. God, she, and "the absurd" commune is laughter. In her final words she gives thanks to God for "that untamable, eternal gut-driven ha-ha / and lucky love." The resolution, as the poet herself knew, goes beyond poetry to belief. Yet even as poetry, *The Awful Rowing Toward God* is an effective piece of work, despite some characteristic unevenness. In its best passages, emotions are communicated with powerful intensity, and part of the world we have made and live in is revealed to us, as if for the first time.

Sexton excels at what I would tentatively term the "bourgeois image." Plymouth fenders, salad anchovies, batter, Coke bottles, tension headaches, Cannon towels, frozen haddock, pantsuits and names of hotel chains comprise the sensuous surface of this verse. These images are sometimes used satirically, but more often straightforwardly. In an age in which obscenities are part of the orthodox poetic diction, Sexton has daringly enlarged the resources of our literary tradition by including the truly quotidian, thus ratifying the importance of our everyday existences. In these poems, the extraordinary occurs in the language of the ordinary. Sexton's God leaves baskets covered with Cannon towels. Any list of the best poems in *The Awful Rowing* would probably include "Rowing," "The Witch's Life," "The Sickness Unto Death," "The Wall," "Is It True?," "Frenzy," and "The Rowing Endeth." It is consoling to know—and to think that she herself knew—that in these poems written at the end of her life Anne Sexton was writing as well as she ever had written.

"That Awful Rowing"   Katha Pollitt*

Like Sylvia Plath, with whom she is often paired, Anne Sexton arouses strong feelings of popular adulation and critical unease. How could it have been otherwise? At a time when American poetry was nearly as male-dominated as football, she wrote frankly, extravagantly and without apology about the experience of women. Scarcely less important, she was a democrat practicing the most snobbish of arts. While most of her colleagues were scholars and critics and translators with university affiliations, she was a junior-college dropout and suburban matron who began writing poetry after watching a television program called *How to Write a Sonnet*. With her recurrent bouts of madness, her suicide attempts (she finally succeeded in 1974), her flamboyant sexuality and her vibrant physical presence on the poetry-reading circuit, she fit as no poet since Dylan Thomas the popular stereotype of the self-destructive genius—beautiful, damned and oh-so-

*Reprinted with permission from the *Nation* 233 (21 Nov. 1981): 533–37.

sensitive. It was a role she exploited to the hilt. Her books, exhaustively documenting her painful childhood, difficult marriage and mental break-downs, sold 20,000 copies and more; she published poems in *Playboy;* she gave readings to packed auditoriums with a rock group backing her up. Lowell, Jarrell and Snodgrass had readers; Sexton had fans.

Time has muted the appeal of this image. Suicide and madness are less voguish these days, for one thing—perhaps the public self-destruction of so many postwar poets, male and female, has been a cautionary lesson. Then, too, the progress of feminism has made the suicide of gifted women seem less a romantic triumph of the will than a sorry failure of the same. (The women's movement came too late for Sexton, who admired its goals but could not internalize its values, a combination of attitudes succinctly expressed in the nickname she gave herself: Ms. Dog.) The 16-year-old girl who slept with Sexton's poems under her pillow in 1972 is probably in law school today.

Finally, thanks largely to Sexton's own influence, it is no longer shock-ing for a woman to write poems about menstruation or her uterus or abortion—or, for that matter, about erotic joy, of which Sexton also had her share. No doubt many critics still wince in private at women poets who claim for themselves the sexual frankness long ago claimed by their brothers, but they are much less likely to wince in print, and when they do they look squeamish rather than authoritative. When Patti Smith can be compared to Rimbaud in the *New York Times Book Review,* anything goes.

As if to ratify that cultural shift, here is this eminently respectable-looking tome, a whopping 600-plus pages containing the eight books Sexton prepared for publication, the two posthumous collections edited by her daughter Linda Gray Sexton, six hitherto uncollected poems and a graceful, sympathetic and intelligent introduction by the poet Maxine Kumin, who was Sexton's close friend. If you are a fan or a library, you will doubtless want to rush out and get your copy. If you are a lover of poetry or a book reviewer, you may try to read your way straight through. I caution against this, though. There are many beauties here—Sexton wrote as many tight, precise, bril-liantly associative and emotionally subtle poems as any number of poets with more secure reputations. But she also wrote dozens and dozens and *dozens* of poems that are histrionic, verbose, flaccid, mechanical, sentimental, man-nered and very, very boring. While this melancholy ratio is not surprising, or even, perhaps, very interesting—it's *hard* to write a good poem—the sheer quantity of inferior work does tend to dull one's response to the gems. One puts down this enormous book with the nagging feeling that all along a slim volume of verse was trapped inside it.

And yet, the gems are there. Sexton's poems about her hospitalizations, for instance, are sadder, humbler, less literary than Lowell's—closer, one feels, to the inmate's sense of infantilization in the face of psychiatric author-ity and the madness itself. There are no night watchmen reading "The Mean-ing of Meaning" in Sexton's dreary mental wards:

> Wait Mister. Which way is home?
> They turned the light out
> and the dark is moving in the corner.
> There are no sign posts in this room,
> four ladies, over eighty,
> in diapers every one of them.
> La la la, Oh music swims back to me
> and I can feel the tune they played
> the night they left me
> in this private institution on a hill.
>   ("Music Swims Back to Me")

The sheer range of Sexton's voice is impressive. There is the restrained, formal grief of "The Double Image," with its delicate probings of mother-daughter connections; the dazzling purity of "The Starry Night"; the sardonic, precise diction of "Wanting to Die":

> Even then I have nothing against life.
> I know well the grass blades you mention,
> The furniture you have placed against the sun.
>
> But suicides have a special language.
> Like carpenters they want to know *which tools*
> They never ask *why build*.

She could be witty, too, as in "Housewife":

> Some women marry houses.
> It's another kind of skin; it has a heart,
> a mouth, a liver and bowel movements.
> The walls are permanent and pink.
> See how she sits on her knees all day,
> faithfully washing herself down.
> Men enter by force, drawn back like Jonah
> into their fleshy mothers.
> A woman *is* her mother.
> That's the main thing.

All the poems I've mentioned come from her first three books, *To Bedlam and Part Way Back* (1960), *All My Pretty Ones* (1962) and *Live or Die* (1966), for which she won a Pulitzer Prize. Most of Sexton's memorable work is to be found in these early books: "The Moss of His Skin," "In the Deep Museum," "The Black Art," "Her Kind," "And One for My Dame," "The Wedding Night," "Little Girl, My String Bean, My Lovely Woman." The list goes on and on. And most of this good work pays homage, however faintly, to some sort of traditional form.

Like most poets of her era, Sexton began as an apprentice to poetic tradition. She was a daring rhymester ("The Double Image" gives us *Glouces-ter / lost her* and *cancer / answer*) and, on occasion, a brilliantly colloquial reworker of classical forms and themes—see her biting sonnet on the Icarus myth, "To a Friend Whose Work Has Come to Triumph." Sexton moved away from form as she matured, as most poets do, but without having worked out ways of achieving in free verse what form makes so easy: the use of structure and sound to delimit a drama, intensify emotion and clarify meaning. With some notable exceptions—"Housewife" or "In Celebration of My Uterus," with its high-spirited echoes of "I Hear America Singing"—Sexton's free verse, early and late, is lax and rambling and self-indulgent. She starts a poem pages before announcing its subject, or she starts on one theme and wanders off into another. She uses language carelessly, relying on repetition, that bluntest of instruments, instead of on aural patterns—assonance, off-rhyme, half-rhyme, rhythms and pauses. Rather than use images that relate so as to deepen them all, she uses arbitrary, throwaway similes reminiscent of Roethke at his most annoying ("I . . . brought forth young girls / to grunt like fish"; "My long brown legs, / sweet dears as good as spoons").

Consider this passage, toward the end of "Pain for a Daughter," whose central event is the crushing of her daughter's foot by a beloved horse:

> Blind with fear, she sits on the toilet,
> her foot balanced over the washbasin,
> her father, hydrogen peroxide in hand,
> performing the rites of the cleansing.
> She bites on a towel, sucked in breath,
> sucked in and arched against the pain,
> her eyes glancing off me where
> I stand at the door, eyes locked
> on the ceiling, eyes of a stranger,
> and then she cries . . .
> *Oh my God, help me!*

This is purest bathos. Note the clumsy repetitions, the loose grammar, the language at once inflated and bland ("blind with fear," "performing the rites of the cleansing"), the ploddingly literal recounting of action, like instructions from a first-aid manual (First, sit on the toilet and balance the foot over the washbasin. Next, apply hydrogen peroxide). All this in a poem that has already taken time to inform us that Sexton's daughter "visits the neighbors' stable, / our acreage not zoned for barns"! It's as though Plath had begun "Cut," her poem about cutting her thumb while slicing an onion, with a description of a trip to the supermarket and ended it with a recipe for onion soup.

Speaking of Plath, what about "Sylvia's Death," surely one of the most florid acts of self-promotion ever written under cover of an elegy for a friend:

> Thief—
> how did you crawl into,
>
> crawl down alone
> into the death I wanted so badly and for so long. . . .

"Pain for a Daughter" and "Sylvia's Death" are not late poems, as it happens, and the faults they exemplify multiply wildly after *Live or Die*. Sexton was a prolific writer—Kumin is careful to point out that Sexton often revised painstakingly, but she also tells us that she frequently dashed off three or four poems in a single day—and much of her late work reads like first drafts, at once unfocused and glib.

Even here, though, there are moments. *Transformations*, Sexton's Freudian-suburban-chic modernizations of fairy tales, has humor and verve and images of exquisite strangeness and surreality ("Beauty is a simple passion, / but oh my friends in the end / you will dance the fire dance in iron shoes"). But you don't have to be Christian to be revolted by "The Jesus Papers," an embarrassing farrago of smarmy religiosity and cheap sophistication: "It was the year / of the How To Sex Book, / the Sensuous Man and Woman were frolicking / but Jesus was fasting. / He ate his celibate life. . . ." Ick! Even worse are "The Divorce Papers," which put forward at great length the comparison, borrowed from Plath, of Sexton's husband to a Nazi and herself to a Jew.

The equation of marital failure with the genocide of millions is both monstrous and telling. In the late work, Sexton lavishes the same level of imprecise feverishness on anything and everything, from God to her therapist, from the signs of the zodiac to the Vietnam War dead. And one realizes with growing horror that these vastly disparate occasions really *are* all one for her, for they are all merely the flickering projections of a grotesque and seamless solipsism. In Sexton's case, at least, Sartre was wrong and Milton was right. Hell was not other people. It was herself.

Well, perhaps it is too much to ask that her work be larger-spirited and more stringent than it is. Poetry for Sexton was always a matter of half-art, half-therapy. "I hook into my mood and drain it onto the paper," she wrote of her prodigious output of letters, and she might have said the same thing about many of her poems. If one can see her as an artist who squandered her talent by refusing to discipline it—out of vanity or hunger for easy celebrity or sheer self-absorption—one can also see her as an anguished, mentally ill woman who managed out of her inner chaos to make a few poems that work as literature and as safety valves, a few momentary stays against confusion, not just for herself but for the reader as well.

Both of these assessments are right. Critics often finds themselves quoting F. Scott Fitzgerald's famous remark that there are no second acts in American lives, and Sexton is squarely in the tradition of writers whose careers are a long downhill slide from early achievement. But Jarrell provides a kinder epitaph. "A good poet," he said, "is someone who manages, in a lifetime of standing out in thunderstorms, to be struck by lightning five or six times; a dozen or two dozen times and he is great." Never mind the numbers, or whether they were evenly spaced out over the course of her life. Anne Sexton did her standing out in thunderstorms. Her rain-soaked poems will vanish. The lightning-struck ones will remain.

Poet of Weird Abundance
[Excerpts]
Diane Wood Middlebrook*

When Anne Sexton's posthumous *Complete Poems* came out four years ago, poet Katha Pollitt summarized the negative judgment many critics arrived at in their reviews: "the sheer quantity of inferior work does tend to dull one's response to the gems. One puts down this enormous book with the nagging feeling that all along a slim volume of verse was trapped inside it."[1] Contemporary poets tend to be assessed by the carat: prized for glitter, expense, durability and for scale that permits resetting in an anthology. As Pollitt says, "the gems are there" in Sexton, too.

Yet the appearance of a complete poems also presents an opportunity to pose questions about a writer whose entire body of work is the necessary critical context. How are the gems related to surrounding poems? Is the un-gemlike work inferior as art, or does it represent different artistic goals? Sexton's method of writing, which she referred to as "milking the unconscious,"[2] often produced a loosely-structured poetry dense with simile, freaked with improbable associations. In a poem addressed to James Wright, Sexton herself acknowledged she knew the effect offended certain tastes: "There is too much food and no one left over / to eat up all the weird abundance" ("The Black Art"). Weird: uncanny, magical, unconventional. While some of Sexton's most admired poems work, like little machines, on well-oiled armatures of rhythm or rhyme (such as "All My Pretty Ones," "The Starry Night," "Wanting to Die"), others equally powerful depend on manic or despairing or ecstatic cascades of association ("The Furies," "O Ye Tongues") that flow like an open spigot. The gems, or closed forms, tend to be early; the looser style, later. In this collection, the reader can watch Sexton evolve her second style as a way of exploring a changing relation to her subject matter.

Sexton's *Complete Poems* is a compilation of the eight books she saw into print, plus an edited collection of work left in manuscript at the time of her death; Sexton's good friend Maxine Kumin supplies a valuable introduction. The early poetry (*To Bedlam and Part Way Back*, 1960; *All My Pretty Ones*, 1962) holds up very well. But as this volume shows, Anne Sexton made bolder exploration of her lifelong subject—her experiences of madness—in later work, beginning with the volume *Live or Die* (1966). Mining the realm of the unconscious as she had been taught by both psychotherapy and contemporary writing, after 1962 Sexton became increasingly preoccupied with the psychological and social consequences of inhabiting a female body.

Because Sexton's writing seems so personal she is often labeled a "confessional" poet and grouped (to her disadvantage) with poets such as Lowell, Berryman, Roethke, and Plath. But Sexton resisted the label "confessional";

*Reprinted with permission from *Parnassus* 12, no. 2; 13, no. 1 (1985): 293–96, 301–2, 305–6, 308, 312–14.

she preferred to be regarded as a "storyteller."[3] To emphasize that she considered the speaking "I" in her poetry as a literary rather than a real identity, Sexton invariably opened her public performances by reading the early poem "Her Kind." These are the first and last stanzas:

> I have gone out, a possessed witch,
> haunting the black air, braver at night;
> dreaming evil, I have done my hitch
> over the plain houses, light by light:
> lonely thing, twelve-fingered, out of mind.
> A woman like that is not a woman, quite.
> I have been her kind.

> . . .

> I have ridden in your cart, driver,
> waved my nude arms at villages going by,
> learning the last bright routes, survivor
> where your flames still bite my thigh
> and my ribs crack where your wheels wind.
> A woman like that is not ashamed to die.
> I have been her kind.

No matter what poetry she had on an evening's agenda, Sexton offered this persona as a point of entry to her art. "I" in the poem is a disturbing, marginal female whose power is associated with disfigurement, sexuality, and magic. But at the end of each stanza, "I" is displaced from sufferer onto storyteller. With the lines "A woman like that . . . I have been her kind" Sexton conveys the terms on which she wishes to be understood: not victim, but witness and witch.

The witch-persona of Sexton's poetry is the voice Sexton invented to tell the story of her changing relationship to a severe, incurable, but apparently undiagnosable malady. She was born in 1928 in Wellesley, Massachusetts, and lived all her life in the suburbs of Boston. Married at age nineteen to a man in the wool business, Sexton had two daughters. Severe depression following the birth of her second child deepened into a permanent mental illness for which she was treated by psychiatrists for the rest of her life. She died by suicide of carbon monoxide poisoning in 1974. Her professional interest in poetry began during the first phase of her illness, in 1956. Intensified by the death of her parents in 1959, the illness was the fixed point of reference by which she measured the reality of love, the practice of poetry, and the possibility of spiritual redemption.

Sexton's *Complete Poems* yields most when read as if it contained a narrative: an account of a woman cursed with a desire to die. Why is she different from other women? Where did the curse come from? A story line with a beginning, middle, and end takes shape in *Complete Poems* as Sexton systematically exhausts a set of culturally acceptable explanations for the condition of her kind. These are, first, a psychiatric explanation; later, a sociological explanation; and finally a spiritual explanation.

The story begins with the discovery of the poet in the sick person. The narrator of Sexton's first book is a woman " part way back" from Bedlam—that is, not yet restored to the family home as wife and mother—contemplating what took her to the mental hospital: the preference for suicide over motherhood as she had learned that role from her own mother ("The Double Image"). Bedlam has been a school which taught a valuable lesson: the power of signs.

> I tapped my own head;
> it was glass, an inverted bowl.
>
> . . .
>
> if you turn away
> because there is no lesson here
> I will hold my awkward bowl,
> with all its cracked stars shining
> like a complicated lie.
> ("For John, Who Begs Me
> Not to Enquire Further")

From now on, she will be a poet of the tapped head: the mad housewife.

Condensed into the metaphor of the broken kitchen bowl are most of the meanings Sexton associates with her own liberation into poetry. Before she tapped meanings from her head, the bowl—her womanly identity—revealed but enclosed her (like Plath's bell jar); only through costly breakage did the identity begin to shine with complex significance. Breakage ruined the bowl for kitchen use but endowed it with a more precious moral utility. Further, the act of offering her own breakage as a gift shifted her relation both to her suffering and to the beholder. In the metaphor of the bowl whose cracks become stars, Sexton avows belief that her experience has been redeemed by its transformation into the social medium of language. "Star" in her personal mythology will from now on designate that place—the poetic symbol—where the language of private suffering grows radiant and magically ambiguous.

Sexton began writing poetry as a form of therapy, at her doctor's suggestion. In her first two books, she uses a good many references to this therapy and occasionally speaks of herself almost objectively as a case history. These are her most admired books. They are also her most "confessional" books in that they establish that her maladjustment as a woman is to be her subject as a poet.

By 1962 Sexton's poetry had won a respectful audience. But as a psychiatric patient she had experienced many setbacks and relapses. She had changed as an artist; as a sick woman, she did not change: repetition of destructive patterns was one of the symptoms of her illness. To survive as a poet meant to attain another, a less reportorial relation to the subject of her pathology. Beginning with poems written for her third volume, *Live or Die*, Sexton gradually abandoned the polarity sick / well which gives underlying structure to the poems of *Bedlam* and *Pretty Ones*. In the poetry of *Live or Die* Sexton begins to explore the suspicion that what she suffers from is femaleness itself, and is probably incurable. "—I'm no more a woman / than Christ was a man," she says in a dream ("Consorting with Angels," *Live or Die*). Behind this claim are questions that eventually dominate her last, religious poems: what kinds of social significance has *her* suffering? Is it too specifically female to contain spiritual meaning? Can a woman speak for Man? More and more for Sexton the problematic will not lie between being insane and being healthy, but within being female. To be female is to be defective. . . .

In my reading of Sexton's *Complete Poems*, *Love Poems* (1969) and *Transformations* (1971) form a dyad. *Love Poems* exposes the dilemma of the female poet trying to write within the conventions of the literary genre of love poetry; *Transformations* explains this dilemma by situating sexual love in its social context: the marriage contract that stabilizes the social order. Both have an unsettling, masochistic tone. The speaker of *Love Poems* experiences her body as a hoard of attributes, desirable only in dismemberment. "Love" is the anxious energy she feels as her body parts come to life under the prospective or actual gaze of a man:

> For months my hand had been sealed off
> in a tin box.
>
> . . .
>
> It lay there like an unconscious woman
> fed by tubes she knew not of.
>
> . . .
>
> Oh, my carpenter,
> the fingers are rebuilt.
> They dance with yours.
> They dance in the attic and in Vienna.
> My hand is alive all over America.
>
> ("The Touch")

The woman in sexual relation to a man becomes his construct. Heart, hand, clitoris, breast, mouth, womb become, under a man's attention, "households" ("That Day"), "cities of flesh" ("Mr. Mine"), "the boards, / the roof, the removable roof" ("You All Know the Story of the Other Woman"). Between her legs, "the woman / is calling her secrets, little houses, / little tongues that tell you" ("Barefoot").

Transformations also presents women as some of their parts; but since Sexton adopts here the plots of fairy tales from Grimm, by which children are instructed in the repression and displacement of libido, the consciousness is perhaps more acceptable than it feels in the radically masochistic *Love Poems*. The tale-teller of *Transformations* is "a middle-aged witch, me"—the woman who has done her hitch over the plain houses but is not a woman quite. She designates as the chosen auditor of these stories a boy of sixteen ("He is sixteen and he wants some answers. / He is each of us") who has found a gold key and is about to learn the use of it.

> Its secrets whimper
> like a dog in heat.
> He turns the key.
> Presto!
> It opens this book of odd tales.

These narratives are adapted directly from Grimm; what Sexton underscores in retelling is the phallic key. The wisecracking witch supplies prologues which emphasize roles and strategies within the system of exchange where sexuality is the coin circulated among the generations to replenish the family and define differences between masculine and feminine identities. As in "Cinderella:"

> Cinderella and the prince
> lived, they say, happily ever after,
> like two dolls in a museum case
> never bothered by diapers or dust,
> never arguing over the timing of an egg,
> never telling the same story twice,
> never getting a middle-aged spread,
> their darling smiles pasted on for eternity.
> Regular Bobbsey Twins.
> That story.

Sexton said *Transformations* was "as much about me" as any of her first-person lyrics, and it is. Yet in neither *Love Poems* or *Transformations* is the pathological conceived as merely personal. If Sexton's *Complete Poems* can be read as a woman's story of her wish to die, these explore the death wish as a response to the emptiness of sexuality experienced as a commodity—its repetitiousness, its fetishes.

In the last three books Sexton saw through publication, another appetite emerges: the hunger for redemption. Sexton reformulates, this time in religious terms, her oldest questions about the origins and meaning of her wish to die. The dyad of mother and daughter, and the oedipal triangle, scrutinized psychiatrically in earlier work, return to these volumes as potential sources of grace. In one of Sexton's most imaginative inventions, regression becomes a metaphor for spiritual quest.

The Book of Folly reintroduces the theme of the mother's power of cursing or curing a sick daughter. Sexton had, in effect, two mothering figures in early childhood, and both have roles to play in Sexton's late poems.

Great-aunt Anna Dingley, the loving "Nana" of Sexton's early childhood, went insane and was institutionalized shortly after Anne told her about kissing a boyfriend at age thirteen. Sexton thus associated her own sexual development with her spinster aunt's decline, and recreated the episode in numerous poems (see, especially, "Some Foreign Letters," "Rapunzel," "The Nana-Hex") as well as in her play *Mercy Street*, in which the maiden aunt witnesses an incestuous episode with the father. In *Folly*, Sexton's yearning to recover the "good mother" lost first to insanity and then to death takes the form of desire for regression to the period before the heterosexual kiss divided them. . . .

In this world both symbolic and real, it is no more innocuous to be male, of course. The three ambitious sequences that end *Folly*—"The Death of the Fathers," "Angels of the Love Affair," "The Jesus Papers"—can be read as progressive confrontations with father figures, motivated by Sexton's defect-haunted sense of herself as a woman. If to mother a daughter is to press her into female roles, so to father a daughter is to expose her to male desire. "The Death of the Fathers" revisits old subject matter—young Anne Harvey's tender fascination with her father Ralph Churchill Harvey—treated in the elegiac lyrics of the earlier volumes, most poignantly in "All My Pretty Ones," "Young," "And One for My Dame." But by the time of writing *Folly*, Sexton has reduced the dead father to a mere symbolic shadow of himself. In *Folly*'s "Death of the Fathers," he stands for the unattainable object of desire, the lover who might give her both safety and sex. But above all, he is the man she can't have: first because he's her father; again because he's a drunkard; then because he's dead; and now, when Sexton is 42, because his authenticity has been challenged by a usurper, a man claiming to have been her mother's lover. By 1971, of course, Sexton's memory of Ralph Churchill Harvey has been much mediated by years of psychotherapy. But in any case by age 42 a woman's relationship to her father, even a relationship disfigured by memories or fantasies of incest, takes its place in a social realm larger than family life.

In *The Book of Folly* this realm is theological. Sexton's most inventive explanation of femaleness in the scheme of things occurs in "The Jesus Papers," the sequence of nine poems that ends *Folly*. . . .

In Sexton's version of Christian theology, Christ's death, like her own deathwish, is meaningful to others as a source of symbolisms. For God does not dispense meaning. He dispenses in infancy the hunger for meaning, and he endows the earth with meaning-makers. In Sexton as in Christ the sufferer and the symbol-maker meet: she is the hungry woman we eat as we read her words.

These, in any case, are the symbolisms carried over into Sexton's last two books: *The Death Notebooks* and *The Awful Rowing Toward God*. The baby drawn "out of the hollow water," above, returns in *Death Notebooks* as "the death baby." Found, shockingly, in the refrigerator "between the mayonnaise and the bacon," later put among dogs as their food, the death baby is

Sexton's symbol for her identity as a poet at this time. Most obviously, it represents her suicide wish, born horribly within the conventions and controls of a quiet family life in the suburbs. As horribly, the death baby represents the marketing of poetry expressing her suicide wish: it puts food on the table. Beyond these, it stands for her spiritual hunger, the desire for connection expressed in offering the breast and in taking the breast. Particularly in the sequence titled "The Death Baby," but throughout this volume, the speaker is alternately infant and mother fused in an act of rocking, symbolizing both the rhythms of maternal care and the rhythms of the poetic lines which are Sexton's sacrificial offering. . . .

Sexton's firmest poems in the volume *The Death Notebooks* are built on the symbolisms radiating from this infant identity condensing hunger / sacrifice / poetry. In both the "Death Baby" sequence and, further on, in the "Furies" sequence, the successes arise from the startling originality and intelligence with which Sexton draws on regression as a source of imagery. "The Furies" appears occasionally to owe something to Theodore Roethke's sequence "The Lost Son," and the final sequence, "O Ye Tongues," is modeled after Christopher Smart's "Jubilate Agno." In both cases the models are structural, and have served to free Sexton's characteristic strength: access to the matrix of symbolism, the infant psyche from which she retrieved her subject matter throughout life. . . .

Arriving at the end of Sexton's *Complete Poems* brings me to the question of merit. Sexton was in many ways an interesting writer; but was she an inferior poet?—Inferior, say, to her mentor W. D. Snodgrass, her teacher Robert Lowell, her friends James Wright and Sylvia Plath, her Boston peers Adrienne Rich and Denise Levertov?

As I have been suggesting, I find Sexton a startlingly original and valuable artist. But Sexton differs from members of this group in two important ways that make it difficult to rank her among these other writers. First, she was not an intellectual. Sexton had only a high school education; she got her training as a poet in workshops. Though she had a quick mind and read widely, her thinking was intuitive rather than systematic. She did not identify herself with a literary tradition, she did not measure herself in terms of precursors, she did not acquire a critical language by which to classify and discriminate. Hers is not a poetry of ideas—aesthetic, political, philosophical, or historical.

Second, she stopped writing the kind of short lyric that remains coin of the realm in American poetry: the lyric of perfect economy composed according to an exacting formal standard, whether in meter or free verse. Critics still praise Sexton's early work for its control of the materials of disorder by means of formal effects she dismissed as "tricks." Manuscripts of early poems reveal that Sexton often began by setting herself a design problem: a stanza template with rhyme positions designated "a, b, c," etc.; then she would write a poem into the mould. She continued this practice, with good results, through 1962: her workshop years.

As I have been arguing, Sexton's later style developed out of the demands of her subject matter: accounting for madness. The exploratory, associational method she devised gave priority to the implacable structure of unconscious processes. This method is most successful in such poems as "O Ye Tongues," "The Jesus Prayers," "The Furies," "The Death of the Fathers," "The Death Baby," *Transformations*—works where the traces of a narrative adumbrate a boundary of reference within which to rationalize the flow of association. For much of Sexton's *Complete Poems*, the horizon or story line is, of course, autobiographical, focused on Sexton's attraction to death. Sexton's *Complete Poems* might be described as a psycho-narrative in verse, to which each poem is a contribution.

Moreover, the type of poem Sexton evolved was probably an inevitable creation in mid-century American poetry. It articulates the dilemma of a female recipient of certain ideas about women's place in the social order; it invests this dilemma in a single persona, a performing voice. The contemporary writings of Sylvia Plath and Adrienne Rich offer perhaps the closest analogues to Sexton's work, since their own dilemmas were equally privileged and middle class. As young *women*, all three had embraced prevailing ideologies about women's roles. All three of them seem to have been excessively susceptible to highly conventional expectations, tormented by questions about whether they were "good" daughters, students, mothers, wives. As young *artists* they had to gain recognition in a prestige system condescending to women, and the conflicts they experienced between the roles of woman and artist fueled their development. In fact, the gender specificity of much of their poetry helps us see how specifically "masculine" were the concerns of peers such as Lowell, Snodgrass, Berryman, Wright, Roethke, Ginsberg—who struggled to attain spiritual authority in the postwar consumer society littered with unusable masculine stereotypes.

But for Plath and Rich, the male-identified literary tradition eventually suggested models for transcendence uncongenial to Sexton. Both Plath and Rich essentially revised, for women's use, the poetics of romanticism which centers the poem in a visionary ego. Plath adopted the voice of a maenad; Rich evolved a powerfully personal voice of informed social criticism.

Sexton's voice remained unembarrassedly domestic. She tested notions about self and God against feelings schooled in repression, and her poems do not transcend, they explore this repression. Sexton's art celebrates word-magic, buffoonery, regression, "milking the unconscious," as inexhaustible sources of resistance to the deadly authority of the stereotypes constraining adult women's lives. Sexton's artistry was to achieve a mode of expression for this particular female consciousness, expression at once intimate and theatrical. Her audiences, mostly women, responded to that voice as the manifestation of a condition they had previously felt to be wholly personal and interior. Suddenly, poetry had expanded to acknowledge a whole new citizenry: the middle-class American woman beginning to seek liberation from confinement in domestic roles. As American poetry slowly incorporates a feminist consciousness, Sexton's work seems uncannily ahead of its time. It seems bound to endure at least as long as the social and psychological dilemmas that inspired her.

Notes

1. *The Nation*, November 21, 1981, p. 534.

2. To Barbara Kevles, for an interview in *Paris Review*, 1968, Sexton remarked, "The poetry is often more advanced, in terms of my unconscious, than I am. Poetry, after all, milks the unconscious. The unconscious is there to feed it little images, little symbols, the answers, the insights I know not of." This interview is reprinted as "The Art of Poetry: Anne Sexton" in *Anne Sexton: The Artist and Her Critics*, ed. J. D. McClatchy (Bloomington: Indiana University Press, 1978), p. 5.

3. Ibid., *passim*.

Essays

The Achievement of Anne Sexton

Greg Johnson*

> When we must deal with problems, we instinctively resist trying the way that leads through obscurity and darkness. We wish to hear only of unequivocal results, and completely forget that these results can only be brought about when we have ventured into and emerged again from darkness. . . .
>
> —Carl Jung, *The Stages of Life*

I

At the heart of Anne Sexton's poetry is a search for identity, and her well-known infatuation with death—the cause of her rather notorious fame, and the apparent reason her work is often dismissed as beneath serious consideration—has little to do with this search; in her best work, in fact, it is most often an annoying irrelevancy, however potent it seems in its occasional command of the poet's psyche. Quite simply, Sexton's poetry is a poetry of life, and if her work is "confessional" at times, or even most of the time, this does not mean that the poet's confessions (the word itself is misleading) necessarily describe experiences ridden with guilt or pain. This is where Sexton's poetry diverges so dramatically from that of Sylvia Plath, of whom she is frequently seen as a kind of epigonic follower. Plath mythologizes death with great power and succinctness, and places herself at the center of a myth whose message is "blackness—blackness and silence"; her vision is brutally nihilistic, and she embraces it willingly. Plath's struggle is that of the mythmaker—primarily artistic rather than personal, since the personal self is mercilessly pared away in her poetry (as are all other selves) in deference to the controlling myth. Anne Sexton, on the other hand, speaks longingly and lovingly of a world of health, of childlike wholeness—a world toward which she struggles valiantly and against insuperable odds. To understand her poetry as a record of this struggle, and as a testament to its value and importance, is to appreciate its special relevance to the contemporary world, a world of increasing disjunction between personal and social selves and one

*Reprinted with permission from the *Hollins Critic* (June 1984): 1–13.

whose chaotic, literally "maddening" effect on the individual mind Anne Sexton manages to convey with that blend of craft and vulnerability that is her special magic.

Unlike Plath, and certainly unlike Robert Lowell—with whom her name is also frequently and pointlessly linked—Sexton is a Primitive, an extraordinarily intense artist who confronts her experience with unsettling directness, largely innocent of "tradition" and privately developing an idiom exactly suited to that experience. As Louis Simpson remarked after the publication of her first book, "This then is a phenomenon . . . to remind us, when we have forgotten in the weariness of literature, that poetry can happen." The reader's sense of the direct and seemingly spontaneous quality of Sexton's earliest volumes—*To Bedlam and Part Way Back* (1960), *All My Pretty Ones* (1962) and *Live or Die* (1966)—can partially be explained by noting that she first began writing poetry, at the age of twenty-eight, as a form of personal therapy, a way of formalizing past traumas and of coping with an increasing sense of disorientation in her conventional role of suburban wife and mother. Her emotional instability, including her suicidal impulses, contributed to the immediacy, rawness and power of much of the poetry. This kind of therapy no doubt helped the poet in her personal life, but what is heroic in Sexton's case, and particularly relevant to her readers, is the earnestness and scrupulosity with which she mastered her craft, developed her highly original voice, and set about the task of communicating her experience to others. That Anne Sexton herself later succumbed to the "weariness of literature"—her later work, on the whole, is distinctly inferior to her early poetry, and verges at times on self-parody—and finally to her own destructive impulses, does not diminish the value and irresistible power of her finest achievements, which speak to us in a voice by turns inspired and beleaguered, joyful and aggrieved, lost in the confusions of self but found, ultimately, in her masterful articulation of her experience as a whole, a complex experience which serves as a painfully truthful mirror of the age.

II

Sexton's first two volumes have much in common, both in their multifaceted handling of the identity theme and in their adherence to rather strict poetic forms. In both there is a constructive relationship between the deeply painful, inchoate materials—experiences in a mental institution, the loss of the poet's parents, and unceasing struggle to define her own selfhood—and the restraining, masterful form of the poems themselves. There is little sense that the poet is arbitrarily forcing her experiences into rigid, inappropriate shapes, primarily because she convinces us that she has pierced to the core of those experiences to discover shapes inherent in them; the formal, measured quality of the verse not only indicates the poet's necessary caution in dealing with her turbulent materials, but also establishes a crucial distance from which she may safely view her continuing struggle and present it to her readers in palatable form. Yet the controlled, meditative voice of these early poems is frequently mingled with an openly vulnerable, "confessional" voice, one which conveys genuine, childlike experiences of pain and terror. The poems are neither songs of innocence nor experience, but continually oscillate between conflicting states of mind, admitting continued disorientation while simultaneously creating an impressive poetic order.

An important difference between the first two books should be recognized, however. *To Bedlam and Part Way Back* comprises an ordering of a specific, urgent experience—the descent into madness and a partial return—while *All My Pretty Ones* broadens from this painful but rich experience to consider more general themes of loss (especially the loss of parents) and upon an explicit need to define the poet's self in terms of the world. Although Sexton's books describe an ongoing personal development and flow naturally one into the other, each of the early volumes has a distinct identity and merits separate discussion. As Geoffrey Hartman has noted, *To Bedlam and Part Way Back* is not merely a collection of poems but "truly a *book*," and there is ample evidence that Sexton organized the volume with meticulous care. The shorter lyrics in Part One deal with a cluster of obsessive themes, all related to the poet's search for identity, while the pair of long, meditative poems in Part Two achieve a tentative but emotionally satisfying resolution.

Anne Sexton expresses concern about her female identity in a way which links her, especially in her first book, to other American female poets. Many of these poets initiate the search for identity by complaining, in strikingly analogous language, of an original and mysterious feeling of loss. "A loss of something ever felt I," wrote Emily Dickinson in only one of her many expressions of this idea, and Sylvia Plath, in her long poem "Three Women," voices a similar lament: "What is it I miss? / Shall I ever find it, whatever it is?" Sexton's tone, however, is not wistful but strident, calmly determined "to question this diminishing" ("Funnel"); in "The Lost Ingredient" she laments the seeming futility of her search:

> Today is made of yesterday, each time I steal
> toward rites I do not know, waiting for the lost
> ingredient, as if salt or money or even lust
> would keep us calm and prove us whole at last.

"Am I still lost? Once I was beautiful," she says in a poem addressed to her psychiatrist ("You, Dr. Martin"). The revealing *non sequitur*—a familiar device in Sexton's work—raises another major concern in this first volume: her identity as a conventional woman (a "beautiful" wife, a devoted mother) has proved to be only a partial one; it is this recognition that has precipitated the speaker's crisis, but which may also lead to full self-realization, a recapturing of the "lost ingredient."

By far the majority of poems in *To Bedlam and Part Way Back* explore the poet's identity in terms of other women. There are poems about being buried alive ("The Moss of His Skin"), paralysis within a marriage and its "pantomime of love" ("The Farmer's Wife"), the literal paralysis of the goddess Diana, changed forever to a laurel tree and noting in despair that "blood moves still in my bark bound veins" ("Where I Live in This Honorable House of the Laurel Tree"). In one of the most moving of these poems, "Unknown Girl in the Maternity Ward," Sexton dramatizes the relationship between a mother and her daughter with a typical mingling of tenderness and a hopeless sense of estrangement. The mother can only consider her child a "fragile visitor," her "funny kin," and the reason is the mother's lack of her own selfhood, since she is, after all, "unknown":

> I touch your cheek, like flowers. You bruise
> against me. We unlearn. I am a shore
> rocking you off. You break from me. I choose
> your only way, my small inheritor
> and hand you off, trembling the selves we lose.

The lost self, in this case, is one which fails to emerge even in the most basic relationship between a mother and child. Sylvia Plath, in a more direct and angry protest at this failure, says to her own child, "Off, off, eely tentacle! / There is nothing between us"—the child is envisioned as a mere hindrance to the achievement of the ruthlessly independent, mythologized self of *Ariel*. But Anne Sexton yearns back toward human connections, and her madness rises from her sharp awareness that these connections are lost, and that the loss is irrevocable.

In seeking to define her own identity through poetic fictions about other women, and about relationships between women, Sexton merely sees her own identity as inferior and finds that genuine relationship is unavailable. Later volumes will explore the causes behind her failure to "connect" meaningfully with others, but in *To Bedlam and Part Way Back*, her failure leads directly into madness. Although she pictured herself, wryly, as "a secret beatnik hiding in the suburbs in a square house on a dull street," any pride she might have taken in her role as poet seems cancelled by this image of herself as a misfit, someone who did not live in that "good world" she envied her great aunt and could not create for herself. One senses that Anne Sexton felt herself forced into poetry, that her inability to find satisfaction in a conventional role made the pose of a "secret beatnik," a rebel—in the sense that both poetry and madness are forms of rebellion—her only means of survival. Unlike Emily Dickinson, who felt that "Much Madness is divinest Sense" and whose extreme self-sufficiency (however "mad" it might have appeared to her Amherst contemporaries) was the sign of a fully realized identity, Sexton desperately needed the approval of others: "I want everyone to hold up large signs saying YOU'RE A GOOD GIRL." Her belief that she had failed to be "good," and that she had no way of finding a "good world," led to a madness that was not divinest sense but hellish chaos, a threatened disintegration of selfhood.

This linking of madness with evil, with the inability to be "good," recurs in Sexton's poems dealing with her experiences in mental instititutions. She continues to lament her sense of loss and disorientation: "They lock me in this chair at eight a.m. / and there are no signs to tell the way" ("Music Swims Back to Me"). In the first stanza of this poem she pictures herself as an orphan seeking the way home:

> Wait Mister. Which way is home?
> They turned the light out
> and the dark is moving in the corner.
> There are no sign posts in this room,
> four ladies, over eighty,
> in diapers every one of them.
> La la la, Oh music swims back to me
> and I can feel the tune they played
> the night they left me
> in this private institution on a hill.

These lines, like Ophelia's mad speeches, blend irreality and the absence of sequential thought with a terrifying, sane intuition; immersed in a surreal, abandoned world, the speaker nonetheless understands her need to escape, to find "sign posts" back toward health.

Does Sexton imagine any way out of this impasse, any way to escape the debilitating terrors of a consciousness plagued by a conviction of its own evil? One possibility is to replace self-loathing with an open acceptance of evil—even admitting the likelihood that she is "not a woman." What is remarkable, however, is not this admission itself but the lively, almost gleeful tone in which it is uttered:

> I have gone out, a possessed witch,
> haunting the black air, braver at night;
> dreaming of evil, I have done my hitch
> over the plain houses, light by light:
> lonely thing, twelve-fingered, out of mind.
> A woman like that is not a woman, quite.
> I have been her kind.
>
>   ("Her Kind")

"A woman like that is misunderstood," Sexton adds wryly, but the poem is a serious attempt to understand such a woman—her sense of estrangement, her impulse toward death—by internalizing evil and giving it a voice: a chortling, self-satisfied, altogether amiable voice which suggests that "evil" is perhaps the wrong word after all. Sexton's witch, waving her "nude arms at villages going by," becomes something of value to the community, performing the function Kurt Vonnegut has called the "domestication of terror." Unlike Plath's madwoman in "Lady Lazarus"—a woman at the service of a private, unyielding anger, a red-haired demon whose revenge is to "eat men like air"—Sexton's witch is essentially harmless. Although she remains vulnerable—"A woman like that is not afraid to die"—she rejects anger in favor of humor, flamboyance, self-mockery. She is a kind of perverse entertainer, and if she seems cast in the role of a martyr, embracing madness in order to domesticate it for the rest of the community—making it seem less threatening, perhaps even enjoyable—it is nevertheless a martyrdom which this aspect of Sexton accepts with a peculiar zest.

Poems like "Her Kind" and "Music Swims Back to Me" help create the famous, fatally glamorous mask of Anne Sexton—part lovable witch, part helpless madwoman—for which she became famous, and which is often discussed as if it were the only self present in Sexton's poetry. Denise Levertov, in her well-intentioned, somewhat patronizing remarks on Sexton's suicide, suggested that Sexton was "too intensely troubled to be fully aware of her influence or to take on its responsibility. Therefore it seems to me that we who are alive must make clear, as she could not, the distinction between creativity and self-destruction." But Sexton did take on a personal responsibility for the interest her work aroused—she sent cheerful, supportive letters, for instance, to the countless victims of mental illness who wrote to her—and much of her poetry, from the first volume onward, expresses anguish over her destructive impulses, with an awareness that they are threatening to her poetry as well as to her personal well-being.

Part Two of *To Bedlam and Part Way Back* contains only three poems, but they are long, reflective works which attempt to take stock of the poet's progress, to state a rationale for her kind of poetry, and especially to acknowledge lifelong conflicts that have prevented a healthy development of self. These goals are directly addressed in the volume's longest and finest poem, "The Double Image." Here the poet gathers all her themes into a single autobiographical narration, seeking that "certain sense of order" through a careful, measured recounting of her seemingly chaotic and random experiences. Like many of Sexton's more somber, reflective poems, "The Double Image" is addressed to her daughter, establishing the crucial dynamic between the poet's desire for an affectionate, healthy relationship with the child, and her yearning toward the madness that threatens to separate them. The poem's tender, carefully modulated voice is firmly aligned on the side of health, but the poet remains aware of her continued vulnerability. She sees her madness as an unknown, demonic force, an "ugly angel" whose voice enchants the poet—much like the "disquieting muses" in Plath's analogous narrative. After giving way to madness and losing her child, Sexton has returned as a "partly mended thing," still unable to assume a healthy identity:

> I had to learn
> why I would rather
> die than love, how your innocence
> would hurt and how I gather
> guilt like a young intern
> his symptoms, his certain evidence.

The poem's title refers to Sexton's mother and daughter, seen as potent forces pulling her simultaneously in two directions. Sexton's mother (certainly a cold, uncaring figure in this poem) represents "the stony head of death," while the final lines speak of the daughter's inestimable value for the poet's present self, not only as a symbol of the life-force but as a hopeful foreshadowing of her own developing selfhood:

> We named you Joy.
> I, who was never quite sure
> about being a girl, needed another
> life, another image to remind me.
> And this was my worst guilt; you could not cure
> nor soothe it. I made you to find me.

In the volume's concluding poem, "The Division of Parts," she admits that she cannot escape her dead mother, now a "god-in-her-moon," and she rehearses the religious guilt that will become an increasingly potent theme in her later work; but with the flowering of her poetic gift in a remarkable first volume, the birth of a daughter named Joy, and a general rise of self-esteem in her success as a woman of letters, Sexton makes a heroic effort to put Bedlam behind her, finding solace in the attempt to appreciate—and record—the complexities of her experience.

In Sexton's second volume, *All My Pretty Ones* (1962), she broadens her scope from consideration of the specific, urgent experience of madness to consider more universally comprehensible forms of loss. Sexton's parents died in 1959, and though she insisted at the time that she would not write poems about them, she later changed her mind. The first part of this volume contains "The Truth the Dead Know," "All My Pretty Ones" and "Lament," poems dealing with her parents' deaths and among the finest she ever wrote. Not surprisingly, the ostensible theme of bereavement is mingled with an examination of the poet's continuing struggle toward identity. In that strange, bitter elegy, "The Truth the Dead Know," Sexton seems to eschew the common rituals of mourning: "Gone, I say and walk from church, / refusing the stiff procession to the grave"; she prefers, instead, to "cultivate myself" and to avoid such a powerful intimation of mortality as the death of both parents within a few months. The poem ends, however, by emphasizing not her own refusals but those of the dead, and into her voice creeps something like envy:

> And what of the dead? They lie without shoes
> in their stone boats. They are more like stone
> than the sea would be if it stopped. They refuse
> to be blessed, throat, eye and knucklebone.

A far gentler, more nostalgic poem like "Young" recalls the poet's innocence as a "lonely kid" whose relationship to her mother was not yet perceived as a "funnel"; and in "Old Dwarf Heart" she creates a separate, mythical self—

again resembling Plath's disquieting muses—who insists upon "the decay we're made of": "When I lie down to love, old dwarf heart shakes her head." Sexton can never escape this destructive self ("Where I go, she goes"), which is perceived as having originated in a vicious Oedipal "tangle," but the loss of her parents does give her a kind of grim new beginning, and the rest of the volume explores various avenues of escape.

In her attempt to counter the truth the dead know with a gentler, more humanizing truth, Sexton seeks out two major sources of comfort: religious belief and domestic love. Her early cluster of religious poems, forming Part Two of *All My Pretty Ones,* initiates a theme that will recur throughout her work—especially in her posthumous volume, *The Awful Rowing Toward God* (1975)—but she seemed to find little solace in her religious ponderings; at times, in fact, they only increase her sense of guilt. In "With Mercy for the Greedy," addressed to a Catholic friend who tried to convert the poet, Sexton says with childlike sincerity: "I detest my sins and I try to believe / in the Cross. I touch its tender hips, its dark jawed face, / its solid neck, its brown sleep." Unlike Emily Dickinson, who saw herself locked in a battle of wills with God the Father, a Puritan Nobodaddy who threatened her own sense of self, Sexton was drawn toward the image of a gentle, redemptive Christ, a God who was palpably human. But she concludes, ruefully, "Need is not quite belief," and explains, with typical Sexton wryness, "I was born doing reference work in sin . . . ." In Part Three, which consists of a single poem, "The Fortress," Sexton insists that the love between herself and her daughter has greater redemptive power than any religious belief. The poet has a sense of her own value, however fleeting, in her protectiveness toward her daughter: "What ark / can I fill for you when the world goes wild?" Although she knows that "Life is not in my hands" and cannot promise that her daughter will find happiness, the poem emphasizes their tender domestic alliance, the "fortress" their togetherness forms against the "bombs" of experience.

In one of the volume's most impressive poems, "Letter Written While Crossing Long Island Sound," Sexton makes an ordinary boat ride into the occasion of an optimistic, even transcendent spiritual vision. Although the ocean seems "without miracles or rage / or unusual hope," she sees four nuns sitting together "like a bridge club," and in a long, striking passage, half prayer and half fantasy, she imagines them rising up from the poet's depressed vision of reality, her incalculable "sadness," to serve as messengers of hope. The poem mingles Sexton's gift for whimsical description and her ability to convey her own dire state of need. She sees "these four nuns / loosen from their leather boots / and their wooden chairs," and then:

> There go my dark girls,
> their dresses puff
> in the leeward air.
> Oh, they are lighter than flying dogs . . .
> They are going up.

See them rise
on black wings, drinking
the sky, without smiles
or hands
or shoes.
They call back to us
from the gauzy edge of paradise,
good news, good news.

Sexton yearns toward the gauzy edge of paradise, she hopes for good news,
yet she remains surrounded by the "whitehearted water" of "The Truth the
Dead Know," and that despairing truth affects even her most hopeful visions.
Exercising her "black art" in a wide range of poetic styles and voices, giving
definite form to hope as well as to despair, Sexton had yet to confront the
most basic question of her poetic and personal lives.

III

With two accomplished volumes behind her, with a blossoming career
and innumerable devoted readers, she summoned the courage to bluntly
question the value of living—to decide whether, in fact, the pain of life does
not outweigh its rewards. In "The Black Art" she insisted: "A woman who
writes feels too much, / those trances and portents!" Her decision to explore
fully those excessive feelings, to relate her mysterious "trances and portents"
to her central concerns of identity, poetry and survival, helped her toward
Live or Die (1966), winner of a Pulitzer Prize and the finest achievement of
her career. The volume's title represents an ultimatum; the poems themselves, arranged in chronological order and reading, as Sexton herself noted,
like a "fever chart," show the poet moving toward a stark confrontation with
her suicidal impulses and with her "portent" that life as a whole—not only for
her, but perhaps for everyone—is simply not worthwhile. And yet, as one
astute reviewer, Thomas P. McDonnell, noted at the time *Live or Die* was
first published, Sexton gives us more than "impulses": "(this) is not a poetry
or spasmodic revelation or of occasional incident transformed from similitude
to artifact: in its continuing wholeness one perceives the suggestion of a
journey." It was a journey, as *Live or Die* makes clear, upon whose outcome
rested her life itself, and one she approaches with great courage and her
developed artistic powers.

Carl Jung, discussing the obstacles to personal growth, notes that ven-
turing into "obscurity and darkness" is absolutely essential in the quest for a
new stage of development, a higher individuation of self. For Anne Sexton,
there were two kinds of "darkness"—her madness, which represented personal defeat; and that agonizing uncertainty about her life and her identity
which could only be eased through poetry and whose resolution—even if
temporary—could represent significant progress toward mental stability and
a secure sense of self. In *Live or Die*, Sexton has greatly matured as woman

and as poet: she does not glorify madness, setting herself apart from the rest of humanity, but rather perceives it as an ignoble escape and, most of all, as a colossal waste of time. The most fearsome "obscurity and darkness," Jung suggests, lies in a sane, ego-centered approach toward personal problems, not in a surrender to the chaotic promptings of the id. In her third volume Sexton recognizes this truth, and the recognition helps produce some of her finest poetry.

In her long, moving description of yet another confinement in a mental institution, "Flee on Your Donkey," the poet betrays little of her former fascination with madness; now the asylum is "the scene of the disordered senses," a place where she has wasted some of her best years:

> Six years of such small preoccupations!
> Six years of shuttling in and out of this place!
> O my hunger! My hunger!
> I could have gone around the world twice
> or had new children—all boys.
> It was a long trip with little days in it
> and no new places.

She now sees that her doctor represented a kind of crutch, someone who "promised me another world / to tell me who / I was." The poem concludes that madness is merely "the fool's disease," a way of "allowing myself the wasted life," and the poet finally exhorts herself: "Anne, Anne, / flee on your donkey, / flee this sad hotel . . . ."

Sexton, refusing the descent into madness, must now attempt to deal rationally with her nearly irresistible impulse toward suicide. Many poems in *Live or Die* deal explicitly with this subject: "To Lose the Earth," "Wanting to Die," "Suicide Note," and "Sylvia's Death," a poem about the suicide of Sylvia Plath. "The Addict" describes the part of Sexton that is a "death monger": "I'm an expert on making the trip / and now they say I'm an addict." What has not been remarked about these poems, however, is that their imagery, tone, and often their explicit argument speak *against* suicide; Sexton is not flirting with death but attempting to exorcize personal demons, to understand her impulses and thereby transcend them. In "Wanting to Die" she addresses an unnamed "you"—perhaps the rational, questioning part of the poet's own psyche—and her voice seems rueful, melancholy. The poem's first stanza is one of the finest Sexton ever wrote:

> Since you ask, most days I cannot remember.
> I walk in my clothing, unmarked by that voyage.
> Then the almost unnameable lust returns.

Here the desire for suicide is a "lust," and therefore love—as the poem's final line claims—can only represent an "infection." Sexton emphasizes not only this perversity in the suicidal impulse but also its blatant irrationality: "suicides have a special language. / Like carpenters they want to know *which tools. /* They never ask *why build.*" Summoning up her own former persona, the glamorous witch of her earlier volumes, Sexton realizes that she had "possessed the enemy," had "taken on his craft, his magic," but that this represented an erroneous course, a capitulation to destructive forces. In "Suicide Note" she admits that "I am only a coward / crying *me me me*" and in "Sylvia's Death," despite her acknowledged envy of Plath ("I know at the news of your death / a terrible taste for it"), Sexton emphasizes Plath's defeat. She gained nothing through her sucide, Sexton implies, since death is nothing but an "old belonging," and she finally refers to Plath's diminishment, her new identity as a mere "blonde thing" who has relinquished her own "special language" and received nothing in return.

In "Wanting to Die," Sexton notes that her own body, her essential physical self, is only a "bad prison" that should be emptied of breath, of life. Through poetry she sought liberation from this cruel and unnecessary prison, a liberation that could come only through a compassionate acceptance of her own flawed but redeemable self. Thus her emphasis in *Live or Die* is not upon "confession," with its implication of guilt, but upon compassion for herself and for all those who have influenced her personal existence. Seeking out the origin of her illness in childhood traumas and inadequate relationships with her parents, she is not interested in assigning blame but in bringing to light the dismal facts themselves; there is a new, strong impulse to face past realities and to assess their impact on the present. If this produced only a partial liberation, at least it represented an *earned* freedom that could directly affect the poet's life—acting as a form of therapy—and intensify the honesty of her art as well.

"They put me in the Closet," Emily Dickinson wrote, "because they liked me 'still' "—but the poem focuses upon her elders' inability to imprison the poet's spirit (defined as inhering in her poetic faculties) even in childhood. Anne Sexton is far less confident than this; she lacks Dickinson's firm sense of mission, she frequently distrusts her own creative excitement, and she cannot conceive of her identity—even in its aspect of poetic creativity— as having sufficient strength to withstand external constraints. Her typical reaction to her own analogous experiences is one of fear. "Imitations of Drowning," for instance, includes this bleak reminiscence: "I was shut up in that closet, until, biting the door, / they dragged me out, dribbling urine on the shore." The poem concludes: "in the end it's fear that drowns you." In her superb long poem, "Those Times . . . ," she elaborates upon the sufferings of her childhood:

> I was locked in my room all day behind a gate,
> a prison cell.
> I was the exile
> who sat all day in a knot.

Although this situation may recall that of Plath's "Daddy," in which the poet recalls living under her father's domination like a foot trapped inside a black shoe," poor and white, / Barely daring to breathe or Achoo," Sexton's poem lacks vindictiveness or even anger; it simply tells what happened.

The poem's description brilliantly conveys her early terror and help-lessness:

> The closet is where I rehearsed my life,
> all day among shoes,
> away from the glare of the bulb in the ceiling,
> away from the bed and the heavy table
> and the same terrible rose repeating on the walls.

Locked in her bedroom, the child retreats into an even smaller cell, her closet, but one whose conditions she could control. There she "rehearsed" her life, as if unconsciously attempting to ignore the distorting influences of her present experience. When her stern, punishing mother "came to force me to undress"—the phrase contains an unmistakable suggestion of rape—Sexton says that she "lay there silently, / hoarding my small dignity." Certain phrases recur throughout the poem, testifying to the child's ignorance: "I did not question it," "I did not ask," "I did not know." The poem is remarkable for its withholding of judgment: it creates sympathy for the mother as well as for the suffering child. As so often in Sexton's work, the true villain seems to be life itself, whose tragic process insists upon the movement away from innocence toward unending pain, and its resulting tragic awareness.

Live or Die is Sexton's first volume, after all, which simply arranges the poems in chronological order, as if surrendering to the flux of experience, its chequered pattern of elation and despair. Yet there are many elements which form a constant, hopeful strand in the fabric of Sexton's continued pain: humor and tenderness, the recognition of madness as a waste of time, a caustic, disapproving attitude toward suicide, and a remarkable development of the poet's artistic powers. The volume frequently celebrates personal relation-ships, and it exalts the artist's autonomy and necessary solitude. The poem "Live," which Sexton chose to conclude the volume, represents a new, mature attitude, a recognition of these positive elements as a possible starting point for a new stage of personal development. It ends with a positive, infectious excitement:

> The poison just didn't take.
> So I won't hang around in my hospital shift,
> repeating The Black Mass and all of it.
> I say *Live*, *Live* because of the sun,
> the dream, the excitable gift.

IV

After *Live or Die*, Sexton's personal evolution began to seem increas-ingly frenetic and directionless. In her later volumes she assumes various effective guises—the witty lover of *Love Poems* (1969), the ribald folklorist of *Transformations* (1971), the religious seekers of *The Awful Rowing Toward God* (1975)—but never again does she achieve the immediacy and fullness of *Live or Die*, a book that shows her largest, most personal issue examined with her utmost energy and clarity. In a sense, her later books are elaborate footnotes to that volume, developing ancillary themes and exploring areas of existence which become important once Sexton has made her crucial decision to live. And, as many critics have noted, she began to abandon the careful craftsmanship so evident in the early volumes, producing a larger number of poems but letting their quality suffer a noticeable decline. Increasingly uncertain about the direction of her career, Sexton began to rely on the familiar, melodramatic voice of her earlier work, frequently repeating herself and no longer seeming able, or willing, to hone that voice through a rigorous attention to form, or to deepen its implications through fresh or surprising insights. As an artist, in short, she seems to stop growing. As a result, the American literary myth that a writer is only as good as her last book has been extremely damaging to Sexton, as expressed in the form of harsh or dismissive reviews of her last volumes. The recently issued collected edition of her work, however, should force readers to take another look, and especially to rediscover the value of Sexton's important earlier work.

In a letter written a few weeks before her death, Sexton remarks upon the famous closing poem of *Live or Die:*

> I do not know how I feel about such an old poem as "Live" in *Live or Die*. The poems stand for the moment they are written and make no promises to the future events and consciousness and raising of the unconscious as happens as one goes forward and does not look backward for an answer in an old poem.

A typically breathless, headlong statement, one which contains—with the advantage of hindsight, we can see it easily—a veiled warning, as well as a surprisingly harsh contempt of "old poems" representing experiences that are past, dead, no longer available to the poet (and, it would seem, no longer interesting to her). On the surface it also suggests an unwillingness to *learn* from experience, to assimilate past insights into the vulnerable present consciousness as talismanic reminders, if not as forms of positive moral instruction. But actually the statement is consistent with Sexton's poetry as a whole, and merely states once again the darker side of her belief: one cannot go backward, and the poet can "make no promises" that artistic resolutions can remain valid beyond the experience of a particular poem. "Experiment escorts us last," as Emily Dickinson wrote, and Sexton shared this frightening awareness of the uncertain, friable nature of personal evolution, of the pitfalls lying in wait at every turn of experience. What remains for us, after her death, is to admire her spirit in facing that experience, to rejoice in her momentary triumphs and to recognize, in the poems themselves, her ultimate survival.

The Sacrament of Confession

Paul A. Lacey*

To distinguish the Robert Lowell of *Life Studies,* Anne Sexton, W. D. Snodgrass, and Sylvia Plath, among others, as "confessional" poets has been useful primarily for calling attention to a subject matter and attitudes toward it. After a generation of criticism which insisted that the "I" of a poem was not to be identified with the writer, the *real* John Keats, T. S. Eliot, or W. B. Yeats, but was to be seen strictly as a persona in the poem, we have returned—in some of our most vital poetry—to first-person utterances which are intended to be taken as autobiographical. Thus M. L. Rosenthal speaks of Lowell's "Skunk Hour" and Sylvia Plath's "Lady Lazarus" as true examples of confessional poetry because "they put the speaker himself at the center of the poem in such a way as to make his psychological vulnerability and shame an embodiment of his civilization,"[1] and he goes on to speak of how the poems show us Lowell's sickness of will and spirit, or Sylvia Plath's self-loathing, leading on to her suicide.

Of course, the relation between the writer and his persona in a poem is still as complex as ever. Though some critics have cited the passage in "Skunk Hour" where the speaker tells of spying on lovers in their cars as evidence of Lowell's illness, the incident, in fact, comes from one of Walt Whitman's letters.[2] Similarly, readers have been so persuaded of the factual foundation for Anne Sexton's "Unknown Girl in the Maternity Ward," that they have assumed the poet herself must have had an illegitimate child— which she has not. The dramatic lyric or monologue still sets up some distance between writer and character; but a new openness, a willingness to make poetry of experience unmediated by such doctrines of objectivity as the mask, the persona, or the objective correlative, a preoccupation with extraordinary experiences—mental breakdown, infidelity, divorce—these are some of the hallmarks of "confessional poetry." And, with deep gratitude for the lessons in close reading taught us by the criticism which insists that we must read each poem as "a little world made cunningly," without reference to biography, history, or the body of work created by the same artist, we must nevertheless apply those lessons in new ways, especially when confronted with writers who consciously refuse to write within that critical canon. "There is always an appeal open from criticism to nature," said Dr. Johnson.

To interest us for very long, poetry must offer more than the *frisson* of shocked pleasure which accompanies our learning that someone else acts out our fantasies; it must be more than a casebook example of abnormal psychology; and it must make more demand on our attention than that—in the words of many novice writers—"this really happened to me!" Which is to say that, whatever the adjective "confessional" tells us about subject matter, the noun it

*Reprinted with permission from Paul A. Lacey, *The Inner War, Contemporary Poets in Review* (Philadelphia: Fortress Press, 1972), 8–31.

modifies, "poetry," points us once more to the questions of style and form. A poem gives shape to experience so that both the experience itself, in all its density and complexity, with whatever tastes, sights, feelings, and textures are peculiar to it, and the "meanings"—the insights, reflections, consequences, emotional and spiritual implications of the shaped experience— become available to us.

When we write poetry, we do so in order to re-live or celebrate experience, to put things that have happened to us together with others that have not—things we have imagined or appropriated from our reading, our observations, or our friends. But we also write poetry to play with language, to obscure or mediate experiences through words, images, and rhymes. Starting perhaps with an emotion we wish to preserve, we become concerned with how things sound or look, how the rhythm builds or breaks, how emotions are generated and channeled by what we are saying. Looking for release or discovery, we also become interested in making the poem *work*, in saying things well. The poem, then, looks two ways, toward expression and toward communication. It organizes our responses as we write, but it also organizes responses in the audience we begin to imagine.

As readers of poetry we look for the signals from the poem which organize our responses, which tell us we are reading aright and confirm our satisfactions in seeing what is really there. The poem creates its own frame of reference, establishing the norm—ethical, emotional, social, personal—by which we understand it. The poem tells us how to regard its statements, how to read a pattern of metaphors, when the stance is ironic, when it is successfully or unsuccessfully finished. It leads us to make judgments by comparing it with other works in its genre, or with a similar theme or tone.

What organizes our responses, whether we are writing or reading poetry, and leads us to satisfaction or dissatisfaction with the final result, is form, what Robert Frost calls "the figure a poem makes."

> . . . There is a big change after you write a poem. It's a marvelous feeling, and there's a big change in the psyche, but I think you really go into great chaos just before you write a poem, and during it, and then to have come out of that whole, somehow is a small miracle, which lasts for a couple of days. Then on to the next.[3]

The satisfactions Anne Sexton speaks of have to do with moving from and through chaos into wholeness. They are both aesthetic and psychological, both impersonal and highly personal, and they come together in the process of finding adequate form, or, to put it another way, in exerting control over the chaos and making it yield up meaning. "For one lyric poem I rewrote about 300 typewritten pages. . . . You have to look back at all those bad words, bad metaphors, everything stated wrong, and then see how it came into being, the slow progress of it, because you're always fighting to find out what it is you want to say."[4]

The pleasures of writing poetry are not the same as those we anticipate in reading it, however, and while most poets might speak in a similar fashion about the pains and pleasures of composition, the reader of "confessional" poetry seems faced with a particularly complex set of claims on his responses. What are his satisfactions? What entrée does he have into the poem? If the reader is being addressed in some special "confessional" sense, what is his role? Is he hearing confession like a priest, granting or withholding absolution? Is he the client-victim of such a judge-penitent as the narrator of Camus's *The Fall* or Coleridge's *Ancient Mariner*? Do we overhear an unwitting confession, as we do in "The Bishop Orders His Tomb" or "My Last Duchess"? Or are we suddenly drawn into the life of the poem by a violation of the distance established by the form, as Eliot draws us into the action of "The Waste Land": "You! hypocrite lecteur!—mon semblable,—mon frere!"

Equally important, what protection does the poem offer the reader from too much harrowing, too dangerous an evocation of psychic material within himself? The content of any confession is likely to be threatening to one who hears it. If it occurs in a context where one cannot imitate the detachment of a priest, or where the response demanded is too revealing, one may only withdraw or block all response. A reader is at once the most defenseless and the most powerful of men; he may be moved and manipulated by every intonation and gesture the poet gives, but he may also close the book and go away.

All these are questions which must be raised about most poetry, but asking them about Anne Sexton's poetry leads us directly to problems of poetic form as she has faced them.

It has been relatively easy for some critics to dismiss Anne Sexton's poetry by concentrating on its subject matter. Reviewing her first book, James Dickey begins:

> Anne Sexton's poems so obviously come out of deep, painful sections of the author's life that one's literary opinions scarcely seem to matter; one feels tempted to drop them furtively into the nearest ashcan, rather than be caught with them in the presence of so much naked suffering.[5]

Hayden Carruth speaks of a mind almost in control of her material; Denis Donoghue speaks sympathetically of the experiences Anne Sexton has gone through, but he concludes that she has tried too hard to make the material into poetry. Carruth, again, argues that the literary qualities of her poems are impossible to judge, that they are still documentaries of experience which might be starters for other poems where images and ideas "may be strengthened and consolidated in more fully objectified, imagined poems."[6] Flatness, lack of concentration, an unfinished quality to the poetry, or, alternatively, works which try too hard to be poems: these are the standard criticisms of Anne Sexton's works.

But a careful reading of her four books of poetry reveals, not the lack of form which these critics emphasize, but a continual preoccupation with both thematic and technical means for giving significant shape to her poetry.

Many of the poems have elaborate rhyme and metrical patterns. Each of the books is shaped by ruling themes, carefully chosen epigraphs, or a chronological or developmental pattern. The title *To Bedlam and Part Way Back* precisely indicates the arc which the book describes, and which each poem is designed to advance: from sickness toward health; from possession by the ghosts and demons of guilt toward exorcism; from disownment toward inheritance. The book's epigraph describes the method by which the way back can be won: making a clean breast of it in the face of every question; pushing the inquiry further, even in the face of appalling horror.

All My Pretty Ones announces the themes of the book, total loss and the affliction of memory: "I cannot but remember such things were, that were most precious to me." And, just as for Wordsworth recalling emotion and experience under the control of artistic creation brings new health and strength, the aim of remembering for Anne Sexton is to learn to exorcise the evil and celebrate the good. The book's second epigraph, taken from a letter by Franz Kafka, tells us what to expect in the way of method and goal for the poetry, which will "act upon us like a misfortune," and "serve as the ax for the frozen sea within us." The epigraphs do not promise the satisfactions of resolution or the sense of a completed journey. At the most, they promise to take us to the edge of things, the boundary situation, where, for good or ill, the frozen sea within us begins to break up.

Live or Die is the appropriate next stage of development in the poetry. The choice announced by the title is real for the poet, but the poems, printed in the order of their composition from 1962 to 1966, do not simply move from death- to life-wish. "Live or die, but don't poison everything," says the epigraph, and the poems enact the process of throwing off the poison which makes them read, as Anne Sexton says, "like a fever chart for a bad case of melancholy." In the final poem, "Live," she gathers up the ruling words, images, and themes of the book to express a new equilibrium.

> So I won't hang around in my hospital shift,
> repeating the Black Mass and all of it.
> I say *Live, Live* because of the sun,
> the dream, the excitable gift.

Finally, in *Love Poems*, she quotes from a Yeats essay about the teaching of Mohini Chaterjee, "Everything that has been shall be again." The poems affirm the body in a way not to be found in her earlier poetry. Whereas in the first three books the body is apt to be described as a prison cell or a house inhospitable to its occupant, in this last book the whole body and its separate parts are celebrated and delighted in. Images of the lover as architect, builder, and kneader abound. The poetry asserts the creative power of love and is less self-conscious of its own nature. The eternal cycle described by Mohini Chaterjee brings a sense of peace to the poems gathered in this book.

This brief examination of one means by which Anne Sexton has shaped her collections of poems does not argue that carefully chosen titles, epigraphs, and influences will improve or justify a particular poem, any more than showing that a poem is a perfect Petrarchan sonnet, or in terza rima proves that it is a successful work. What may be argued from such conscious shaping of her books, however, is first, that we must read and evaluate each poem in its larger context, just as we read each line or extended image of a poem in the context created by the whole poem; and second, that the confessional mode requires such shaping influences to give both the distance and familiarity a reader needs for handling the material. Speaking of *All My Pretty Ones,* May Swenson notes:

> Her method is as uninhibited as entries in a diary or letter . . . , the diction seems effortless, yet when we examine for form we find it solidly there, and its expertness is a pleasureable thing in contrast to the merciless *debridement* taking place in the content.[7]

Just as any confession must provide signals telling us how to respond and protections from too much danger, confessional poetry must balance horror with comfort, threat and relief, merciless *debridement* with pleasure, in order to keep us engaged. So the wrenching loss described in "Unknown Girl in the Maternity Ward" and the claustrophobic terror of "The Moss of His Skin" are lightened by the hopeful ritual of "The Lost Ingredient" and the lyrical self-control of "For John, Who Begs Me Not to Enquire Further":

> Not that it was beautiful
> but that I found some order there.
> There ought to be something special
> for someone
> in this kind of hope.

To convince us that we have experienced something true, and that we can live *by* and *with* what we have experienced, is the supreme accomplishment of art. Anne Sexton has said, "I think all form is a trick in order to get at the truth." The remark underlines the importance for her of shaping the lived or imagined experience into the truth. She says in her interview with Patricia Marx that in the poems which are hardest for her to write, she imposes some exceptionally difficult metre or rhyme-scheme, which *allows* her to be truthful. "It works as a kind of super-ego. It says 'You may now face it, because it will be impossible to get out!' "

The *content,* it must be insisted, does not make the poem truthful. Even the most autobiographical poet distorts or suppresses *facts* for the sake of making a fiction which will tell more of the essential truth. To reach its readers, the poem must persuade us that the truth it tells is worth the price it exacts; it must lead us to appropriate and satisfying reactions. Form operates to say to the reader what it says to Anne Sexton: this is a pattern which allows you to be truthful.

The thematic and technical forms she uses in the books establish the distance from the material which allows us first to contemplate it and then to approach it more closely. The Greek tragedians were able to handle the most psychically dangerous material we know—incest, parricide, and matricide—precisely because the stylized language, acting, masks and costumes established sufficient distance between the protagonist and the audience that the latter could have its fear and pity tempered by the pleasure of seeing an action imitated. The playwrights of our own time who handle equally volatile materials have adapted many of the same ritualistic elements for their plays; the reduction of dialogue to ritual or its parody in Beckett, Pinter, Ionesco, and others; the nonrealistic acting styles of many absurdist plays—all have as their purpose setting distance between audience and play. The poets who handle the most dangerous materials are also most concerned with poetic form. Anne Sexton says:

> I used to describe it this way, that if you used form it was like letting a lot of wild animals out in the arena, but enclosing them in a cage, and you could let some extraordinary animals out if you had the right cage, and that cage would be form.[8]

Anne Sexton employs a great variety of thematic and technical shapers on her poetry, so many, in fact, that it might be more accurate to criticize her unsuccessful poems for having too much rather that too little form. Thematically her poems are often built around such paired contrasts as guilt and love, truth and falsehood, mobility and fixity, illness and health. Other themes develop incrementally from poem to poem: the double image, the mirror and the portrait—all used to speak of the past and present confronting each other, the conflicts of parent and child, or the testing of identity by measuring it against family history; sin, guilt, belief, grace, and love worked through a number of poems about Christ or traditional Christian faith; the connection of writing to finding health.

One preoccupation in her poetry which acts as an informing principle for both theme and technique is ritual. This preoccupation expresses itself in her use of words or images commonly associated with rituals—"sacrament," "ceremony," "rites," "ritual," "magic," "exorcise," "communion." These, and words with similar connotations, occur frequently in enough of the poems to indicate at the very least a kind of compulsive pattern by which the poet tries to make sense of what she is saying. Similar effects come from poems built on the rhythms of children's rhymes which, as M. L. Rosenthal says, "catch the note of the self reduced to almost infantile regress."[9] These patterns provide a framework in which irrational acts can be understood or order imposed on chaos.

More important in the poetry, however, is the making of rituals, or the discovery of ritual meaning in an ordinary action. Without claiming to exhaust or fully distinguish all the rituals in Anne Sexton's poetry, we may speak of three kinds which predominate: rites of *mastery,* in which power is tested or exorcised; rites of *initiation* or *cleansing,* in which the poet looks for confirmation of a new insight or stage of growth, or experiences testing, purification, or absolution; and rites of *communion,* where some gesture or order of words opens up a sense of oneness with others.

"You, Dr. Martin," the first poem in her first book, is about power, but this subject is explored by acting out rites of mastery. The poem is addressed to a therapist under whose power the hospital inmates stand. He represents order, "God of our block, prince of all the foxes." The inmates "stand in broken lines," awaiting "the shibboleth" which will open the gates and let them go to dinner, where they "chew in rows." The images emphasize the helplessness and childishness of the patients and the false connections of words and ideas which characterize madness—"the frozen gates of dinner," "we move to gravy in our smock of smiles." But they also illustrate the meaninglessness of this order; the rows and broken lines lead to nothing, the order is for its own sake. Because it demands helplessness and childishness, the poet perceives this order as judgment. The doctor has a "third eye," a magical way to see into lives; it is "an oracular eye in our nest." Dr. Martin symbolizes power. In his name the shibboleth is pronounced, the intercom calls; his eye is the oracle which both sees and speaks. And the poet responds "of course, I love you"—an act of submission and abnegation.

Another power is present in the poem, however, and it is also evoked in ritual terms. This is the power of submission and childishness: the unraveled hands, the foxy children who fall. The poet asserts herself as "queen of this summer hotel" and even "queen of all my sins / forgotten." The power has no channel or focus yet, "we are magic talking to itself," but it is more genuine and capable of meaning than the perfect order imposed by the hospital. "Once I was beautiful. Now I am myself," and it is from that standpoint that she asserts her power in the rituals she makes out of naming and counting.

"We are magic talking to itself" introduces a connection between therapy and making poetry. In "Said the Poet to the Analyst," the poet says, "My business is words. . . . Your business is watching my words." Where the analyst wants to make words refer to facts or events so he can determine whether they correspond to the truth, the poet speaks of words as "like swarming bees," alive and vital, creating their own shape. They do not tell the truth, they control it; they are ritual or magic.

In "The Black Art" the theme is repeated. The events of life are never enough, either as experience or as meaning.

> A woman who writes feels too much,
> those traces and portents!
>
>   .   .   .
>
> A man who writes knows too much,
> such spells and fetishes!

The poem is not concerned primarily with distinguishing women from men or feeling from knowing; instead, it separates these ways of entering and valuing experience—each conceived of as magical—from the trivial data of experience itself. A writer is a spy or a crook, one who discovers or steals secrets, in the poem. He is also a perverter of order for the sake of nature. "With used furniture he makes a tree."

"You, Dr. Martin" is concerned with two kinds of power—the power of the therapist-parent who imposes a mechanical order on the patient, and the power of the patient-child, who discovers a deeper order or a more meaningful disorder through madness and poetry. Many of the other poems explore other kinds of power and sources of order. Sometimes our perception of the triviality of order comes through a poem's rhythm. "Ringing the Bells" develops like the final verse of "The House that Jack Built," in one long run-on sentence where no event or impression is subordinate to any other. Neither causality nor chronology matters as a means of explanation; "and" or "who" introduce each new element in the poem to operate at the same dead level.

> And this is the way they ring
> the bells in Bedlam
> and this is the bell-lady
> who comes each Tuesday morning
> to give us a music lesson. . . .

Patients, attendants, and music therapist become automatons, revealed by the childlike telling of the verse, which continues in one sentence for twenty-eight and a half lines, until the whole illusion of meaningful pattern and activity is demolished in the last lines of the poem:

> and although we are no better for it,
> they tell you to go. And you do.

Settling family estates and disposing of the remains of history provide the narrative peg for several of Anne Sexton's poems. Here putting things in order becomes a weighty ritual action which issues in either an exorcism or a benediction. In some of the poems, the poet expresses her love simply by retracing the steps of a relative or ancestor. "Tonight I will learn to love you twice," she says in "Some Foreign Letters," addressing the old maid aunt whose letters reveal her secret sins and desires. In "Walking in Paris" she reenacts the youthful past of the old aunt, measuring herself against that other life as though she were the old woman's twin:

> You are my history (that stealer of children)
> and I have entered you.

In "Funnel" she makes yet another ceremony of meeting the ancestors, in this case celebrating the richness and openness of the past, the mouth of the funnel.

> I sort his odd books and wonder his once alive
> words and scratch out my marginal notes
> and finger my accounts.

Sorting becomes the chief ritual of mastery in these poems. "Funnel," "All My Pretty Ones," "Elizabeth Gone," "Divison of Parts" begin or end with the act of sorting and arranging the relics of the past. From this imposed, perhaps arbitrary, order, remembering, forgiving, and releasing can follow.

"All My Pretty Ones," generated and sustained by old documents and photographs, becomes a meditation on inheritance—on how to "disencumber" the dead father and the living child from past failures. Sorting means putting proper value on the past and knowing what may be discarded, and what must be kept "to love and look at later." The father's nature—"my drunkard, my navigator/my first lost keeper"—must be affirmed, and so the poet keeps a three-year diary which documents the father's alcoholism, for

> Only in this hoarded span will love persevere.
> Whether you are pretty or not, I outlive you,
> bend down my strange face to yours and forgive you.

Discarding the past does not disencumber us. Moving back through one's history means painfully untying each of its knots all over again, forgiving one's past and the actors in it. On the surface, *sorting* is simply the method anyone uses for making the judgment whether to keep or discard, but as it becomes the process by which the poet relives the past, celebrates times, places and people, and arrives at conclusions, it takes on some of the characteristics of *sortilege*, omen-reading or casting lots, a word to which it is etymologically close.

For M. L. Rosenthal the successful confessional poem must achieve a fusion of "the private and the culturally symbolic," and be more highly charged than other poems.[10] One strategy for achieving such a fusion is to turn private idiosyncratic gestures into formal rituals or to play the private rite off against the public one.

An exceptionally rich poem which brings together ordering, exorcising, and the traditional patterns of Christian observance is "The Division of Parts," where things which are simultaneously "debts," "obstacles," and "gifts I did not choose," must be sorted. Against that action proceeds the observance of Good Friday and the anticipation of Easter, in which a similar working out of debts and unchosen gifts occurs on the public level. *Dividing* is a key to the poem: making the distinctions which separate gifts from debts and performing the acts which turn debts into gifts are the acts which disencumber the past and allow the poet to claim her real inheritance. Two kinds of inheritances are at issue, the effects left by the dead mother— money, "letters, family silver, / eyeglasses and shoes,"—and the complex of attitudes, emotions, doubts, and guilts with which children must also come to terms as their heritage. In this poem that second kind of inheritance is symbolized by "The clutter of worship" taught the poet by the mother, of which she says:

> I imitate
> a memory of belief
> that I do not own.

The poet must come to terms with both her mother and with Christ, and in both cases this means asserting her adulthood in defiance. Defiance causes guilt, but it also opens the way for genuine grieving. Or, to put it in the terms established through the rituals in the poem, the mother, described variously as "sweet witch," "worried guide," and "brave ghost," must first be exorcised before she can be invoked. The poet must "shed my daughterhood," an image sustained by a series of references to inherited clothes, the coats, stones, and furs which "settle on me like a debt." The same cluster of images establishes an identity between Christ and the mother.

> And Christ still waits. I have tried
> to exorcise the memory of each event
> and remain still, a mixed child,
> heavy with cloths of you.

In an earlier stanza the poet has identified the mother and Christ in images recalling the crucifixion—the thieves and the casting of lots for Jesus' garments—but also establishing the complex relationship between guilt and grief.

> I have cast my lot
> and am one third thief
> of you. Time, that rearranger
> of estates, equips
> me with your garments, but not with grief.

Daughterhood, the heavy cloths, the clutter of worship must all be shed until they can be "owned," both acknowledged and possessed. The poet must reject the "dangerous angels" who call on her to convert and the tempting image of Christ, on whom so many have "hitched" in trouble, and find another way which is her own. It is not the way of conversion but the way of deprivation, imaged by Jesus, the "ragged son" of Easter. Her way, tentative and incomplete even when the poem is finished, is suggested by the exorcism-invocation of the last stanzas. The poet has a dream while wearing her mother's nightgown, a dream which reenacts the struggle for mastery which is at the heart of the poem and the particular ritual patterns which shape it. What greater power can there be than the power over spirits which characterizes Jesus in the Gospel of Mark? The mother, "divided," climbs into the daughter's head, only to be cursed and expelled, *Dame / keep out of my slumber, / My good Dame, you are dead.* Recalling this at noon on Good Friday, the beginning of Christ's agony on the cross, the poet sums up her ambivalence by speaking of both cursing and summoning her mother through her "rhyming words." And indeed, the entire next to last stanza in Part IV of the poem is made up of epithets by which the mother is invoked, celebrated, and finally laid to rest. The grief, which would not come when the poet "planned to suffer," because it was blocked by guilt, flows now into the phrases of invocation and benediction:

> my Lady of my first words,
> this is the division of the ways.

The conjunction of the dream and the hours of sorrow commemorating the crucifixion recalls the journey to the underworld to meet the parents which is so often found in ancient myth and epic. The hero goes to meet the past, calls up his parents to learn about the future, and then returns to the world in which he is about to meet his most important adventures. Surely it is not strained ingenuity to see the same psychological pattern being worked out in "The Division of Parts," the ritual acting out of the passing of power from parent to child. The child asserts maturity, now, by taking an independent course. And, because the relationship with Christ has also been one of childlike dependence, or a temptation to "convert" to another's expectations, He too must be taken leave of, so that the poet can come into the real inheritance from Him. Therefore the last stanza of the poem shows us Christ fastened to His crucifix, still the ragged son and sacrifice, not the triumphant Lord who might demand obedience. The poet identifies with the tormented man, not with a theology of sin and salvation which might keep her a child. Christ remains on the cross "so that love may praise / his sacrifice / and not the grotesque metaphor." And as Christ has no power over her, neither has the mother, now only a "brave ghost" who *fixes* in the poet's mind, incapable of giving or withholding "praise / or paradise," but by that very incapacity setting the poet free to enter and affirm her real inheritance.

What we have called rituals of mastery occur elsewhere in the poems. Typically, they shape either the poet's response to the guilts of the past or to the making of poetry as a way of imposing order on life. In "A Story for Rose," for example, the poet controls memory and fear of death on an airplane ride by making a story of them. In "Mother and Jack and the Rain," the tensions of the poem revolve around the "haunting" and "cursing" of the rain outside and the "affirming" of the room and the "endorsing" of the poet's womanhood by her memories; but the tensions are resolved by the making of poetry, by the poet's "conjuring" her daily bread. The thematic and formal significances of rituals of mastery come together:

> With this pen I take in hand my selves
> and with these dead disciples I will grapple.
> Though rain curses the window
> let the poem be made.

Whereas the rites of mastery tend to dramatize conflicts with the God-like authority figures of doctors and parents, those of initiation and cleansing tend to dramatize the poet's role as mother to her children, or to be concerned with moving from shame for the body to affirmation of it. Such a statement of the case is too schematic to be true, of course, but it separates out a tendency in the poetry which rewards close examination.

Houses, rooms, cells, caves, and other images indicating close confinement symbolize the body, especially in the volumes *All My Pretty Ones* and *Live or Die,* as though the self were an unwelcome inhabitant in a hostile environment. "Housewife" develops this pattern of imagery most clearly, opening with the assertion "Some women marry houses. / It's another kind of skin . . . ," and closing with "A woman *is* her mother. / That's the main thing." Here two equivalences, woman equals house, and woman equals her mother, establish the sense of entrapment against which the rituals of cleansing or initiation work, for their effect is to help the poet find escapes from the trap for herself or her daughters. In "Those Times" the poet describes a "bedtime ritual," "nightly humiliations" when she was "spread out daily / and examined for flaws," at the age of six. She describes her body as "the suspect / in its grotesque house," locked all day in her room, behind a gate. In defense against a mother who keeps her a prisoner to prevent divorce, the poet withdraws even further, withholding herself from the mother's breasts, from the well-made dolls, retreating into the closet, "where I rehearsed my life." Rehearsing fantasies becomes planning growth into womanhood "as one choreographs a dance"; meanwhile, she acts out another kind of fantasy, "stuffing my heart into a shoe box." The poem exploits images of testing and probing, especially through the bedtime ritual on the bathroom tiles, to express guilt and shame for being female. There is no cleansing or release here, though the poet looks forward to the time of maturity, when "blood would bloom in me / each month like an exotic flower . . ." and children "would break from between my legs. . . ." The poem, though it speaks of rituals, and shows us a child making ceremonies to protect herself, does not lead us to a resolution in those terms. Instead, menstruation and parturition become the adult counterparts of or fulfillments of the shameful rituals.

"Those Times" can serve as a gloss for other poems where the ceremonies are efficacious. "The Lost Ingredient" is one such poem. It deals with many kinds of loss—the lostness of the past, of the salt sea which was our beginning, of "rites," and of the "ingredient." The word "lost" appears six times in the twenty-four line poem, all but once at the end of a line, and is echoed in the near-rhymes "last," "loosed," and "lust" which close four other lines. "Steal" or "stole" and its near-rhymes end seven more lines. These two key words, "lost and "steal," shape not only its rhyme but also the poem's thematic development. The gentle ladies in Atlantic City bathe in salt water to gain "impossible loves," "new skin," or "another child," but they sit in bathtubs, "smelling the stale/harbor of a lost ocean." In the second stanza the poet swims in the Salt Lake, "to wash away some slight / need for Maine's coast," and to "honor and assault" the Salt Lake "in its proof." As the gentle ladies of the first stanza wished to recapture lost rites, the poet makes her own washing an evocation of something she calls "proof," some confirmation of the self. She goes on to associate this with Reno, where she also performs the ceremonies of gambling for the sake of a "better proof." This evidence, or lost ingredient, must be wrested from life, from time, from the salt sea; the rite becomes the way into this evidence, a gamble to "keep us calm and prove us whole at last." But in the poem the ingredient stays lost, not even identified in its absence; all we know is that salt, money, or lust have no power to uncover it. The poet has made a ritual action out of ordinary events, and we are aware of the enormous organization and control which informs the poem, but the reader remains aware only of loss and mystery.

Initiation into being a woman, which the poet calls being twice-born, controls the action of the poem "Little Girl, My String Bean, My Lovely Woman." The child, poised on her twelfth year, inhabits a body which is about to be possessed by the new powers of fullness and ripeness. The poet speaks of the daughter's body as a "home" or "place" about to be entered by the ghost hour, noon, when the sun is at its zenith. The images work together to hint at magic and mysterious powers, a divine possession of the soon-to-be-fruitful girl, but the poem also associates this new becoming with the original birth, when the child was "a world of its own / a delicate place." The change in the body does not come from outside, however, but from within; even so, it must be greeted with an act of initiation, and on that account the girl is described as separated from her body, needing to let it into her self:

> Oh, darling, let your body in,
> let it tie you in,
> in comfort.

To be initiated is to learn some new truth by having it acted out before or with one. So it is here; the body's changes are confirmed and celebrated— "there is nothing in your body that lies. / All that is new is telling the truth." Initiation rites often have to do with possessing something; and here too the poem provides confirmation. The daughter is not an alien in the house of her body; at the end of the poem she possesses it, and the poet urges her to "stand still at your door, / sure of yourself, a white stone, a good stone." Let the noon hour in, let the sun in, let the body in, let newness and the truth in, then stand at the door, in possession of the house: so the ritual of initiation goes in the poem.

Perhaps the best example of the ritual of cleansing and initiation—and a fine poem—is "Pain for a Daughter." The title itself suggests some of the meanings working in the poem—the daughter's pain, the poet's pain on behalf of the daughter. The poem grows out of the contrast between blindness in several metaphorical senses and seeing or knowing. The daughter is described variously at the beginning of each stanza as blind with love, then with loss, pain, and fear. As she moves through these feelings, from love to fear, she loses her mastery over situations in return for knowledge. In the first stanza, blind for love of horses, she overcomes her squeamishness to treat her pony's distemper, draining the boil and "scouring" it with hydrogen peroxide. In this case her love makes her blind to the distastefulness of the job and lends her a capacity she did not have. "Blind with loss," she asserts her mastery over the neighbor's horses, but is injured and returns home, hurt and frightened. Here her father performs "the rites of cleansing" on her injured foot, cleaning it with hydrogen peroxide, and, for the first time, her eyes are mentioned: "eyes glancing off me," "eyes locked / on the ceiling, eyes of a stranger." Though the eyes do not see, they are an index to her *knowing* in the face of her pain. She cries to God for help, where a child would have both cried to and believed in her mother. The rites of cleansing have introduced her into the adult world, symbolized not by a cry of hope but by one of despair. Her seeing parallels her mother's, who sees her daughter's life stretched out, her body torn in childbirth:

> and I saw her, at that moment,
> in her own death and I knew that she
> knew.

Anne Sexton speaks of writing as putting things in place, having an ordering effect on her own life. "I mean, things are more chaotic, and if I can write a poem, I come into order again, and the world is again a little more sensible and real. I'm more in touch with things." It is not surprising, seeing how the poems work, that Anne Sexton thinks of form as a kind of magic for discovering the truth.

> I'm hunting for the truth. It might be a kind of a poetic truth, and not just a factual one, because behind everything that happens to you, every act, there is another truth, a secret life.[11]

Nowhere do we see her commitment to the discovery of the secret life behind things more clearly than in those poems, many of them dealing directly with the figure of Jesus or the traditions of Christianity, built around rites of communion, prayer, and gift-giving. These poems are her most complex work, for they do not simply rest on traditional forms of words and actions to counterpoint or frame the struggle for peace or unity, they explore a profound ambivalence about the Christian understanding of life. Christianity, in the full force of its explanation of human existence, entices her, as the epigraph from Guardini in *All My Pretty Ones* indicates: "I want no pallid humanitarianism—if Christ be not God, I want none of him; I will hack my way through existence alone. . . ." The prayers or acts of communion in the poems, then, are neither ironic parodies nor secularized ceremonies; they are, rather, expressions of the deepest human needs in the full consciousness that "need is not quite belief."

"With Mercy for the Greedy" illustrates the point. It is addressed to a friend who has urged the poet to ask a priest for the sacrament of confession and has sent her a cross to wear. The poet prays, not to the cross, but to its shadows, detesting her sins and trying to believe in the cross. But what draws her is the crucified man—"I touch its tender hips, its dark jawed face, /

its solid neck, its brown sleep"—just as in "The Division of Parts" she affirms the sacrifice and not "the grotesque metaphor." The cross around her neck taps like a child's heart, "tapping secondhand, softly waiting to be born," but it cannot come alive for the poet precisely because it represents so complete and final an answer. As Yeats resolves the debate between Soul and Heart in the Heart's favor—"What theme had Homer but original sin?"—Anne Sexton chooses the sacrament of poetry over the sacrament of confession. Or rather, she chooses the particular kind of sacrament of confession which poetry is, its kind of mercy, its wrestle with words, and meanings.

We cannot know whether prayer, confession, or communion would lack efficacy for the poet; we only know that she cannot permit herself to yield to them. When they occur, they are magic incantations or childish pleas for a miracle, as in "The Operation."

> Skull flat, here in my harness,
> thick with shock, I call mother
> to help myself, call toe of frog,
> that woolly bat, that tongue of dog;
> call God help and all the rest.

Here is an implied answer to the pious believers who brag that there are no atheists in the trenches; one will believe or try anything, if only the fear is great enough, but it will be in shame at the reversion to such immaturity. In "Letter Written on a Ferry While Crossing Long Island Sound," the poet pleads for a comic miracle, that God should let four nuns break loose from the pull of gravity and float through the air, doing "the old fashioned side stroke," and then she imagines it happening, with the four nuns crying out "*good news, good news*," as well they might.

"For the Year of the Insane" is subtitled "a prayer," and addressed to Mary, but order and form are fragmented; "There are no words here except the half-learned, / the *Hail Mary* and the *full of grace*." The beads lie *unblessed*, and hammer in on her like waves as she counts them, for the poet knows herself an unbeliever. The words and beads associated with the worship of Mary do not convey a sense of grace but of further condemnation, as the poet moves further into silence and madness. The fragmented prayer gives way to an equally fragmented holy communion, where the bread and the wine also become images of damnation; the wine burns, and the poet says "I have been cut in two." Mary does not respond, the bread and the wine do not change, no communion occurs. The prayer for grace, for "this crossing over" is denied, and the poet remains "in the domain of silence."

Communion occurs both between man and God and between man and man; and the efficacious ritual symbolizes and facilitates both kinds of communion. It is not accidental or arbitrary that such rituals include eating and drinking. They represent what Philip Wheelwright calls "assimilative ritual," which he says "consists in reaffirming and attempting to intensify man's continuity and partial oneness with nature, or with the mysterious creative force behind nature."[12]

The hunger for communion is the hunger for assimilation, oneness with others, and with what Anne Sexton has called a "secret life" behind things, and for self-transcendence, getting out of oneself and "in touch with things." In "For the Year of the Insane," no one but the poet appears; she is handed wine, and she invokes Mary, but the prayer for self-transcendence only confirms her isolation.

> O little mother,
> I am in my own mind.
> I am locked in the wrong house.

"Hunger" is a ruling word in *Live or Die*. In "Flee on Your Donkey" and "Suicide Note" the same line appears, "O my hunger! My hunger!" The former poem describes madness as a kind of hunger, and the poet finally turns, not to answers to save her, but to her hungers, exhorting them to turn and "For once make a deliberate decision." In "Suicide Note" we are told that "Once upon a time / My hunger was for Jesus," but again there was no fulfillment. Roman Catholic theology speaks of taking communion in a state of sin as eating and drinking damnation, precisely what "For the Year of the Insane" commemorates. So does "Wanting to Die," where a suicide attempt becomes a kind of black mass, a perverted communion service aimed at overcoming the enemy, who is both life and death.

> Twice I have so simply declared myself,
> have possessed the enemy, eaten the enemy,
> have taken on his craft, his magic.

The hunger for death in Anne Sexton's poems is equally a hunger for meaningful life, for choice, and for affirmation. Being hungry need not mean there has been no communion, only that it was not enough for the speaker's appetite; so she can say of the suicide attempt, "To thrust all that life under your tongue!— / That, all by itself, becomes a passion." "The Addict" further elaborates images of communion to speak of the lure of suicide. The pills are "a mother," "loaves," and "a diet from death," but they also keep the speaker in practice for another attempt to die. This addiction to "goodnights" is "a kind of a marriage / . . . . a kind of war"; it is a ceremony and a sport, filled with rules, and taking the pills demands

> . . . a certain order as in
> the laying on of hands
> or the black sacrament.

All these images work to suggest the complexity of the hungers to be met by this communion service, for the ritual brings together the best and worst relations human beings have with one another—war and marriage—

and tries to make sense within those limits. The poet takes the pills and lies on her altar, "elevated by the eight chemical kisses." No consecration occurs on this altar, however, just as no love or affection come with the chemical kisses. We know what the poet wants, what the ceremony tries to evoke, only by their absence: self-acceptance, "I like them more than I like me," maturity, "I'm a little buttercup in my yellow nightie," and a sense of love and sacramental order. The final lines are a child's jingle, mocking the longings which shape the poem.

A suicide attempt means taking one's life in one's own hands, being responsible for it; this addiction parodies suicide and gives up responsibility for one's life. In many of her poems Anne Sexton tries to impose order on events by inventing ceremonies or insisting that something is a rite, that a bed or a stretch of beach is an altar, that irrational gestures or forms or words could hold off events, as in "Lament," or gain forgiveness, as in "Christmas Eve." Rituals, like symbols, grow out of their own inner principles, however; we cannot invent meaningful rituals, we can only discover them. In Anne Sexton's poetry there are a great many rituals which do not work *as rituals*, though many of them help the poems work.

That distinction may seem forced and arbitrary, since poetry has always been close to, when not a form of, magic, and the connection between prophet, priest, and poet is as real as it is ancient; nevertheless, distinguishing the effects of ritual, especially that rooted in traditional Christianity, from those of the poetry which supports or grows out of it, in Anne Sexton's poetry, is essential. For of the three kinds of rituals discussed here, those which most closely depended on traditional Christian imagery and gestures were also those in which the meaning of the poems was most widely separated from the meaning of the rituals. What I have called rituals of mastery, where the poet struggled for ascendency over the God-like doctor, the authoritarian parent, or the chaos of past history, succeeded in and through the poems, on the two levels demanded by Rosenthal, the personal and the culturally symbolic.

Poems which employed ritual language to speak of cleansing, initiation, prayer, or communion often succeeded in being culturally symbolic precisely to the extent that they revealed an isolation and anxiety on a personal level which was not to be relieved by rituals. The poet's intense attraction to Jesus, the man who suffers for others, and Mary, the perfect and all-forgiving mother, always stands at odds with the worship which attends both those figures. Anne Sexton's poetry chronicles a struggle to come of age: to work through the conflicts with the parents in order to forgive and be forgiven; to break free from the guilts and inadequacies of the past and become open to others; to become the kind of parent who sets her children free and thus breaks the cycle of guilt and shame which has marked her family history. If we are to believe some theologians, the need of our time is also to come of age, to set aside the comforts of cult and ceremony and live affirmatively in a totally secular world. "Need is not quite belief," Anne Sexton has said, and that is a kind of gloss on our times. So is the description of Protestants she puts in an eight-year-old's mouth in "Protestant Easter":

> Those are the people that sing
> When they aren't quite
> sure.

A. R. Jones says of Anne Sexton's poetry that "her framework of reference is ultimately religious,"[13] that is, that the values she insists on are traditional religious ones. The argument of this chapter is that her poetry is largely shaped by attempts to enlarge a traditional Christian framework which has been a chief source of the psychological suffering she has endured. It would be a mistake to say that she is working her way out of that framework, since the same issues, questions, and answers have a way of recurring over and over in a lifetime, and her first play, *Mercy Street*, takes place during a celebration of Holy Communion, but the evidence of *Live or Die* and *Love Poems* supports the opinion that the poetry has worked its way to a new level of apprehension of that framework. *Live or Die* closes significantly with the poem 'Live,' which gathers up most of the major themes and preoccupations of her previous work and looks ahead to the affirmations of her last book, *Love Poems*. Surveying the course of her life, as it has been charted in the book, the poet acknowledges how things have been distorted by her "dwarf-heart's doodle," and how turned inward and entrapped she has been. The attempts to tell the truth became lies; the body was naked, even when she dressed it up. Now she asks a question whose answer implies a judgment on her strategies for making sense of things, especially the psychological, social, and personal rituals she has invented, "Is life something you play?"

Now, however, life opens up within her; the sun, which has been an important image in a number of earlier poems, where it has gone from being a threat to being benign, now shines from within, purifying her. This inward change is confirmed by the love of her family, who replace her ceremonies and rituals with games and playfulness.

> If I'm on fire they dance around it
> and cook marshmallows.
> And if I'm ice
> they simply skate on me
> in little ballet costumes.

Love Poems by its very title leads us to expect a change from the earlier books of poetry, and the poems bespeak the self-acceptance toward which "Live" has moved. Even unhappy love and the sorrow of being the other woman exist in the context of hope. Truth and the secret life do not now come through obscure or tortured rituals; things are their own meanings— the pleasures of physical love, delight in the human body, trust in the lover, pain and anger at loss. Whereas many earlier poems seemed to impose meaning by insisting on the sacralization of things, the ceremonies of *Love*

Poems are all playful, desacralized, celebrating the simply human. A ritual completes some kind of action and confirms its meaning by referring to the secret life underlying ordinary life. Making, constructing, building, harvesting, all of them key terms in *Love Poems*, are ordinary human occupations; they complete actions, too, but according to a plan or blueprint. When these terms become metaphors for lovemaking, they take us into a new way of creating ceremonies. "But your hands found me like an architect." "I am alive when your fingers are." "Oh, my carpenter, / the fingers are rebuilt." "He is building a city, a city of flesh."

In her work so far, Anne Sexton has penetrated deeply into chaos and has tried a number of strategies for working her way through it. In some of these strategies therapy and poetry have come together; confession has brought relief by putting things in order in the process of sharing the shame and suffering; the devices which protect the reader from too much reality also protect the writer. And if these ways of handling her material have narrowed the range of her themes, that may be a necessary price to pay for the depths she has reached. If, as seems to be the case, the poetry *has* been therapy, and the fever chart now points toward greater health, a major index of this—and perhaps something of a cause as well—is the movement from the tight confinement which rituals of mastery, initiation, and communion are attempts to break to the playful games of lovemaking which characterize Anne Sexton's last book of poems.

It is no disparagement of those earlier poems to say that *Love Poems* shows more health than the previous three books, since without them no such change can be imagined. They are the record of spiritual struggles which have issued, however tentatively and provisionally, in new degrees of self-acceptance and affirmation of love and human communion. They are also testimonies to the power of poetic forms to give point and substance to spiritual struggles. As Anne Sexton says, in speaking of what constitutes the truth in her poetry, "The effort is to try to get to some form of integrity when your write a poem, some whole life lived, to try to present it now, to give the impact."[14]

Notes

1. M. L. Rosenthal, *The New Poets: American and British Poetry Since World War II* (New York: Oxford University Press, 1967), p. 79.

2. Robert Lowell, "On 'Skunk Hour'," in *Robert Lowell: A Collection of Critical Essays*, ed. Thomas Parkinson (Englewood Cliffs, N.J.: Prentice-Hall, 1968), p. 133.

3. Patricia Marx, "Interview with Anne Sexton," *Hudson Review* 18, no. 4 (Winter 1965–66): 570.

4. Ibid., p. 562.

5. James Dickey, "Five First Books," *Poetry* 97, no. 5 (February 1961): 318–19.

6. Hayden Carruth, "In Spite of Artifice," *Hudson Review* (Winter 1966–67): 698.

7. May Swenson, "Poetry of Three Women," *Nation* (February 1963): 165–66.

8. Marx, "Interview with Anne Sexton," p. 568.

9. Rosenthal, *The New Poets*, p. 134.

10. Ibid., p. 80.

11. Marx, "Interview with Anne Sexton," p. 563.

12. Philip Wheelwright, *The Burning Fountain* (Bloomington, Ind.: Indiana University Press, 1954), p. 179.

13. A. R. Jones, "Necessity and Freedom: The Poetry of Robert Lowell, Sylvia Plath and Anne Sexton," *Critical Quarterly* 7 (1965): 25.

14. Marx, "Interview with Anne Sexton," p. 564.

The Witch's Life: Confession and Control in the Early Poetry of Anne Sexton

Jeanne H. Kammer [Neff]*

With her death in 1974, Anne Sexton confirmed for many readers her place among the group of confessional, suicidal poets (Berryman, Plath, and Lowell, for example) who inhabit and invest with their prophetic presence the troubled decades of the middle century. Approaches to her poetry are often correspondingly handicapped by the voyeuristic interest which followed her last volumes toward their inevitable outcome. There is more interest in the substance of her writing, it seems, than in its craft—and the limbo area where art touches life appears more ill-defined than ever. In order to see more clearly what she became as a poet, it is helpful to return to the place where she began—to the first collections, whose strongest poetry has settled securely into the American tradition, and by which she was first known to the current generation of students and scholars.

The most striking aspect of her first book, *To Bedlam and Part Way Back*, is the regularity of form which characterizes most of the poems in it. In a sequence marked by recurrent themes of grief and loss, explicit in its depiction of physical and emotional distress, the horror of the institutional experience, Sexton's use of reiterated stanza patterns and complex rhyme schemes comes as a surprise to the reader expecting a "free" confessional narrative. Some of this may indeed be therapeutic; "the ingenuity of shape," says Richard Howard, "has something of the basket-weaver's patience about it, it is the work of a *patient*."[1] But it is also true that, like her literary predecessors and with her strongest contemporaries, Sexton perceived the general dilemma of the woman artist as characterized by the culture ("A woman who writes feels too much . . ."), along with her personal vulnerabil-

*Reprinted with permission from *Language and Style* 13 (Fall 1980): 29–35.

ity as a poet inclined to the confessional mode. She responded to both conditions, in the early years of apprenticeship and reputation-building, by imposing upon the stuff of her experience the boundary and counterpoint of intense poetic control.

"You, Doctor Martin," the opening poem of the collection and one of the strongest, is a good example of her technique and can stand close scrutiny. The voice of the "queen of the summer hotel" is full of the gleeful, murderous, placating tones of the inmate/patient, held in check by an orderly visual pattern. Sexton's habit is to allow an initial stanza to take its own shape, then to repeat that form in the ones that follow. Here, the visual enclosure is tidy and symmetrical:

> You, Doctor Martin, walk
> from breakfast to madness. Late August,
> I speed through the antiseptic tunnel
> where the moving dead still talk
> of pushing their bones against the thrust
> of cure. and I am queen of this summer hotel
> or the laughing bee on a stalk
> of death.

The apparent symmetry of the stanza is opposed, however, by the run-on lines and the failure of the whole to be, in the end, self-contained. The form is both an ironic extension and a contradiction of the content: it swings, like Doctor Martin and his patients, "from breakfast to madness," a ritual pacing, a pushing of the "bones against the thrust of cure." At the same time there is a denial of motion; the "moving dead" only *talk* of resistance, and the final pun on "stalk" (contrasting with Dr. Martin's free "walk" in the first line) conveys the speaker's double sense of herself as aggressor and victim, "queen" and prisoner.

Walk / talk / stalk—rhyme is an important element in Sexton's early poetry, because it is a game played against visual uniformity even as the appearance of regularity is maintained: the patient's riddle and the witch's web. While the shape of the stanzas may remain consistent throughout a poem as an element of visual control, the rhyme shifts, doubles back, deceives the eye. In the later stanzas of "You, Doctor Martin," for example, the dominant walk / talk of the first is moved to a secondary position, then buried in syntax and masked by spelling variations and half-rhyme. It persists, nevertheless, as a reminder of the poem's main axis: the attempt of the individual to move, to speak, to escape, opposed by the immobility, silence, inexorable sameness, and containment of the institutional group.

By the end of the poem the same rhyme is acting (like Denise Levertov's "horizon note") as a constant in the background which centers theme and tone. "Doctor," after all, has sounded the initial note, which becomes "god of our block" in stanza four, to be echoed again in "foxes / boxes" and the "foxy children." Near the end of the poem, the block / smock sound softens to frost / lost, but we find "talking," "forgotten," and "moccasins" reflecting and repeating earlier terms. It is a painful sound, repeated over and over, sometimes sharp and sometimes muffled, cut off even as it begins—an appropriate vehicle for the speech and the feeling of Bedlam.

Other patterns of internal rhyme support the poem's core of control and feeling: the sequence, for example, of "moving / pushing / laughing / cutting / breaking / talking" emphasizes the contradictory doubleness of the human-but-confined; the repetition of "moving / move / moves," is poignantly linked to "love" in the fourth stanza; there is a humorously punning opposition of "I" and "eye" (patient to doctor) stretched to a painful edge in the echoes of lines / smiles / whine / knives / lives / sky / lights / cry / *life*"; the casual "breakfast / thrust" of the first stanza reappears sarcastically, desperately in the last ones as "most / best / nest / twist / frost / *lost*." The total effect, says Richard Howard, is of rhyme slightly off-balance, "roughed-up, abandoned when inconvenient, psychologically convincing" (445).

It is Howard's last phrase which is important to an understanding of Sexton's poetic choices, where matters of form and style are involved. Control, for Sexton, is not simply an antidote to autobiography, but also a vehicle for communicating the individual experience. It is a means of making strong poems—sturdy baskets—while telling the truth. Nearly all the pieces in this first collection exhibit a similar use of set, visually repetitive stanza forms with varying sorts of contrapuntal, expressive sound activity. They range from the self-generated shape and patterns of "You, Doctor Martin" to a thick, 16-line unit with heavy end-rhyme in "Some Foreign Letters" to the childlike litany of "Ringing the Bells." "Elizabeth Gone" is composed of two sonnets, and "Her Kind" employs a rhythmic, incantatory stanza and refrain. The poet's technical concern, in all of these, deflects the imagination from the pain of direct confrontation and denies the temptation to self-pity, even as the experience is relived and named. In her later work, even as she moves beyond the visual security of the reiterated stanza form and loosens her grip on meter and syntax, Sexton preserves this early discipline of internal control.

The *Bedlam* poems, after all, do not simply represent the therapy of intricate weaving, the "counting of moccasins," although that element is certainly present. Rather, the riddle—the game of order in disorder, structure in chaos—is an important aspect of their peculiar stance: dramatically unstable, but determined to have an authority which form and style alone do not create. One source of that authority is found in another aspect of control in Sexton's work which is more difficult to dismiss as therapeutic in origin or mechanical in nature. By the time of her second volume, *All My Pretty Ones*, her instinctive sense of the striking opening phrase is matched by her knack for a closure which is powerful and precise. In both cases, the principles of understatement and economy are uppermost, and rooted in the placement of sharp images within tight, often minimal sentences.

Here is the first stanza of "The Operation":

> After the sweet promise,
> the summer's mild retreat
> from mother's cancer, the winter months of her death,
> I come to this white office, its sterile sheet,
> its hard tablet, its stirrups, to hold my breath
> while I, who must, allow the glove its oily rape,
> to hear the almost mighty doctor over me equate
> my ills with hers
> and decide to operate.

"Recall if you can," says Peter Davison, "The opening of any recent poem to match that for economy, fullness, and power in setting a scene."[2] We may notice once again the strong presence of rhyme; the most painful or shocking words are saved for the ends of lines and joined firmly, faced up to. At the same time, they comment ironically on one another: "Sweet. . . . sheet," "rape . . . equate . . . operate." The play of the long line against the short, the enclosure of present details within a hazier past and future, intensify the emotional stress. From the deceptively "sweet promise, the summer's mild retreat," we come quickly to a catalogue of horrors: "this white office, its sterile sheet, its hard tablet, its stirrups. . . ." "To hold my breath," in the center, is a temporary death, imaging the mother's even as it is an ironic acting out, in a hostile setting, of the "little death" of sexual fulfillment ("the glove's oily rape"). "My ills," in line 8, is more than a literal, physical term—encompassing as it does a span of seasons, generations of fear and grief. The effect of the stanza's shape and movement is to focus all our attention on the last word: "operate" is both abstraction and image, familiar and ominous, flat and charged with emotion. The patient is exposed in her vulnerability even as the artist remains supreme in her control.

Other poems demonstrate the same capacity in Sexton to summon to opening lines the emotional core of an experience while economically setting forth its key images and issues. In "The Truth the Dead Know," she provides a head-note with the dates of her parents, who died within months of each other, then begins with these blunt lines:

> Gone, I say, and walk from church,
> refusing the stiff procession to the grave,
> letting the dead ride alone in the hearse.
> It is June. I am tired of being brave.

"Letter Written on a Ferry While Crossing Long Island Sound" opens with the sarcastic, understated strength of this declaration:

> I am surprised to see
> that the ocean is still going on.

"The Starry Night" in swift strokes recalls to mind the painting which occasions the poem and at the same time recasts it in the speaker's private images and emotional landscape:

>The town does not exist
>except where one black-haired tree slips
>up like a drowned woman into the hot sky.

Sexton's impulse to crisp, direct statement is a way of not appearing over-emotional, where the subject is highly personal and intensely felt. It is also a tactic that invites the reader's recognition and curiosity, and demands a close attention. So, too, in her endings. The effectiveness of poetic closure is often a means of distinguishing between the gifted and the merely competent writers, the interesting poetry and the great. In the *Bedlam* volume, the endings of Sexton's poems are for the most part unmemorable, except for the few that set up a complex resonance and mark the best pieces:

>A woman like that is not ashamed to die.
>I have been her kind.
>("Her Kind")

>Go, child, who is my sin and nothing more.
>("Unknown Girl in the Maternity Ward")

>Allah will not see
>how I hold my daddy
>like an old stone tree.
>("The Moss of His Skin")

By the time of *All My Pretty Ones,* however, she is hitting the mark more consistently; many poems end with phrases that strike us as singularly appropriate, collecting the poem's force in a few well-placed final words. There is humor in "Woman With Girdle:"

>straightway from God you have come
>into your redeeming skin.

tenderness in "I Remember:"

>and what
>I remember best is that
>the door to your room was
>the door to mine.

Death and pain are met with characteristic understatement and irony:

>The supper dishes are over and the sun
>unaccustomed to anything else
>goes all the way down.
>("Lament")

>and run along, Anne, and run along now,
>my stomach laced up like a football
>for the game.
>("The Operation")

Rhyme remains a strong element in Sexton's closure, even if camouflaged or postponed; the last phrases are kept deliberately minimal, isolated carefully—apparently artless, but powerful in their simplicity. Again, the structure of lines and sentences causes us to focus on the final image each time, which provides the testimony of the senses for what has been said.

It should be apparent by now that the structural means by which Sexton maintains a firm command over material which is nakedly personal are consistently supported, in these volumes, by a texture of language which is often as lean and cryptic as that of an Emily Dickinson. Yet James Dickey, in reviewing the *Bedlam* poems, comments that "they lack concentration, and above all the profound, individual linguistic suggestibility and accuracy that poems must have to be good;"[3] and Barbara Howes, from the opposite corner, complains that Sexton "has a habit, which may be mere carelessness, of using verbs ungrammatically or of wrenching them away from their usual meaning, and sometimes she twists words cruelly. . . ."[4] Some of this critical scoring may be explained in its context; Sexton suffered in the early 1960s from competition (almost book for book) with Denise Levertov, a more widely recognized and experienced poet, and with such "delicate" poets as Katherine Hoskins, noted for her coolness and restraint.[5]

Nevertheless, carelessness and lack of concentration are hardly terms which may apply to Sexton in these volumes, particularly where language is concerned. She employs a diction that is characteristically simple, strong, and colloquial, in what Richard Howard accurately terms a "lucid obstruction to sentimentality" (447); a good example is found in "The Operation":

> There was snow everywhere.
> Each day I grueled through
> its sloppy peak, its blue-struck days, my boots
> slapping into hospital halls, past the retinue
> of nurses at the desk, to murmur in cahoots
> with hers outside her door, to enter with the outside
> air stuck on my skin, to enter smelling her pride,
> her upkeep, and to lie
> as all who love have lied.

The "ungrammatical" use of "grueled," the coinage of "blue-struck," the unusual sense of "upkeep" are all part of the effort to portray accurately the distorted hospital world, to preserve the delicate balance of feeling and saying required of patients, staff, and visitors.

Language in general for Sexton appears bound up with the act of *seeing*, of accurate observation and naming—truth sought out and confronted, reflected in the solidity of the printed word, the appropriate image. "Perception," says the poet Marvin Bell in a recent essay on the art, "Has two meanings: sight and insight. I believe that both sight and insight derive from fierce consciousness, whether it begins in looking at a small object or in paying attention to all of the implications and resonances of an idea or image."[6] For Sexton a "fierce consciousness" of the real world as well as of the individual word was inextricably linked with self-consciousness as we find it in her literary ancestors: Dickinson, H.D., Marianne Moore.

"*See* how she sits on her knees all day," she says in "Housewife"; "let us consider the *view*," in "From the Garden"; "*see* them rise on black wings" in "Letter Written While on a Ferry. . . ." And the loon (crazy, ridiculous among birds) landing awkwardly in "Water" goes under "calling, I have *seen*, I have *seen*." The contemporary need, of which Bell speaks, to *get closer to* rather than to accumulate more of poetic detail (38) is strong in Sexton and in the peculiar sort of confessional tradition associated with poets like Dickinson: the self revealed in the craft of the poem even more than in its content. It is also an effort to escape both self and outer world by getting *through* the image in the word—the same attempt described in Gerard Manley Hopkins' process of "inscape" and celebrated by Denise Levertov in the poetry of H.D.—to a still place of clarity and peace.

In these early books, however, the habit of seeing and of finding the precise words to articulate insight is primarily another means of control in a world which otherwise appears subjective, inchoate. In her later books, sight intensifies to vision, and is coupled with an increasingly oracular *persona* and images which take on archetypal, mythic dimensions. With *Live or Die*, unity of volume becomes the most apparent controlling factor in Sexton's poetry; the individual poem begins to be subsumed in the larger movement of which it is a part. And with *Transformations*, Suzanne Juhasz argues, Sexton is able to abandon her tight control of meter, rhyme, and syntax because she is in command of the poem at a different level.[7]

Without denying the effect of these developments in Sexton's poetry (longer, more prosaic poems and the use of poem sequences, for example) we may still pay attention to the means of its technical success—and find that the early discipline hangs on in the continuing love of the challenge of set forms (the sonnet sequence "Angels of the Love Affair," in *The Book of Folly*); the subtle internal control of rhyme ("Doctors," in *The Awful Rowing Toward God*, may be profitably compared with "You, Doctor Martin"); and the urgent effort to approach and enter the image / word which, at its best, allows us to see as she sees.

The outspoken, confessional poet of "The Abortion," "Menstruation at Forty," and "The Fury of Cocks" remains throughout her career a determined and beguiling shaper of words in the best tradition of the art. To see that her work, in Philip Legler's words, is in fact "crazily sane and beautifully controlled,"[8] is to understand that the witch's life has more solidity to it than fetishes and spells, and that the exploration of the self does not preclude the mastery of speech. It is an important lesson for those who read and teach Anne Sexton's poetry; it is even more important for those others who would practice that black art.

Notes

1. "Some Tribal Female Who Is Known But Forbidden," *Alone with America: Essays on the Art of Poetry in the U.S. Since 1950* (New York: Atheneum, 1969), p. 444.

2. "The New Poetry," *Atlantic*, November 1962, p. 88.

3. "Five First Books," *Poetry*, 97, 5 (February 1961), 319.

4. Review of *Bedlam* poetry in *New York Herald Tribune* Lively Arts Section, December 11, 1960, p. 37.

5. See, for example, Louis Simpson, "The New Books," *Harper's*, August 1967, p. 91.

6. "Homage to the Runner," *American Poetry Review*, 7, 1 (January-February 1978), p. 38.

7. *Naked and Fiery Forms: Modern American Poetry By Women—A New Tradition* (New York: Harper & Row, 1976), p. 127.

8. "O Yellow Eye," *Poetry*, 110, 2 (May 1967), p. 127.

Embracing Life: Anne Sexton's Early Poems
Cheryl Vossekuil*

Contrary to critical perceptions of Anne Sexton as a death poet, her first three collections—*To Bedlam and Part Way Back* (1960), *All My Pretty Ones* (1962), and *Live or Die* (1966)[1]—show her to be life-affirming, struggling with the temptation of death, but choosing life—at least for a time. All three collections are written in the voice of a single persona— a female who is wife and mother as well as poet, and who questions much in her life, immediately disclosing her dissatisfaction with her current life, a half-life of stasis and inactivity. She sees her life as a prison, and herself as a being for whom fulfillment and growth are an ever-receding dream. Despite the elusiveness of this dream, however, through the first three books, she persistently searches for a life conducive to growth. For Sexton, however, growth is a process that inevitably leads to and is present in death as well as in life, and so the poet must choose between the two. Either involved life or death offers escape from the static condition she sees as poisoned, and after careful consideration, by the end of *Live or Die*, Sexton's choice is to live.

Throughout the first three collections, Sexton argues that she must escape from her current life. In "Cripples and Other Stories" (*Live*, 162) she reveals her feelings of ugliness and her repulsion at her life, as well as her inability to disguise those feelings: "My cheeks blossomed with maggots. / I picked at them like pearls. / I covered them with pancake. / I wound my hair in curls." The perception of decay just under the surface, barely hidden from view, is indicative of the persona's entrapment between life and death; like a

*This essay was written specifically for this volume and is published here for the first time by permission of the author.

snake shedding its skin, she must "strip away a dead self"—her poisoned self.[2] A quotation from Saul Bellow serves as an epigraph to *Live Or Die:* "Live or die, but don't poison everything . . ." (94). As Sexton explains, "Saul Bellow had given me a message about my whole life. That I didn't want to poison the world, that I didn't want to be the killer; I wanted to be the one who gave birth, who encouraged things to grow and to flower, not the poisoner."[3] Sexton's determination not to poison becomes the resolve to escape the "menacing flat accent of life-in-death."[4]

The stasis that Sexton loathes is well-illustrated in poems such as "The Farmer's Wife" (*Bedlam* 19). The persona has little life of her own—and that life is a passive one; she is described as "her husband's habit," as he urges her toward sex, saying, "honey bunch let's go." "Honey bunch," a pet name as easily used for a child as for a lover, intimates that he treats her as less than an equal: one cannot grow in such a relationship. Additionally, Sexton's use of "habit" here is studied. Nunlike, the farmer's wife wears her role like a habit; she is almost asexual, for though she participates physically in the love act with her husband, she is mentally chaste. The only knowledge one has of this woman is in her responses to and relationships with others, as the title suggests; she is trapped in her life as a reflected image. There is a sense, however, that animosity is building and that the passive wife might act "as her young years bungle past." The persona recognizes her life of stasis, represented by the sexual act without fruition, so that a potentially life-giving act becomes a life-denying act: after all, it is simply a habit. She wishes her husband "cripple" or "dead" to complete the life-denying concept; he is already dead emotionally. Or she wishes him "poet"; poetry for Sexton is a life-affirming act. In an interview with Barbara Kevles, Sexton observed than "Suicide is, after all, the opposite of the poem."[5]

Sexton regularly explores the theme of poetry as life. The inability to act or to grasp the fullness of life is described in "For the Year of the Insane" (*Live*, 132): "My body is useless. / It lies, curled like a dog on the carpet. / It has given up." Here, the nonmovement of the body indicates the lethargy of the entire person, who exists only on a basic physiological level. As automatic as breathing, even the words used within this state of torpor are routine, rote: "the 'Hail Mary' and the 'full of grace.' " Too late, the speaker realizes that she has entered "the year without words." A poet unable to use her words is essentially dead, but if she is still living physiologically, there is a conflict, because she is dead creatively: this is an intolerable situation. Sexton aligns herself, in this state of living–nonliving, with "people who stand at the open window like objects waiting to topple" ("The House," *Pretty*, 75). Standing is, figuratively, inactivity, and the coupling of standing with waiting alludes to an eventual crisis. The poet often describes such arrested movement, as in "The Operation" (*Pretty*, 58): "I wait like a kennel of dogs / jumping against their fence." These lines elicit the restlessness (and possibly the kindling aggression) of the trapped animal and the understanding of motion without gain, as well as a mounting sense of tension.

Concurrent realities of life as death are clear in "The Double Image" (*Bedlam*, 35), in which the persona is split into two personalities she cannot unite—one of substance, the other a mirrored reflection. Since the mirrored image is a reflected one, and is consequently dependent upon the other for its existence, it only partially represents reality. This notion is reminiscent of Socrates' "Parable of the Cave," in which he discusses reflections cast on the cave wall by a fire, concluding that to the observers of these reflections, "the [apparent] truth would be nothing but the shadows of the images."[6] One sees a "shadow" in the mirror, not one's true self. She who is reflected exists independently of her mirror-image, and not vice-versa. Therefore, the mirror imperfectly portrays life because it captures only a part of reality. The persona is stymied between the two images—reality and doppelganger—as between life and death: "And this was the cave of the mirror, / that double woman who stares / at herself, as if she were petrified / in time."

The double woman exists within photographs and portraits as well as within mirrors. Sexton uses these images to evince the duality of that which records life and thereby renders it immortal, yet also stops the action and therefore freezes it. The doppelganger in the portrait represents ultimate life without motion—the woman who is forced to remain living, yet is motionless, dormant, for eternity. In "The Double Image" Sexton herself is the woman in the portrait, describing her life with her mother and her retreat into inactivity—the portrait—when she wants to avoid conflict: "I cannot forgive your suicide, my mother said. / And she never could. She had my portrait / done instead . . ." (36). Because the mother cannot understand the daughter's "suicide," she withdraws from her, preferring to keep her idealized view of her daughter intact through the portrait. As mother and daughter, the two women mirror each other as well; the mother–daughter relationship is a continuum, especially as the persona later gives birth to her own daughter, thereby creating another set of dualities—a virtual fun-house hall of mirrors—images within images within images—inwardly spiraling, creating multiples rather than mere doubles. Suzanne Juhasz also contends that there is a continuum: " 'I made you to find me,' says the poet [Sexton]. And why not, because surely in some ways I am you and you are me, a girl child that I have made in my woman's body; and in other ways you are not me, I am not you, for I am mother while you are child. We are a double image."[7] As the daughter attempts to kill herself—the primary image—so too the reflective image of her mother nearly dies. Interestingly, the persona uses the term "suicide" rather than "suicide attempt": obviously the persona could not have committed suicide since she is alive to speak through the poem. For the mother the mere attempt has killed the daughter. Additionally, the poet both participates in and perpetuates flawed mother–daughter relationships—she is at once daughter and mother.

Photographs also represent frozen life in allowing the dead to live on. "A Little Uncomplicated Hymn" (*Live*, 150) describes her daughter's "school portrait / where you repeat third grade, / caught in the need not to grow— / that little prison—." While the photograph preserves life, one can only

preserve that which is already dead. A photograph is always "past tense"—
the reality of the moment vanishing as quickly as the shutter is snapped—
and is yet another example of the duality and coexistence of life and death.

This vision of preserved, if petrified, life—life that Sexton struggles to
escape—occurs throughout her poetry. Because much of the landscape
within the poems is the landscape of institutions, one notes there the duality
of life and death: the lack of freedom in institutions limits the inmates' lives
to half-lives. Sexton refers to the mental institution as a "hierarchy of death"
("Flee on Your Donkey," *Live*, 104) and to the inmates as the "moving dead"
("You, Doctor Martin," *Bedlam*, 31). Having surrendered their identities,
the broken people are counted at the "frozen gates of dinner," one by one,
like sheep. Frozen in their incarceration, the inmates cannot grow.

In addition to the prison that is external, Sexton reveals the internal
prison of her own mind and body in "Wanting to Die" (*Live*, 142); "[death]
waits for me, year after year, / to so delicately undo an old wound, / to empty
my breath from its bad prison." One of the ways in which the persona escapes
this self-described imprisonment is through medication, drugs. The imagery
of pills and needles represents both release and avoidance in Sexton's poetry.
While the drugs provide comfort, in the form of calm or sleep, they also numb,
so that a sleeping pill becomes "a splendid pearl [which] floats me out of
myself" ("Lullaby" [*Bedlam*, 29]). The very title "Lullaby" connotes something
soothing, and the juxtaposition of sleeping pill and lullaby conjures an elemental sense of comfort—the mother who rocks her child to sleep. And indeed,
"the pills are a mother, but better" ("The Addict," *Live*, 165). Additionally, the
proliferation of white images suggests a purity, a return to the state of loved
daughter and a life of possibility, but the images also elicit the elusiveness of a
dream: only in a dream is such singularity of color possible.

Despite her reliance on these medications, despite their capacity to
keep her "on a diet from death," the persona realizes the danger inherent in
her "addiction": "I like them more than I like me . . . / It's a kind of marriage
/ It's a kind of war / where I plant bombs inside / of myself" ("The Addict,"
Live, 165). Furthermore, the poet's ambivalence toward the drugs is evident
as she praises them as "eight chemical kisses," yet admits she is slowly killing
herself. In numbing her, the pills are also a kind of poison: they prevent her
from fully experiencing life.

Because the poet knows that she cannot continue much longer on her
present course before the "bombs" she has planted explode, she recognizes
the need to change. Or, to follow the plentiful Christian symbolism, an
escape from sin—salvation—is warranted. "With Mercy for the Greedy"
(*Pretty*, 62) declares "I was born / doing reference work in sin, and born /
confessing it."

Another Christian image Sexton uses is the garden. The poet wills a
return to the garden, that is, innocence, so that things would only grow, not
die, for the concept of death began with the first sin: the death of innocence.
In "Little Girl, My String Bean, My Lovely Woman" (*Live*, 145), Sexton

maintains that her prepubescent daughter, "at eleven / (almost twelve), is like a garden." In her gardenlike state Sexton's daughter remains untainted, yet a change—represented here as "high noon"—is imminent. At high noon the persona's daughter is nearly at the zenith of her life, both as adult and as woman who has the possibility of new life within her; she is the very embodiment of growth: "The summer has seized you, / I think even of the orchard next door, / where the berries are done / and the apples are beginning to swell." Despite the fruition, however, growth will continue: she has only begun to ripen. The poet also seems to be in awe of having given life to this child, finding hope and affirmation in the thought:

> If I could have watched you grow
> as a magical mother might,
> if I could have seen through my
> magical transparent belly,
> there would have been such ripening within:
> your embryo, . . .
> a world of its own. . . .

Because growth in the form of continuance comes through children, the persona feels reborn as she watches her children grow. As her daughters live, so too will she.

However, growth inevitably leads to, and is present in, death as well as life. The process of dying begins at the moment of conception, for "death too is in the egg" ("The Operation," *Pretty*, 56), and death "was in the womb all along" ("Menstruation at Forty," *Live*, 137). Therefore, the processes of life and death are interchangeable. Juhasz describes Sexton's view of life as a continuum:

> One is born with one's death inside oneself, like an egg, or a baby. Through the process of living one transforms oneself into one's own death, through a process of hardening, stiffening, freezing. Each birth only hastens the process, so one grows from baby to child to daughter to mother: in the last act of birth, a mother gives birth to her own death, a death baby. . . . I give birth to my own death. I am my mother's baby; I am my mother's death; I am my mother; I am my baby; I am my death.[8]

Growth that leads to death is present in another form as well: cancer. In several poems Sexton portrays this growth that leads not to fruition, but to death. She speaks of her mother in the poem "The Operation" (*Pretty*, 56): "[Cancer] grew in her as simply as a child would grow, / as simply as she housed me once, fat and female. . . . [an] embryo of evil." Whereas here cancer is represented as a naturally growing malevolent thing—a "death baby," a twin to the poet—in a later poem written about John Holmes, her first writing instructor ("Somewhere in Africa," *Live*, 106), Sexton describes cancer with language and imagery that border on lushness in detailing growth: "cancer blossomed in your throat, / rooted like bougainvillea into your gray backbone, . . . / The thick petals, the exotic reds, the purples and whites. . . ." The cancer finally causes Holmes to blossom through death into a state of rebirth, of innocence, as he is welcomed by a female who is the very embodiment of fertility, of the earth mother, of Eve: "a woman naked to the waist / moist with palm oil and sweat, a woman of some virtue / and wild breasts, her limbs excellent, unbruised and chaste."

In addition to the growth of cancer that leads to death, growth comes out of death itself. After death the body continues to grow, in that the nails and hair seem to lengthen, and mold, decay, and the growth of bacteria set in. "The Moss of His Skin" (*Bedlam*, 26), a dramatic monologue in the persona of a young girl entombed, by ancient custom, with her dead father, presents this process: "daddy was there, / . . . his hair growing / like a field or a shawl. / I lay by the moss / of his skin until / it grew strange. . . ." The father's body begins to decay, and so gestates anew in the womb-like interior of the tomb. Were the body in the ground, it would give life through its decomposition, returning nutrients to the soil.

While some growth through death—life that comes out of death—is physical in nature, the poet also implies repeatedly that the dead have a consciousness, and so continue to live after death, albeit in a diminished capacity. In "Letter Written During a January Northeaster" (*Pretty*, 89), Sexton writes: "It is snowing, grotesquely snowing, / upon the small faces of the dead. . . . / The dead turn over casually, / thinking . . . / Good! No visitors today." As she argues the choice between life and death, Sexton makes a strong case for her belief in life and movement after death, perhaps revealing why the choice is a difficult one—both offer possibilities for growth.

In addition to showing growth through theme, the poet uses imagery to detail movement. Movement, growth, and freedom are the opposite of a static, poisoned life; the many images that detail movement foreshadow and reinforce Sexton's strong attraction to life. Representing escape and control—a seeming paradox—bird imagery is used often through these first three books. The persona admires the birds' ease of movement, appreciating their sense of freedom, strength, volition, and power: "I planned such plans of flight, . . . / I planned by growth and my womanhood / as one choreographs a dance" ("Those Times," *Live*, 119). The poet remembers herself during childhood as she dreams of her adult life. Only during dreams, it happens, will innocence and control occur for her now, as in childhood she could fly only in dreams; even so, the poet must try to regain her sense of innocence, her zeal for life.

The movement that leads out of the stasis in the persona's life is represented in much other imagery as well. That movement is detailed through fish, for example, as they move through water, the life force, though there is also the understanding that water kills things by drowning. Other symbols of growth—trees, for example, which grow though standing still—and much plant and animal imagery are prominent and plentiful in the poetry. One of the most interesting sets of images is the bells that mark progression of time and life-passages as they are tolled at christenings, marriages, and deaths; yet

Sexton also uses the bells to represent life that is in stasis—motion without gain: "And this is the way they ring / the bells at Bedlam . . . / and this is always my bell responding / to my hand that responds to the lady / who points at me, E flat . . ." ("Ringing the Bells," *Bedlam*, 28). Here the persona functions perfunctorily as the extension of a bell, meekly submissive to the director of the bell choir.

The movement and growth that lead the persona out of stasis, then, must result in a choice of either life or death. As "Live," (170) the final poem in the collection *Live or Die*, makes clear, Sexton's choice is against death. Just as prisoners leave their cells either by returning to the mainstream of life or by dying, so too the poet must make a choice that allows her to escape from the poisoned state. Robert Boyers observes, "Miss Sexton's propensities are similarly violent and suicidal [to Plath's], but she convinces herself, and her reader, that she has something to live for. We are grateful to Miss Sexton as we can be to few poets, for she has distinctly enlarged and enhanced the possibilities of endurance in that air of lost connections which so many of us inhabit."[9] Appropriately, "Live" ends Sexton's first three books, emphasizing her positive choice:

> Today life opened inside me like an egg
> and there inside
> after considerable digging
> I found the answer. . . .
> I say 'Live, Live' because of the sun,
> the dream, the excitable gift.

Clearly affirming life, the poet discovers that the potential for growth (the sun as an "egg"), or for hope (daily possibility of renewal), is reason enough to keep living. It is possible to change. Boyers finds "Live" to be:

> a triumph of determination and insight, a final resolution of irreconcilabilities that had threatened to remain perpetually suspended and apart. Miss Sexton's affirmation represents a rebirth of astounding proportions, a veritable reconstruction of her self-image in the face of a corrupt and corrupting universe.[10]

Sexton herself insists that she consciously chose to keep living; as she finished writing *Live or Die* she came to realize—when unable to kill a litter of puppies—that "I could let me live, too, that after all I wasn't a killer, that the poison just didn't take."[11]

Sexton chooses to examine life fully, in all its contradictions and restrictions, and then to embrace it fully. It is all too easy to misinterpret her early, clear-sighted and yet unflinching examination of life as a decision against life. However, in the epigraph to *The Awful Rowing toward God* (1975), Sexton quotes Thoreau: "There are two ways to victory—to strive bravely, or to yield" (417). And, in these early poems Sexton undeniably chooses "to strive bravely," to embrace life. Her explicit hope for growth, her belief in life-cycles, will admit to no other choice. In contrast to those who maintain that

Sexton is an unwavering death poet, her early poetry clearly shows that she chooses life, albeit after much struggling and soul-searching. Although she will prove to be only "part way back,"[12] she *did* embrace life for a time. As Boyers observes: "Miss Sexton's decision to live, with her eyes open, and the responsibilities for human values planted firmly on her competent shoulders, is a major statement of our poetry."[13] Anne Sexton, for a while at least, proved herself without a doubt to be a life-affirming poet.

Notes

1. Anne Sexton, *The Complete Poems*, ed. Linda Gray Sexton (Boston: Houghton Mifflin, 1981). Henceforth, any references to the first three volumes within *The Complete Poems* will be included parenthetically within the text using the following abbreviations: *To Bedlam and Part Way Back: Bedlam; All My Pretty Ones: Pretty; Live or Die: Live*.

2. Barbara Kevles, "The Art of Poetry: Anne Sexton," in *Writers at Work: The Paris Review Interviews*, Fourth Series, ed. George Plimpton (New York: Viking Press, 1976), 397–424; rpt. *Anne Sexton: The Artist and Her Critics*, ed. J. D. McClatchy (Bloomington: Indiana University Press, 1978), 6.

3. Kevles, "Art of Poetry," 15.

4. J. D. McClatchy, "Anne Sexton: Somehow to Endure," in his *Anne Sexton: The Artist and Her Critics* (Bloomington: Indiana University Press, 1978), 256.

5. Kevles, "Art of Poetry," 12.

6. Plato, *The Republic*, Third Edition of the Jowett translation, ed. Charles M. Bakewell (New York: Charles Scribner's Sons, 1956), book 7, 273–74.

7. Suzanne Juhasz, *Naked and Fiery Forms, Modern American Poetry by Women: A New Tradition* (New York: Harper & Row, 1976), 123.

8. Ibid., 137.

9. Robert Boyers, "*Live or Die:* The Achievement of Anne Sexton," in *Anne Sexton: The Artist and Her Critics*, ed. J. D. McClatchy (Bloomington: Indiana University Press, 1978), 205.

10. Ibid., 213.

11. Kevles, "Arts of Poetry," 16.

12. McClatchy, "Somehow to Endure," 264.

13. Boyers, *Live or Die*, 214.

"The sack of time": Death and Time in Anne Sexton's "Some Foreign Letters"

Gwen L. Nagel*

When Anne Sexton chose "Some Foreign Letters" for inclusion in *Poet's Choice* in 1962, she described how her voice would break when she read the

*This essay was written specifically for this volume and is published here for the first time by permission of the author.

poem aloud and how its impact remained "strong and utterly personal": "Because 'Some Foreign Letters' still puts a lump in my throat, I know that it is my unconscious favorite."[1]

The subject of the poem is Anna Ladd Dingley, Sexton's great-aunt and namesake, a woman who had lived for some years with Anne's family in one of the western suburbs of Boston. Sexton once said that unlike her mother, who "was very destructive," the "only person who was very constructive in my life was my great-aunt, and of course she went mad when I was thirteen. It was probably the trauma of my life that I never got over."[2] Nana, as Sexton called her, became deaf, lapsed into senility, and was eventually moved to a nursing home where she died in 1954 at age eighty-six.[3] For a time Sexton blamed herself for her great-aunt's dementia[4] and vaguely associated it with her own physical development: "at thirteen I kissed a boy . . . and I was so pleased with my own womanhood that I told Nana I was kissed and then she went mad . . . ."[5] Sexton writes about Nana in several poems, including "Elizabeth Gone," "Walking in Paris," "The Hex," "Anna Who Was Mad," and "The Hoarder," but it is in "Some Foreign Letters," which Robert Lowell once labeled "one of her finest and quietest poems,"[6] where she most deeply explores her relationship with the woman Sexton called "my best friend, my teacher, my confidante and my comforter."[7]

Sexton once referred to the role that time plays in the poem:

> my special loyalty to "Some Foreign Letters" stems from its dual outlook toward the past and the present. It combines them in much the same way that our lives do—closer to life than to art. It distills a time for me, a graceful innocent age that I loved but never knew. It is, for me, like a strange photograph that I come upon each time with a seizure of despair and astonishment.[8]

This "strange photograph" Sexton creates succeeds in capturing a lost world, a time before Sexton's own birth when the young Anna Ladd Dingley had lived abroad. Sexton's great-aunt had lived for three years in Europe in the early 1890s and while there had written a series of letters home to her family that were later bound and preserved. It is these letters that evoke the poet's response and yield a reassessment of her relationship with the woman. Sexton once wrote of her great-aunt: "I never thought of her as being young. She was an extension of myself and was my world. I hadn't considered that she might have had a world of her own once."[9] The childlike egotism that these lines reveal informs the nature of the relationship between the poet and Nana in the beginning of the poem. But the old maiden aunt the poet knew as a child, like other white-haired ladies, had secrets to tell of a past life. The poet's explicit purpose, as she states it in the first stanza, is to re-create Nana's life abroad, to animate that dead world of the past: "I try / to reach into your page and breathe it back."[10] By combining multiple levels of time in the poem, the poet creates a new context for viewing her aunt and a new response to the dead woman.

That Sexton's treatment of time in the poem will be complex is evident from the first lines: "I knew you forever and you were always old, / soft white lady of my heart." Four critical words here evoke time. The past tense, "I knew," suggests the retrospective nature of the poet's relationship with the woman and implies that the relationship has ended. The words "forever" and "always" complicate that idea by suggesting perpetuity and the eternal, a quality outside the realm of real time. The final word of the first line, however, subverts that idea: "old" suggests change and transcience. "Soft white lady of my heart" is an effective second line, for it lends specificity to the abstract quality of the first line by appealing to the senses of touch and sight. "Soft" suggests the tactile quality of the woman. Sexton commented once that her Nana was physically demonstrative: "She cuddled me. I was tall, but I tried to cuddle up. My mother never touched me in my life, except to examine me."[11] The word "white" buttresses the idea of old age and at the same time provides a strong visual image of the woman. Indeed, Sexton refers to Nana's white hair in a later poem, "Letters to Dr. Y," when she writes "Your Nana had white powdery hair, eh?" But "soft white lady of my heart" is more than the poet's warm sentiments about the woman. It, too, relates to time for it subtly implies that the relationship now exists on a plane outside of real time, in the response of the poet.

From the beginning, Sexton subtly yet swiftly introduces the subject of her poem, Nana and the idea of time. What becomes apparent is that what follows will not be a simple chronological narrative about Nana's European travel. The first three sentences of the poem make rapid time shifts as Sexton moves from past tense, to subjunctive, to past tense, and finally to the present tense again, the "I read" establishing the present time of the poem. Such radical juxtapositions occur in four of the five stanzas, with the poet moving from the distant past in Europe, to the more recent past when Nana lived with the poet.

But there is another element of time in the poem as well. The present of the poem is "tonight," a word Sexton uses four times. "Tonight" provides a touchstone in time that Sexton returns to from the journeying she does throughout the rest of poem. Sexton first employs the word in stanza two when she suggests her present conundrum:

> Tonight your letters reduce
> history to a guess. The Count had a wife.
> You were the old maid aunt who lived with us.

Sexton again sets forth many layers of time here as she refers to present, distant past, and more recent past, and in the next line when she writes "Tonight I read how the winter howled around / the towers of Schloss Schwobber," she returns to the present and then immediately begins on the journey into time again, imagining the European experience of the aunt. The poet's response to this created experience, the confluence of the two time periods in her aunt's life, occurs "tonight" and yields a change in her emotional response to the dead woman and to life.

Aside from the numerous shifts in verb tenses and the repeated references to "tonight," the poem contains many other allusions to time, beginning with the explicit comment that the letters were first posted "in the winter of eighteen-ninety." Sexton refers to Lord Mayor's Day in London and to several Wednesdays—in Berlin, near Lucerne, Switzerland in May, in Rome in November. The breakdown at Symphony Hall takes place "one Friday." There are less specific references to the time that the poet shared with Nana: "When you were mine" is repeated in the second and fourth stanzas. The phrase expresses the childlike egotism of possession; the time is not Nana's world as much as it belongs to the speaker as a young girl. That other time never experienced by the poet, unpossessed by her, lies buried in the remnants of her aunt's life, the bound letters. When Sexton takes possession of this lost time by re-creating it, she reinforces the sense of immediacy in the distant past, "breathes" back the lost time, both through evocative sensory detail in her vignettes of Nana's life in Europe as well as through her emphatic use of the present tense. For example, when Sexton writes "This Wednesday in Berlin," "This is Wednesday, May 9th, near Lucerne, / Switzerland, sixty-nine years ago," "this is the rocky path," and "This is Italy" the present tense evokes the instantaneity of her aunt's letters. Another device that Sexton employs to take possession of the lost time occurs in stanza 2 when she says "How distant you are on your nickel-plated skates / in the skating park in Berlin, gliding past / me with your Count. . . ." The line break puts "me" in an emphatic position and underscores the poet's attempts to appropriate these experiences for herself. She pushes outside the boundaries of chronological time here to possess more of her aunt. The motive for doing so, by implication, is that she has lost her. The poet thrusts herself imaginatively in an earlier world, intrudes on experiences she knows only by the letters, and then immediately breaks the spell by asserting: "I loved you last, / a pleated old lady with a crooked hand." This rapid juxtaposition of layers of time is the major device Sexton employs to present her theme of aging and time.

Sexton reinforces the dual quality of time in the poem with a series of contrasting images. Throughout the five stanzas Sexton juxtaposes her great aunt's experiences in London, Berlin, Hanover, Lucerne, Paris, Verona, and Rome with her memories of Nana's life in New England. In each of the European locales Nana is spirited and alive and dominates the activity of the scenes. For example, she guides past the robbers in the slums of London; skates in Berlin; climbs mountains in Switzerland and kisses her count; walks, watches, cheers with the devout in Rome. And she communicates with those around her by learning to speak German and Italian. The older Nana returns to New England where she lives "like a prim thing / on the farm in Maine." In Boston she is inert and restricted by the handicaps of old age, "a pleated old lady with a crooked hand." In London she wears "furs and a new dress"; in Boston she wears an earphone and has no control over herself: "When you were mine they wrapped you out of here / with your best hat over your face." The "best hat" here is a poignant image of shame, of lack of control and loss of self.

It is particularly instructive to compare Nana's activity in stanza 3 with Sexton's last description of her in stanza 5. In the central stanza of the poem Sexton amplifies the sensuous experiences encountered by the "sweet body" of the "yankee girl" in the mountain climbs by providing numerous details suggesting the sensory quality of the experience. For example, the hole in her aunt's shoes, the "rocky path," the "first vertigo / up over Lake Lucerne," the sweating count, the aunt's wading through "top snow," and even the sandwiches and "*seltzer wasser*" suggest a variety of physical sensations. The sensory experiences of the climb culminate when the count holds her hand and kisses her, revealing a side of Nana that Sexton has not experienced by living with her white-haired maiden aunt. Stanza 3 ends with Nana on the move once again, taking a train, catching "a steamboat for home; / or other postmarks: Paris, Verona, Rome."

Sexton contrasts the sensory experiences of the mountain climb and the other European experiences with Nana's more restricted life in America. In the "suburbs of Boston" Nana is passive: she "sees" the world go drunk, watches the children dance (she is no longer capable, is the implication), feels her ears close. And in the stunning image of Nana's breakdown outside of Symphony Hall, Sexton employs images that recall those in stanza 3:

> you will tip your boot feet out of that hall,
> rocking from its sour sound, out onto
> the crowded street, letting your spectacles fall
> and your hair net tangle as you stop passers-by
> to mumble your guilty love while your ears die.

The references to the acute senses in stanza 3 prepare the reader for their dissolution in the final stanza. Here her "boot feet" rock as Nana reels in a spasm of deafness; on the mountains her feet felt the rocky path, and though she feels vertigo, she was surefooted with the help of alpine stocks and the count's steady arm. On the mountain she was alone with her count and had experienced love ("He held your hand and kissed you"), while outside Symphony Hall she is a public spectacle, muttering her "guilty love," her mental derangement conveyed by the falling glasses, the tangled hair net, both evocative images of old age and disorder. And finally, these last lines of the poem counter the sense of endless movement of stanza 3, of the journey going forward to other postmarks. When Nana's "ears die" she is at the end of her journey.

More subtle, perhaps, but no less important, is the contrast between the young Nana's attitudes in Europe and in New England. Sexton once wrote that her aunt came from "a protestant background with a very stern patriarchal father."[12] Although this information is not present in the poem,

Sexton alludes to the austere and even priggish psychological climate that Nana finds at home. Her aunt returns to America "to live like a prim thing / on the farm in Maine" and then moves "to the suburbs of Boston, to see the blue-nose / world go drunk each night." She is a Yankee girl who has had her fling, an affair in Europe with a married count, who returns to a puritanical, prudish world. References to Nana's guilty conscience suggest that her time with her count was not without its cost. With the end of love, Nana is left alone in Rome to absolve her guilt: "You worked your New England conscience out / beside artisans, chestnut vendors and the devout."[13] The relaxed and free woman of the illicit affair becomes the returned Yankee girl who lives "like a prim thing," a woman who might scold the poet for staying up late and reading someone else's mail. That the daughter of the stern Protestant never quite resolved her guilt over this love affair is implied in the description of the beginning of her dementia on the streets of Boston where she is left alone "to mumble your guilty love."

There is one other set of images that provide further contrasts between the created and remembered past. Throughout the poem Sexton refers to the auditory experiences of the young woman. The letters describe, for example, "how the winter howled around / the towers of the Schloss Schwobber, how the tedious / language grew in your jaw." Sexton here underscores the quality of the German, the "tedious / language" Nana learns, by inserting the awkward "towers of Schloss Schwobber." In a more musical, mellifluous line Sexton describes how the young woman in Europe "loved the sound / of the music of the rats tapping on the stone floors." In the more recent past, however, Nana "wore an earphone." There are other such contrasts. For example, the aunt skates to a Strauss waltz played by a military band in stanza 2, but by the last stanza she merely watches "the handsome / children jitterbug." Other words convey the sense of sound and are a part of the world of hearing, such as the lines describing how Nana "rattled / down on the train" and "cheered with the others" at the Vatican. The auditory imagery culminates in the last poignant six lines of the poem, with the poet foretelling Nana's experience outside of Boston's Symphony Hall where she hears only "sour sound." The deliberate, staccato rhythm of "you will tip your boot feet out of that hall," conveys the slowness of the old woman as she moves out into the street where her "ears die."

What emerges from the confluence of these contrasts in places, attitudes, and sensory experiences is the poet's awareness of the effect of time on the life of someone she knew and loved. Essentially Nana's life goes from relative freedom and intensity of sensory response to restriction. She moves from her active journeying and her relative freedom in Europe to the final stasis in a Boston suburb. Life closes in on her, and Nana loses the ability to experience intensely physical and sensory pleasures (as described in the third stanza), the lessening of her senses conveyed most by the loss of hearing in the final stanza. And finally there is the restricted response, from being a free-loving creature to a prim thing in America. Life, which appears to hold out so many possibilities, ends in death. The poet attempts to reverse the unavoidable process in the poem by re-creating the lost time but she ultimately yields to despair and hopelessness: "I try / to reach into your page and breathe it back . . . / but life is a trick, life is a kitten in a sack."

This is the central and controlling image of the poem, and it directly contradicts the sense of eternal time evoked by "forever" and "always" of the first line. When it first appears, the line is hyperbolic. It startles and seems out of keeping with a nostalgic trip back to a lost time. The kitten in the sack image is effective in conveying a sense of youth and innocence doomed to die, but Sexton delineates the aging process that ends in death, concluding the poem with the description of Nana's loss of hearing. Several historical references are portents of death and loss and reinforce the central image. The Europe the young woman knew is "a good world still," unmarked by war, death, or guilty love. It is a world where a Yankee girl can protect her pocketbook in the slums of Whitechapel, where two years before Jack the Ripper had murdered his victims. She can go to a bazaar in Bismark's house in 1890, the year he was forced to resign. Even in the third stanza there are portents of loss in the threats to the safety of the woman, but they go ignored: "You were not alarmed / by the thick woods of briars and bushes, / nor the rugged cliff, nor the first vertigo / up over Lake Lucerne." The references here have a fairy-tale quality about them and suggest a time out of real time. The Lohengrin legend Nana reads in Germany (with the dead geese hanging all around her) ends with the dissolution of the lovers and foretells the end of her own affair. Indeed, in Rome she is alone with her guilt, left to contemplate "the ruins of the palaces of the Caesars," and to observe the silver balloon floating "up over Forum, up over the lost emperors, / to shiver its little modern cage in an occasional / breeze." This is a wonderfully evocative image that reinforces the idea of loss and death. The balloon is lovely and ephemeral as it floats high above the Roman dead. It is as doomed, though beautiful, as the kitten in the sack. The balloon is the sack in disguise. It has its tiny life, but like the lost emperors of Rome, the kitten, and Nana's youth, it is doomed. The loveliness of the balloon's "silver" color gives way to the "shiver," suggestive of cold and death. The balloon imagery even evokes the shape of the sack and reinforces the idea of the sack's confinement. It is filled with breath, with air, but it is a "modern cage." Reliving the youthful life of Nana through the creative process and seeing into the future and how it ended yields the anguish and hopelessness of the kitten-in-the-sack and the cage of the silver balloon images.

These metaphors, along with the radical shifts in time buttressed by images of place and sensory experiences, combine to produce the poet's response to Nana, a response that changes over the course of the poem. In the first two stanzas the speaker actively participates in the life of the dead woman, and especially in stanza 2, where she imagines Nana so intensely that she re-creates history by putting herself back into Nana's life. In the third stanza, however, Sexton seems more detached, only learning the facts of the experience of the mountain climb. In stanzas 1 and 3 she shuttles back and forth in time, from the remembered experiences with Nana to the re-created ones. In stanza 4 she remembers her past responses to the senile woman who was taken away to be institutionalized: "I cried / because I was seventeen. I am older now." The lines suggest age somehow cushions the blows and toughens one to its adversities. But by the final stanza, the poet responds emotionally to her aunt. Because the poet's experience with Nana has been enlarged by her imaginative re-creation of the life in the letters, she needs to respond anew to the woman. Her knowledge of Nana is more complicated now: "Tonight I will learn to love you twice; / learn your first days, your mid-Victorian face." Her experience with Nana is now double and requires a second share of love, of emotional response. The poet also responds a new way: she will take over the parental role by warning her of what is coming: "Tonight I will speak up and interrupt your / letters. . . ." She thus takes an active stance in this relationship; she changes from the young niece Nana would scold if she were alive, to a concerned and loving woman who wants to overthrow the old parent–child relationship. Instead of the prim aunt admonishing the niece for staying up late and reading mail not addressed to her, Nana is cast in the role of the younger one who can benefit by the wisdom of the older poet. The poet attempts to step out of time, to break the boundaries of time to warn the aunt of what is coming. But such intervention is impossible, for the woman is already dead. That she would go to such illogical lengths to step out of time is a measure of the heightened state of the speaker of the poem. Her purpose is to break through time, to do the impossible: "I tell you" becomes incantatory. Sexton warns her aunt "that wars are coming, / that the Count will die," that she will lose her hearing and go mad. What lends the admonitions their tragic weight is their futility. The events have occurred; the poet, caught up in the immediacy of those lost times, Nana's other life in Europe, feels the pain of knowing the future. The futility of the gesture, the attempt at warning her of the future, is finally brought home in the final six lines of the poem, in the description of the aunt's breakdown, the loss of her hearing that marked the beginning of her madness. The finality of "while your ears die" is made more poignant because this is only the beginning of the physical death that is, too, inescapable. She will warn her aunt much as a parent warns a child. But this intervention is impossible. It is too late. Life is a kitten in a sack and the kitten, Nana, is dead.

Part of what Sexton does in the poem is to present the possibility of creating life, if only for a moment, through imagination. The episodes in London, Berlin, Hanover, Switzerland, and Rome portray a living, breathing woman going about life years before Sexton is even born. But this, like life, is a trick. When Sexton writes "This is the sack of time your death vacates" she refers to her own artistic creation. The invented construct of the poem holds out the possibility of breaking through time, for the poem is a kind of envelope or sack of time that contains the invented and re-created life of the dead woman. By pushing beyond real time, by re-creating the intensely experienced moments of life in Europe, Sexton breaks through time and discovers a way of keeping her alive.

"Some Foreign Letters" conveys an attempt to reconcile two layers of past time with the present. The poet dominates time by thrusting herself into the past; she looks into those dead pages of the letters and "breathes it back." And she thrusts forward into the future: "Tonight I will learn to love you twice" and "Tonight I will speak up." But the death of Nana leaves a void, an empty sack, a sack of time, enclosed, impossible to retrieve. What Sexton does is to breathe life into that sack, that dead time, through details that enliven a dead world. She creates living moments and a time when she shares the unknown life with Nana. But what is finally left is the vacant sack, the balloon without air, the dead woman. Then the futility of breathing life into a past that is gone and of avoiding the inescapable end to youth and life is conveyed most poignantly in the empty sack image, for it conveys the emptiness left by the death of the beloved Nana.

The richness of the poem emerges from Sexton's fusion of the imagined past with the remembered past. By juxtaposing a re-created world, the places and times described in Nana's letters, with memories of the older Nana she knew, Sexton achieves in "Some Foreign Letters" a remarkable confluence of period and place, a context from which her new and deeper responses to Nana can emerge.

Notes

1. Anne Sexton, "Comment on 'Some Foreign Letters,' " in *No Evil Star: Selected Essays, Interviews, and Prose*, ed. Steven E. Colburn (Ann Arbor: University of Michigan Press, 1985), 17.

2. Anne Sexton, "With Maxine Kumin, Elaine Showalter, and Carol Smith," in *No Evil Star*, 177.

3. *Anne Sexton: A Self-Portrait in Letters*, ed. Linda Gray Sexton and Lois Ames (Boston: Houghton Mifflin, 1977), 5.

4. Ibid., 41.

5. Ibid.

6. Robert Lowell, "Anne Sexton," in *Anne Sexton: The Artist and Her Critics*, ed. J. D. McClatchy (Bloomington: Indiana University Press, 1978), 72.

7. Sexton, "Comment on 'Some Foreign Letters,' " 16. Nana is also mentioned in "The Death of the Fathers," "45 Mercy Street," "Talking to Sheep," and "The Lost Lie."

8. Sexton, "Comment on 'Some Foreign Letters,' " 16.

9. Ibid., 16–17.

10. Anne Sexton, *The Complete Poems* (Boston: Houghton Mifflin, 1981), 9–11. All further references to the poem are to this edition.

11. Sexton, "With Maxine Kumin," 177.

12. "Interview with Barbara Kevles," in *No Evil Star*, 104.

13. The guilt in this poem does not really carry beyond Nana; in "The Hex," however, the poet's lost purity results in her guilt.

Transformations's Silencings   Carol Leventen*

My subject is the bleak, devastating vision of women's roles that Sexton creates in *Transformations*, her retelling of seventeen of Jacob and Wilhelm Grimm's fairy tales. In these poems Sexton's protagonists are silenced, acted upon, and they acquiesce almost helplessly in continuing silence themselves. The devalued products of patriarchy, of a process of socialization that inscribes male power, are viewed as commodities, as objects—a condition they frequently reify in their acceptance of their curtailed autonomy, their inability to conceive of themselves in active roles, and the difficulties they experience in bonding constructively with one other. At the same time, Sexton also creates, in the stunning and frequently brilliant prologues that introduce each poem, a narrative voice, a dynamic relationship between tale-teller and audience, between teller and tale, that posits but does not fully develop the possibility of an alternative and that reveals, as I shall argue, a problematic ambivalence toward her protagonists in their situation that merits closer attention.

Sexton's best-selling volume, *Transformations*, has found favor with her critics as well as her readers. Generally described as witty, ironic, and acerbic, it has been widely praised for its darkly comic juxtapositions of fairy tale motifs and contemporary references—juxtapositions that underscore the aridity of once-upon-a-time's happily-ever-after resolutions (e.g., her much-quoted parting shot at *Cinderella:* "Regular Bobbsey twins. / That story."[1] Realizing that these poems might be seen as a radical departure from the confessionalism of *To Bedlam and Part Way Back* and *All My Pretty Ones*, she was well aware of their links to her earlier work. She wrote to Kurt Vonnegut, when sounding out his willingness to contribute the introduction for the volume:

> Without quite meaning to I have joined the black humorists. I don't know if you know my other work, but humor was never a very prominent feature . . . terror, deformity, madness and torture were my bag. But this little universe of Grimm is not that far away. I think they end up being as wholly personal as my most intimate poems, in a different language, a different rhythm, but coming strangely, for all their story sound, from as deep a place.[2]

To be sure, many of the poems in *Transformations* articulate the same concerns that inform Sexton's earlier work: no longer justifying herself in response to the imagined criticism or the silencing misgivings of "John, Who Begs Me Not to Enquire Further" (*CP* 34), she confidently proceeds on the premise that "we must have the answers"; in "The Gold Key," her opening poem, she contracts to do much more than merely entertain through her pop art. Like the author, Sexton's Sleeping Beauty seeks, in the "narrow diary of

*This essay was written specifically for this volume and is published here for the first time by the permission of the author.

[her] mind," to articulate unpleasant truths heretofore confined to night-mare; other reinvented tales readdress the problem of unstable boundaries in mother–daughter relationships that dominates what is arguably Sexton's finest poem, "The Double Image."

Sexton implies in "The Gold Key" that the knowledge she is about to impart will be empowering. "I have come to remind you, / all of you," she tells her assembled adult listeners, now "comatose" and "undersea." Suggest-ing that their current condition (for her primary audience turns out to be a group of fellow mental patients) can be ameliorated by unlocking memories of the stories (and ensuing bad dreams) of their childhood, she claims for herself as "Dame Sexton," "a middle-aged witch," a voice powerful enough to elicit secrets that "whimper" to be told. But while the content and context of "The Gold Key" might invite us to anticipate a psychological exploration, a Sextonesque study of the uses of enchantment, just as her epigraph to *All My Pretty Ones* conceives of poetry as an axe for breaking up "the frozen sea within us" (*CP* 48), this is not precisely what occurs: *Transformations* charts the wind-chill factor of the frozen sea around us. To be sure, *Transforma-tions* contains brilliant psychological discoveries (e.g., in many of the pro-logues, in "Iron Hans," "Rapunzel," "The Frog Prince," and especially in her perception of the incestuous father–daughter relationship in "Briar Rose"). But the balance falls elsewhere.

While it has become a commonplace to describe *Transformations* as a transitional volume, nascently macabre and archetypal,[3] that succeeds in "universalizing" the personal focus (by implication a limitation?) of the confes-sional mode, a number of critics have recognized the extent to which it is actually a collection of poems about women's roles and relationships. Such perceptions, however, have yielded contradictory assessments. On the one hand, we read that Sexton gives a voice to the private world of women's experience in these poems, and that her reworkings emphasize the possibil-ity of loving, mutually nurturing relationships between women.[4] On the other hand, these poems' most incisive critics—most notably, Alicia Ostri-ker, Ellen Cronan Rose, and Jack Zipes—concur that Sexton's vision in *Transformations* is grounded in her view of the unequivocally destructive impact on women of patriarchal control of the socialization process. As Zipes observes, "her poems depict how women are used as sex objects and how their lives become little more than commodities or hollow existences when they follow the social paths designed for them. Her utmost concern is with the ways and means women become drained of their energy, creativity, and power."[5] The issues that Zipes, Ostriker, and Rose raise—issues that inform the poems themselves—make it necessary to qualify the assessments of Sex-ton's relation to feminist writing offered by Juhasz and McCabe.

Sexton's interest in the implications and contemporary uses of the liter-ary fairy tale is not unique: *Transformations* belongs to a significant body of revisionist / feminist work, both critical and creative, that is probably more familiar to specialists in folklore and children's literature than to critics of recent American poetry. (In fact, Sexton's version of Sleeping Beauty is included in Zipes's recent anthology, *Don't Bet on the Prince: Contemporary Feminist Fairy Tales in North America and England,* and her "Red Riding Hood" appears in his *The Trials and Tribulations of Little Red Riding Hood: Versions of the Tale in Sociocultural Context.*)[6] This body of work, impressive in its own right, helps to clarify both the conflicting crosscurrents of Sexton's vision in general and the always-vexing question of her debatable feminism in particular. Some of it antedates or is contemporaneous with *Transformations;* some of it was quite literally (and angrily) provoked by Bruno Bettelheim's 1976 neo-Freudian study, *The Uses of Enchantment.*

To put it as simply as possible, Bettelheim reads the fairy tale psychoanalytically, as a fable of human development, in a way that feminist critics have characterized as profoundly insensitive to gender issues. He argues that Cinderella's role is really an active, not a passive one, and that her "psychosocial crises" are actually "steps in personality development required to reach self-fulfillment," and he sees her marriage to the prince (and accession to wealth) as entirely appropriate rewards for the personal growth she has demonstrated.[7] He sees Snow White's comatose stay in the glass coffin as a figure for the latency period, from which she quite properly emerges when ready to be sexually awakened by the right man, and he sees traditional fairy tales in general, which he tends to view as timeless and universal paradigms of unconscious dramas, as therapeutically useful since they mirror psychologically healthy ways of working out issues of separation, individuation, sibling rivalry, and Oedipal conflicts.[8]

This is not the place to debate either the value of various psychoanalytic approaches to the fairy tale or the possible manifestation in those tales of certain psychological processes. What is at issue—and of relevance for Sexton's poems—is the claim of both feminist and materialist critics that such an approach ignores the manifest sociocultural context of the tales—a context, they maintain, that inscribes restrictive social roles for women and that negatively influences women's self-concepts.[9] They argue that the tales perpetuate what Karen Rowe calls "alluring fantasies"[10] in which passivity, beauty, and helplessness are "rewarded" by marriages conferring wealth and status, and in which aggressive women who wield power are "bad" (i.e., wicked witches, wicked stepmothers) and are "punished." Not surprisingly, revisionist critics are appalled by many of Bettelheim's influential assumptions. As Kay Stone puts it in "The Misuses of Enchantment," critics like Bettelheim see fairy tales as "problem-solving stories," whereas feminist critics and readers see them as "problem-creating stories."[11] Countering Bettelheim's claim that gender does not govern the distribution of power and self-efficacy in these stories, and that children do not perceive any gender inequities, Stone quotes an adult woman reflecting upon her own experience of the tales:

> . . . the men seemed to be able to handle themselves, but the women didn't. Lots of things came together to prevent them. Outside forces con-

trolled their lives, and the only way they could solve it was with some kind of magic. . . . if they just got off their ass and thought about their situation they could maybe do something—except for the ones who were already aggressive and mean[12]

Much of Sexton's achievement in *Transformations* stems from her recognition of the impact of the socialization process on women and her decision to focus on the sociocultural context—on the way her protagonists are cast into roles and proceed to play them out—rather than on the exploration of individual psychology we might have expected. Her prologues and anachronisms—sometimes droll and flippant, sometimes savage—anchor her reinventions in a specific here-and-now, a concrete sociopolitical context that she can proceed to anatomize. In adopting this strategy, Sexton almost seems to have uncannily perceived some of what recent scholarship has revealed about the Grimm brothers' social politics, and to have inverted their tactics and methods to serve her own very different ends. In *Fairy Tales and the Art of Subversion*, Zipes says the assumption that the Grimms' tales are set in a timeless, ageless, "archetypal" realm is a misleading illusion fostered by the proliferation of psychological, formalist, and structuralist studies that homogenize the tales, as opposed to social histories of the genre and studies of the tales' production and reception. In his own pioneering materialist critique, which views the tales as "historical prescriptions, internalized, potent, explosive," Zipes analyzes the ways in which the Grimms changed their tales (actually collected from the bourgeoisie, not the peasantry) to reinforce bourgeois norms, including gender arrangements; he demonstrates convincingly, through a comparison of changes made from version to version, that "their entire process of selection reflected the bias of their philosophical and political point of view" (47); and he identifies a critical trend, beginning in West Germany in the sixties, that became increasingly aware of and hostile to the patriarchal norms embedded in the tales, increasingly interested in finding ways to "reutilize" the Grimms' versions for less repressive ends.[13] This perspective has perhaps been diffused to the point where it sounds less than revolutionary—by 1982, Jennifer Waelti-Walters can assert, rather than argue, that "The reading of fairy tales is one of the first steps in the maintenance of a misogynous, sex-role stereotyped patriarchy"[14]—but it was far from a commonplace when Sexton was writing *Transformations*, and the fact that it is now gaining wide currency affords another measure of her pioneering achievement.

Like Stone's anonymous reader, Sexton perceives that "outside forces controlled their lives"; unlike her, though, Sexton does *not* believe that "if they just got off their ass and thought about their situation they could maybe do something." And like the reinterpretations by the Merseyside Fairy Story Collective and Jeanne Desy (for children), Olga Broumas (for adults), or Angela Carter (for both),[15] Sexton perceives the way the Grimm brothers (she does not use Perrault) present women as passive objects with constricted roles; unlike their robust and radical reworkings, however, Sexton does not really conceive of alternatives, and confines herself to dissecting the trivialization and alienation that result from male control of female autonomy and sexuality. Where the fairy tale heroines created by her contemporaries and followers tend either to gain real insight into themselves and their circumstances or to claim self-definition and take control, where their un-equivocally feminist authors really do transform them into self-aware, active protagonists, Sexton's remain silent, passive, powerless victims frozen in—and fated to act out—the prescribed social roles in which her sources cast them. This is no small achievement, and we should not think less of *Transfor-mations* because Sexton's consistency does not permit her to create poems in which individuals have the power to counteract sociocultural forces that Sexton believes to be crushing. The quantitative emphasis of the collection falls on a flat, deadpan, almost minimalist notation of externally observed behavior. Except for "Briar Rose," whose discoveries do not free her from the world of nightmare but make her daylight world "another kind of prison," Sexton rarely allows her readers any insight into her young female protago-nists' minds. Instead, the distanced narrative voice—a real departure from her source, as well as from her earlier work—is entirely consistent with her conception of these young women as commodities, as products rather than people.

Because Sexton emphasizes the aridity that results when young women play out predetermined social roles, she does *not* really give voice to the private world of women's experience. Whereas the Grimms frequently focus on their heroines' feelings—they combine passivity and feelings of helpless-ness with perceptions of threat, fear of abandonment, awareness of their own loneliness and / or isolation and preoccupation with wish-fulfillment (fanta-sies of rescue by either a "good" mother-figure or a prince)—Sexton, consis-tent with her overarching conception of her characters as commodities, con-centrates instead on their market value. The king's eldest daughter in "The Twelve Dancing Princesses" is "the pick of the litter." The real subject of "Cinderella" is not the young girl herself, but the drawing power of "that story," a pulp fiction produced by a tabloid culture to perpetuate a fantasy. Her Snow White, unlike the Grimms' (or Disney's, for that matter), is not a terrified, abandoned child, but a hodge-podge of marketable parts (vin du Rhone, Limoges, cigarette paper, a gold piece) "as full of life as soda pop." A "living doll" like Plath's "Applicant"—"It can sew, it can cook, it can talk, talk, talk. / It works, there is nothing wrong with it"[16]—Sexton's toy virgin "works" by

> rolling her china-blue doll eyes
> open and shut.
> Open to say,
> Good Day Mama,
> and shut for the thrust
> of the unicorn.

Ultimately reduced to an "it," the china doll has become "the glass Snow White— / its doll's eyes shut forever."

Not all are marketable simply because of their doll-like appearance, however: fathers barter daughters to shore up their own inflated egos ("Rumpelstiltskin") or to get themselves off the hook ("The Maiden without Hands"). Indeed, in the latter story, Sexton significantly departs from her source to construct a fable of cruel irony, to suggest that victimization renders women more attractive—for all the wrong reasons. In the Grimms' cozily domestic opening, the father is an inept, dim-witted bungler blind to the trap being prepared for him, but appalled when he realizes its implications for his daughter. The daughter's inventiveness, in turn, protects her temporarily, even in the exigencies of her situation. In Sexton's version, though, the father is arbitrarily cruel, cutting off his daughter's hands to save himself, and the daughter (nameless in both, voiceless in Sexton) is "without resources," "a perfect still life." Sexton's most important change, however, is her emphasis on the usefulness to men of woman as victim, her chilling insistence that women who are victimized and mutilated become more desirable: "The maiden held up her stumps / as helpless as dog's paws / and that made the wizard / want her." And not just the wizard: in the original, the king who rescues her, marries her, loses her, and searches for her is overjoyed when she is restored to him, made whole (apparently) by years of stoic endurance. But Sexton probes more deeply. "Is it possible / he marries a cripple / out of admiration?" she asks sceptically in the prologue, hypothesizing that his motive may be much more self-serving:

> A desire to own the maiming
> so that not one of us butchers
> will come to him with crowbars
> or slim precise tweezers?
> Lady, bring me your wooden leg
> so I may stand on my own
> two pink pig feet.
> My apple has no worm in it!
> My apple is whole!

In the tale proper, "There but for the grace of— / I will take her for my wife," the prince says when first seeing her; later, when she and their child, "both now unfortunately whole," are restored to him, he thinks, Now the butchers will come to *me*, / . . . for I have lost my luck":

> It put an insidious fear in him
> But he was good and kind
> so he made the best of it
> like a switch hitter.

Sexton's maiden is more subtly used, in fact, than by the Brothers Grimm: bad enough to be mutilated by her father, then loved by the king because of her passivity, her silent acquiescence; worse, in Sexton's view, to have one's mutilation used as "a talisman, a yellow star"—the best the maiden can hope for even from a "good and kind" man.

Women unwittingly contribute to their own victimization in "The Wonderful Musician" (an ironic renaming of "The Queer Minstrel"), in which Sexton uses the prologue to conflate women's sexual responsiveness—their response to the seductive "music" of their youth—with the fate of the fable's fox, wolf, and hare:

> My sisters,
> do you remember the fiddlers
> of your youth?
> Those dances
> so like a drunkard
> lighting a fire in the belly?
> Remember?
> Remember music
> and beware.

Ensnared by the capricious, egocentric musician who seeks nothing but a continually new audience to applaud his performance, a musician who first enchants the victims he despises and then abandons them in their traps, they first participate obediently in their own entrapment, then help each other to escape and determine to fight back—"to tear off the musician's / ten wonderful fingers." But they are threatened by a new victim, a poor woodcutter now as captivated as they once were, and they slink away, the status quo restored. Sexton's control of several metaphors is uncertain here: images of Nazi persecution compete with images of Christian crucifixions, a Marxist reading is suggested by the woodcutter's failure to recognize his real oppressor, and all are precariously balanced on the animal fable format. If one message is clear—to fight back against the power structure is to invite death—another is less so: in portraying her victims as vain and greedy, in underscoring their obedient if unwitting participation in their own entrapment, to what extent is Sexton exposing the processes by which women are co-opted and drawn into alliance with the patriarchy, as Ostriker suggests occurs in "Hansel and Gretel,[17] and to what extent is Sexton blaming the victim?

If "The Maiden without Hands" and "The Wonderful Musician," respectively, chart the (ab)uses of passivity and obedience, other poems explore repressive patriarchal responses to any evidence of female autonomy and sexual independence. The ill-fated young girl in "The Frog Prince" is initially self-sufficient, playing with the golden ball that is "Obviously . . . more than a ball"; at the end, she is infantilized by the metamorphosed frog who exerts paternalistic control under the guise of benevolent protection:

> He hired a night watchman
> so that no one could enter the chamber
> and he had the well

boarded over so that
never again would she lose her ball,
that moon, that Krishna hair,
that blind poppy, that innocent globe,
that madonna womb.

The issues are even more clearly drawn in "The Twelve Dancing Princesses." Men marshall all the power at their disposal to regain control over defiant women whose sexuality threatens their authority; fathers prefer to hand over the reins to men of lower status than to accede to their daughters' rebellious independence; and even daughters capable of escaping locked and bolted doors to dance each night "like taxi girls at Roseland / as if those tickets would run right out" will be brutally brought to heel: drained of their vitality, they end up "sagg[ing] like old sweatshirts."

Pursuing Suzanne Juhasz's still-useful distinction between feminine and feminist poets, and affirming Juhasz's judgment that Sexton really belongs to the former group, Jane McCabe asserts in a thoughtful essay that Sexton's rage at the suppression and oppression of women differs qualitatively from the rage of unequivocally feminist poets like Morgan and Wakoski.[18] In fact, McCabe suggests that Sexton's worst enemy may be herself: she is "caught in what is a uniquely feminine trap of simultaneously celebrating herself, exploiting herself, letting herself be exploited, and apologizing for herself."[19] And Sexton's poetry, McCabe says, is the *product* of a society that oppresses women, not a *critique* of it.[20] But while McCabe's view might be arguable in terms of Sexton's oeuvre, it is neither grounded in nor supported by the bulk of the poems that comprise *Transformations*—poems that, as we have seen, do indeed constitute a very conscious criticism of the social order. On the other hand, Sexton's book does reveal a rather subtle contradiction. Her unflinching view of the sheer weight of the socialization process leads her to portray women as empty puppets in a show written, directed, and produced by a patriarchal culture for its own benefit; at the same time, these women's very emptiness, which renders them incapable of claiming autonomy, of countering the patriarchy, and—at times—of perceiving the significance of what has happened to them causes Sexton to distance herself from them.

In "The Wonderful Musician," mothers are gratuitously likened to "little Eichmanns"; in "Hansel and Gretel," they are stereotypic devourers:

Little plum,
said the mother to her son,
I want to bite,
I want to chew,
I will eat you up.
I will spit on you for luck
for you are better than money.
Oh succulent one,
it is but one turn in the road
and I would be a cannibal!

Conversely, she sees daughters—products of the same socialization process—inevitably perpetuating their mother-figures' self-defeating patterns. Her Two-Eyes, the rejected "normal" child, is ultimately crushed in by the "charmed cripples" for whom her own mother "wore her martyrdom / like a string of pearls." And in just four lines, her startling conclusion to "Snow White" reifies the concerns of "The Double Image," extends the discovery in "Housewife" that "a woman is her mother. That's the main thing" (*CP* 77), expands on her punning refrain in "Two Eyes" (mother / eye = mother / I) and anticipates by several years Sandra Gilbert's and Susan Gubar's sophisticated analysis in "The Queen's Looking Glass" of this paradigmatic (step)mother–daughter relationship:[21]

> Meanwhile Snow White held court,
> rolling her china-blue doll eyes open and shut
> and sometimes referring to her mirror
> as women do.

Sexton is hardly sanguine about Snow White's ability to break the cycle. Just as the girl succumbs to the stepmother's proffering of conventionally feminine ornamentation (the laces and the comb), she succumbs to the temptations of the mirror; her future is her (step)mother's past.

Other variants of mother–daughter relationships are either aborted, as when Rapunzel abandons a lesbian interlude with Mother Gothel for the "cesspool" of a heterosexual relationship,[22] or rendered trivial, as in "Red Riding Hood," because of the female characters' shallowness. As Zipes puts it, "she cynically concludes [this] tale with the 'saved' grandmother and Red Riding Hood in a state of social amnesia. By *not* remembering how empty and treacherous their lives had been, they will obviously repeat the mistakes they had made in the past":[23]

> The huntsman and the grandmother and Red Riding
>   Hood
> sat down by his corpse and had a meal of wine and
>   cake.
> Those two remembering
> nothing naked and brutal
> from that little death,
> that little birth,

Whether or not "cynical" is the best description of "Red Riding Hood" 's denouement, the ending's revealing contrast with the prologue does elicit questions. In that prologue, the speaker, focusing on the ubiquity of deceptions, implicitly contrasts herself to the diminished females she depicts. Unlike them, and unlike her comparative shallow, "seemingly respectable" contemporaries who also engage in deceptions, she does so too—but with a twist: "Dame Sexton" retains the capacity to be exquisitely, interestingly *aware* of her own ruses. Figuratively capable of "undergoing open-heart surgery" while playing out her own conventional role at cocktail parties and the like, she retains a center worthy of notice, a "heart, that eyeless beetle, / enormous that Kafka beetle, / running panicked through his maze." But who is to know that Red Riding Hood and her grandmother aren't capable of doing the same—that they don't possess some kernel of awareness that they are allying themselves to the patriarchy after having undergone an experience of violation by the patriarchy? And who is to conclude that they "remember / nothing"? "Every woman who has come to consciousness can recall almost endless series of oppressive, violating, insulting, assaulting acts against her Self. Every woman is battered by such assaults—is, on the psychic level, a battered woman," Mary Daly reminds us.[24]

Although Sexton celebrates her own power to articulate and anatomize, she unwittingly perpetuates many of the gender arrangements of the originals. True, the prologues to "The Frog Prince" and especially "The Twelve Dancing Princesses" ensure the reader's identification with the badly used heroines. "If you danced from midnight / to six a.m. who would understand?" she begins the latter, immediately establishing a bond, a sense of community, among princesses, reader, and people living on the edge, cutting loose; people who'd do anything to escape a draining, confining life; people trapped by circumstances—or themselves; people listening to "the death cricket bleeping." True, she does invest Sleeping Beauty with the power to articulate her discovery of the connection between past dreams and present waking nightmare ("Daddy . . . drunkenly bent over my bed, / circling the abyss like a shark, my father thick upon me / like some sleeping jellyfish"), a discovery that she pieces together despite limited information ("There was a theft. / That much I am told. / I was abandoned. / That much I know. / I was passed hand to hand / Like a bowl of fruit").[25]

But many of her keenest insights and sympathies are reserved for the emotional complexities she attributes to her male characters. Both the prologue and body of "Rumpelstiltskin" do not just depict Rumpelstiltskin's loneliness and unhappiness; they illuminate and universalize the pain of the doppelganger "Inside many of us," the "monster of despair" whose divided nature causes him to self-destruct. If she directs our sympathy toward the dwarf, she also directs it toward the wild man in "Iron Hans"—one of those from whom "you'd turn away"—rather than to the majority of the females who are unable to voice their feelings at being reduced to marketable ciphers because they no longer *have* a voice. The tormented Iron Hans himself, whose bewitchment is likened to the derangement of the patients in the powerful framing prologue, is "transformed" "Without Thorazine / or benefit of psychotherapy" by an act of gratuitous kindness:

> When I was a wild man,
> Iron Hans said,
> I tarnished all the world.
> I was the infector.

> I was the poison breather.
> I was a professional,
> but you have saved me
> from the awful babble
> of that calling.

To render in poetry what it must feel like to come back, or "part way back," from "the awful babble / of that calling" is no small achievement, and one of her consuming tasks. "I am mother of the insane. / Let me give you my children," she says in the prologue to "Iron Hans," setting up a maternal, accepting, compassionate, nurturing relation with the "lunatics" she describes as well as with her primary audience:

> Clifford, Vincent, Friedrich,
> my scooter boys,
> deep in books,
> long before you were mad.
> Zelda, Hannah, Renee.
> Moon girls,
> where did you go?

She can see in them the same humanity—and hence the same possibility of "transformation"—that she sees in the "wild man" but, except for "Briar Rose," she does not extend this potentially healing acceptance to or suggest a similarly nurturing relationship to the young women of the tales at the same time that she celebrates her own power to comprehend and articulate. One effect of this is to perpetuate the mutually exclusive female roles—active, vocal "witch" who breaks free / manipulated, passive girl who stays trapped—that make the tales of her source so problematic for so many female readers. If we are fully responsive to the nuances of Sexton's persona, we too may feel that we are faced with an unsatisfactory alternative: to identify either with silent and silenced women or with the articulate woman who helps us to understand the reasons for their silencing.

This is not to denigrate Sexton's achievement, but simply to understand and accept the extent to which she is indeed caught in Juhasz's classic double bind. Paradoxically, ironically, our recognition of the tenacity with which she pursues her controlling vision of the sociocultural patterns that diminish women, coupled with our appreciation of the pioneering radicalism of her effort, may make us (as female readers) wish that she had seen her power as articulate witch in terms of Daly's "Radical Friendship of Hags":[26]

> Armed with this knowledge, Crones/Hags will make every effort to remove our energy from allegiance to their systems, re-claiming our life force and our hidden, but never totally destroyed, traditions. As we re-create Hagography we will keep clearly in mind the fact that it is the patriarchs' possession and re-definition of "the past" that makes possible their possession of women *by* the male-defined "past.[27]

Notes

1. Anne Sexton, *The Complete Poems* (Boston: Houghton Mifflin, 1981), 258. All quotations from Sexton's poems are from this edition and are cited parenthetically.

2. Linda Gray Sexton and Lois Ames, eds., *Anne Sexton: A Self-Portrait in Letters* (Boston: Houghton Mifflin, 1977), 367.

3. The most interesting study of Sexton as an archetypal *female* poet is Estella Lauter's "Anne Sexton's Radical Discontent" in *Women as Mythmakers: Poetry and Visual Art by Twentieth-Century Women* (Bloomington: Indiana University Press, 1984), 23–46. Lauter says Sexton's "prophetic" work, "based on images that have profound psychological and religious significance for our age," is "best understood . . . in terms of archetypal psychology, as an act of 'soul-making,' " rather than in terms of confessionalism, and that Sexton did not really come to terms with the feminine dimensions of the "fruits" of this enterprise (23–24).

4. Suznne Juhasz, " 'The Excitable Gift': The Poetry of Anne Sexton," in *Naked and Fiery Forms. Modern American Poetry by Women: A New Tradition* (New York: Harper, 1976), 126–27, and Jane McCabe, " 'A Woman Who Writes': A Feminist Approach to the Early Poetry of Anne Sexton," in *Anne Sexton: The Artist and Her Critics*, ed. J. D. McClatchy (Bloomington: Indiana University Press, 1978), 238, 240.

5. *The Trials and Tribulations of Little Red Riding Hood: Versions of the Tale in Sociocultural Context* (South Hadley, Mass.: Bergin & Harvey, 1983), 44.

6. *Don't Bet on the Prince: Contemporary Feminist Fairy Tales* (New York: Methuen, 1986).

7. Bruno Bettelheim, *The Uses of Enchantment: The Meaning and Importance of Fairy Tales* (New York: Knopf, 1976), 275.

8. The most searching critique of Bettelheim is by Zipes (*Breaking the Magic Spell: Radical Theories of Folk and Fairy Tales* [Austin: University of Texas Press, 1979], 160–83); for other useful responses, see James W. Heisig, "Bruno Bettelheim and the Fairy tales," *Children's Literature* 6 (1977):93–114; Kay F. Stone, "The Misuses of Enchantment: Controversies on the Significance of Fairy Tales," in *Women's Folklore, Women's Culture*, ed. Rosan A. Jordan and Susan J. Kalcik (Philadelphia: University of Pennsylvania Press), 125–45; and Jennifer Waelti-Walters, *Fairy Tales and the Female Imagination* (Montreal: Eden, 1982). For less dogmatic Freudian approaches to the fairy tale before Bettelheim, see Julius E. Heuscher, *A Psychiatric Study of Fairy Tales: Their Origin, Meaning and Usefulness* (Springfield, Ill.: Charles Thomas, 1963), and Emanuel K. Schwartz, "A Psychoanalytic Study of the Fairy Tale," *American Journal of Psychotherapy* 10 (1956):740–62. For a Jungian study, see Marie-Louise von Franz, *Problems of the Feminine in Fairytales* (New York and Zurich: Spring, 1976).

9. Marcia Lieberman, "Some Day My Prince Will Come: Female Acculturation Through the Fairy Tale," *College English* 34 (1972):385.

10. Karen E. Rowe, "Feminism and Fairy Tales," *Women's Studies* 6 (1979):237.

11. Stone, "Misuses of Enchantment," 133.

12. Ibid.,

13. In *Fairy Tales and the Art of Subversion: The Classical Genre for Children and the Process of Civilization* (London: Heinemann, 1983), Zipes builds on the work of recent West German critics who, he tells us, "believe that the Grimms' stories contribute to the creation of a false consciousness and reinforce an authoritarian socialization process" (45) and regard the Grimms' tales as " 'secret agents' of an education establishment which indoctrinates children to learn fixed roles and functions within bourgeois society, thus curtailing their free development" (46).

14. Waelti-Walters, *Female Imagination*, 1.

15. All have been anthologized by Zipes. See *Don't Bet on the Prince* for Desy's "The Princess Who Stood on Her Own Two Feet" (39–47), the Merseyside Fairy Story Collective's "Snow White (74–81), and Broumas's "Little Red Riding Hood" (119–20); see *Trials* for Merseyside's "Red Riding Hood" (239–44) and Carter's "The Company of Wolves" (271–80).

16. Sylvia Plath, *Ariel* (New York: Harper), 65.

17. Alicia Ostriker, "The Thieves of Language: Women Poets and Revisionist Mythmaking," *Signs* 8 (Fall 1982): 85.

18. McCabe, "A Woman Who Writes," 218, 224. This is not to say that McCabe ranks Sexton's work below theirs. "Surely the anger of poets like Wakoski, Alta, and Morgan is aesthetically more limiting than Sexton's self-destructiveness," she says; ". . . it may even be necessary to reduce the world and even truth to radical simplicity in order to find ways of leading anger back to its source; but simple anger never was the proper mode for art. We want poetry to be rich in ambiguity, subtlety, and passion. When necessary, we always want to insist on having it both or even several ways. Anne Sexton is inconsistent and contradictory and cannot be stuffed into a single category of writers, and she is consequently a far more interesting poet than Wakoski or Alta or Morgan" (222, 223). For another view of Sexton's anger, see Ostriker's " 'What are patterns for?': Anger and Polarization in Women's Poetry," *Feminist Studies* 10, no. 3 (Fall 1984):485–503, which includes an important discussion of "The Jesus Papers" (495–99). In them, Ostriker says, Sexton's anger is directed at "a patriarchal theology that swallows her alive" (495). The sequence "increases rather than decreases our fear that there is no hiding place for women in religion" (499).

19. McCabe, "A Woman Who Writes," 226.

20. Ibid., 218.

21. Sandra M. Gilbert and Susan Gubar, "The Queen's Looking Glass," *The Madwoman in the Attic: The Woman Writer and the Nineteenth-Century Literary Imagination* (New Haven: Yale University Press, 1979); rpt. Zipes, *Don't Bet on the Prince*, 201–8. The Queen, whom Gilbert and Gubar see as a "plotter, a plot-maker, a schemer, a witch, an artist, an impersonator" (203) but robbed of all outward prospects for exercising these abilities, has internalized patriarchal norms and rules, which "[reside] now in her own mirror, her own mind" (202); thus trapped, she is "driven inward, obsessively studying self-images as if seeking a viable self" (202). "Surely, fairest of them all, Snow White has exchanged one glass coffin for another, delivered from the prison where the Queen put her only to be imprisoned in the looking glass from which the King's voice speaks daily. There is, after all, no female model for her in this tale except the 'good' (dead) mother and her living avatar the 'bad' mother. . . . her only escape from her second glass coffin, the imprisoning mirror" (206). Like the Queen, they continue, she will practice the 'bad' arts through duplicitous schemes and meet the same fate: Her only deed . . . can be a deed of death, her only action the pernicious action of self-destruction" (206). The story of Snow White is frequently read in terms of competition between two generations of women: the older woman, whose own options are limited, becomes consumed with jealousy as her maturing (step)daughter threatens to supplant her. For a fascinating biographical parallel, see Diane Middlebrook, "Becoming Anne Sexton," *Denver Quarterly* 18, no. 4 (Winter 1984):24–34. Middlebrook describes a "family drama in which Sexton had been assigned the role of the dumb daughter" (27) and shows how her emergence as a poet was "linked directly to a struggle with her mother over being a writer" (27). Middlebrook offers evidence that Sexton's mother, a thwarted writer herself, acted to silence her daughter's early verse efforts, going so far as to accuse her of plagiarism at one point (28).

22. The most probing discussion of "Rapunzel" (215–17) is by Ellen Cronan Rose, "Through the Looking Glass: When Women Tell Fairy Tales," in *The Voyage In: Fictions of Female Development*, ed. Elizabeth Abel, Marianne Hirsch, and Elizabeth Langland (Hanover: University Press of New England, 1983), 209–27; see also Juhasz (132) and McCabe (239).

23. Zipes, *Trials*, 44.

24. Mary Daly, *Gyn/Ecology: The Metaethics of Radical Feminism* (Boston: Beacon, 1978), 348.

25. It could be argued that the question of Sexton's ambivalence in giving voice to Sleeping Beauty / Briar Rose but not to other heroines turns in part on whether we read *Transformations* as a collection of poems that stand on their own but share a volume because they represent Sexton's authentic but varied responses to her source, or whether we read it as a sequence (there is no external evidence supporting the latter). In other words, does it make a difference that "Briar Rose" is the *final* poem? The issue is further compounded if we approach the volume with unacknowledged critical assumptions about the value of order and coherence and is, at any rate, beyond the scope of this essay.

26. Daly, *Gyn/Ecology*, 366.

27. Ibid., 349.

Seeking the Exit or the Home: Poetry and Salvation in the Career of Anne Sexton
Suzanne Juhasz*

If you are brought up to be a proper little girl in Boston, a little wild and boycrazy, a little less of a student and more of a flirt, and you run away from home to elope and become a proper Boston bride, a little given to extravagance and a little less to casseroles, but a proper bride nonetheless who turns into a proper housewife and mother, and if all along you know that there lives inside you a rat, a "gnawing pestilential rat,"[1] what will happen to you when you grow up? If you are Anne Sexton, you will keep on paying too much attention to the rat, will try to kill it, and yourself, become hospitalized, be called crazy. You will keep struggling to forget the rat and be the proper Boston housewife and mother you were raised to be. And into this struggle will come, as an act of grace, poetry, to save your life by giving you a role, a mission, a craft: an act, poetry, that is you but is not you, outside yourself. Words, that you can work and shape and that will stay there, black and true, while you do this, turn them into a poem, that you can send away to the world, a testimony of yourself. Words that will change the lives of those who read them and your own life, too. So that you can know that you are not only the wife and mother, not only the rat, but that you are the poet, a person who matters, who has money and fame and prizes and students and admirers and a name, Anne Sexton.

But what about the mother and wife, and what about the rat, when Anne Sexton becomes a poet? This essay is about the end of Sexton's career and poetry, and it looks at the role that her poems played in her life and in

*Reprinted with the author's permission from *Shakespeare's Sisters, Feminist Essays on Women Poets*, ed. Sandra M. Gilbert and Susan Gubar (Bloomington: Indiana University Press, 1979), 261–68.

ours. It is a tale for our times, because it is also about what poetry can do for women and what it cannot do for women. Something we need to know.

Since the recent publication of Sexton's letters, there is now no doubt how conscious she was of the craft of poetry, of the work that it is, and how devoted she was to doing that work. "You will make it if you learn to revise," she wrote to an aspiring poet in 1965:

> if you take your time, if you work your guts out on one poem for four months instead of just letting the miracle (as you must feel it) flow from the pen and then just leave it with the excuse that you are undisciplined.
>
> Hell! I'm undisciplind too, in everything but my work . . . and the discipline the reworking the forging into being is the stuff of poetry. . . .[2]

In fact, for Sexton the poem existed as a measure of control, of discipline, for one whom she defined as "given to excess." "I have found that I can control it best in a poem," she says. "If the poem is good then it will have the excess under control . . . it is the core of the poem . . . there like stunted fruit, unseen but actual.[3]

Yet the poem had another function in her life, the one which gives rise to that label "confessional," which has always dogged her work and is not usually complimentary. Her poetry is highly personal. She is either the overt or the implicit subject of her poem, and the she as subject is the person who anguishes, who struggles, who seems mired in the primary soil of living: the love / hate conflict with mother and father, the trauma of sex, the guilt of motherhood. The person in the poem is not the proper lady and mother and wife who is always trying her best to tidy up messes and cover them with a coating of polish and wax. Rather, it is the rat, a creature of nature rather than culture, who is crude and rude, "with its bellyful of dirt / and its hair seven inches long"; with its "two eyes full of poison / and routine pointed teeth."[4] The rat person, with her "evil mouth" and "worried eyes,"[5] knows that living is something about which to worry: she sees and tells. In form her poem often follows a psychoanalytic model, as I have pointed out in an earlier essay,[6] beginning in a present of immediate experience and probing into a past of personal relationships in order to understand the growth (and the damaging) of personality. As such, the poem for Sexton is an important agent in her quest for salvation: for a way out of the madness that the rat's vision engenders, a way that is not suicide.

Very early in her career, in "For John, Who Begs Me Not to Enquire Further," she presents an aesthetics of personal poetry which is conscious that the poem, because it is an object that communicates and mediates between person and person, can offer "something special" for others as well as oneself.

> I tapped my own head;
> It was glass, an inverted bowl.
> It is a small thing
> to rage in your own bowl.

At first it was private.
Then it was more than myself;
it was you, or your house
or your kitchen.
And if you turn away
because there is no lesson here
I will hold my awkward bowl,
with all its cracked stars shining
like a complicated lie,
and fasten a new skin around it
as if I were dressing an orange
or a strange sun.
Not that it was beautiful,
but that I found some order there.
There ought to be something special
for someone
in this kind of hope.[7]

In such poetry, she warns, there is no "lesson," no universal truth. What there is is the poem of herself, which, as she has made it, has achieved an order; that very order a kind of hope (a belief in salvation) that might be shared. The poem of herself is, however, not herself but a poem. The imagery of this poem attests to the fact, as it turns self into object, a bowl, an orange, a sun, while it turns the poem about self into a coating or covering that surrounds the self. The bowl is like a planet in a heaven of "cracked stars shining / like a complicated lie"; if he should turn from this poem, she promises to "fasten a new skin around" or "dress" her orange, that strange sun.

Of course Sexton was right when she said that there ought to be something special in that gesture her poems made toward others. People responded to her poetry because she had the courage to speak publicly of the most intimate of personal experiences, the ones so many share. She became a spokesperson for the secret domestic world and its pain. And her audience responded as strongly as it did, not only because of what she said but because of how she said it. She was often, although not always, a good poet, a skilled poet, whose words worked insight upon her subject matter and irradiated it with vision.

But what about herself, in the process? What did her poems do for her?

In a letter she speaks of the necessity for the writer to engage in a vulnerable way with experience.

I think that writers . . . must try *not* to avoid knowing what is happening. Everyone has somewhere the ability to mask the events of pain and sorrow, call it shock . . . when someone dies for instance you have this shock that carries you over it, makes it bearable. But the creative person must not use this mechanism anymore than they have to in order to keep breathing. Other people may. But not you, not us. Writing is "life" in capsule and the writer must feel every bump edge scratch ouch in order to know the real furniture of his capsule . . . I, myself, alternate between hiding behind my own hands protecting myself anyway possible, and this other, this seeing ouching other. I guess I mean that creative people must not avoid the pain that they get dealt. I say to myself, sometimes repeatedly "I've got to get the hell out of this hurt" . . . But no. Hurt must be examined like a plague.[8]

The result of this program, as she says in a letter to W. D. Snodgrass, is writing "real." "Because that is the one thing that will save (and I do mean save) other people."[9]

And yet the program is not only altruistic in intent. Personal salvation remains for her an equally urgent goal. As she writes in "The Children," from one of her last books, *The Awful Rowing Toward God* (1975):

> The place I live in
> is a kind of maze
> and I keep seeking
> the exit or the home.[10]

In describing this position of vulnerability necessary for poetry, she tells Snodgrass that a poet must remain "the alien." In her vocabulary for herself, that alien is of course the rat. But there is a serious problem here, because Anne Sexton the woman (who is nonetheless the poet, too) does not like the rat. The existence of the rat obstructs salvation. In "Rowing," the opening poem of *The Awful Rowing Toward God*, salvation is described as an island toward which she journeys. This island, her goal, is "not perfect," having "the flaws of life / the absurdities of the dinner table, / but there will be a door":

> and I will open it
> and I will get rid of the rat inside me.
> the gnawing pestilential rat.
>
> (p. 2)

In the "Ninth Psalm" of her long poem, "O Ye Tongues," an extended description of the state of salvation includes this vision: "For the rat was blessed on that mountain. He was given a white bath."[11]

In other words, Sexton, recognizing at the age of twenty-eight her possession of a talent, turned her mad self to good work (and works): into a writer, an active rather than a passive agent. For she had defined madness as fundamentally passive and destructive in nature. "Madness is a waste of time. It creates nothing . . . nothing grows from it and you, meanwhile, only grow into it like a snail."[12] Yet the rat who is the mad lady is also the poet. To have become a poet was surely an act toward salvation for Sexton. It gave her something to do with the knowledge that the rat possessed. Left to her silence, the rat kept seeing too much and therefore kept seeking "the exit." Words brought with them power, power to reach others. They gave her as well a social role, "the poet," that was liberating. Being the poet, who could make money with her poetry, who could be somebody of consequence in the public world, was an act that helped to alleviate some of the frustration, the impotence, the self-hatred that Sexton the woman experienced so powerfully in her life. The poet was good: how good she was Sexton, as teacher and reader and mentor, made a point of demonstrating.

But the rat was not good; in yet another image of self-identification, Sexton called that hated, evil, inner self a demon.

> My demon,
> too often undressed,
> too often a crucifix I bring forth,
> too often a dead daisy I give water to
> too often the child I give birth to
> and then abort, nameless, nameless . . .
> earthless.
>
> Oh demon within,
> I am afraid and seldom put my hand up
> to my mouth and stitch it up
> covering you, smothering you
> from the public voyeury eyes
> of my typewriter keys. [13]

These lines are from "Demon," which appears in her posthumous volume, *45 Mercy Street*. The poem begins with an epigraph from D. H. Lawrence: "A young man is afraid of his demon and puts his hand over the demon's mouth sometimes." It goes on to show why the demon, though frightening, cannot be covered, smothered, or denied speech: because the demon, exposed, is at the center of her poetry. At the same time the poem, with its bitter repetition of "too often," reveals a hatred, not only of the demon, but of the act of uncovering and parading it. Of the act that is nonetheless essential to making the poem.

Finally, the poem's imagery points to a further aspect of the demon that is for Sexton perhaps the most terrible of all. The demon is crucifix, icon of salvation through death; is dead daisy for which the poem alone provides water; is child which, through the act of the poem, is both birthed and aborted. The demon may begin as something that lives within and is a part (albeit frightening and nasty) of herself; but the poem, in being written, turns the demon into an object separate and alien from herself. This disassociation, this conversion of self into other, is as distressing to Sexton as the self-hatred that she must experience each time she acknowledges the existence of the demon or the rat. Because, as "Demon" makes clear, the self as object, the self in the poem, is dead. To use the self in making poems is to lose the self, for the poem is never the experience that produces it. The poem is always an artifice, as she herself observes in another poem from *45 Mercy Street*, "Talking to Sheep":

> Now,
> in my middle age,
> I'm well aware
> I keep making statues
> of my acts, carving them with my sleep—
>
> (p.7)

The poems can never offer personal salvation for their poet, and she has come to understand why. First, because she defines salvation as a life freed at last from the rat and her pain ("I would sell my life to avoid / the pain that begins in the crib / with its bars or perhaps / with your first breath"[14]), and yet she cannot kill the rat without killing the vision that is the source of her poetry. Second, because the poems themselves are a kind of suicide. She knows that poetry must be craft as well as vision; that the very act of crafting objectifies the poem's content. What has lived within her, externalized and formalized by art, becomes something other than herself; is form but not flesh.

She expresses this new knowledge in the only way she knows, by making poetry of it. In poems like those quoted, or in the following lines from "Cigarettes and Whiskey and Wild, Wild Women," the other side of "For John, Who Begs Me Not to Enquire Further" is revealed: the implications of this aesthetic of personal poetry for the poet herself.

> Now that I have written many words,
> and let out so many loves, for so many,
> and been altogether what I always was—
> a woman of excess, of zeal and greed,
> I find the effort useless.
> Do I not look in the mirror,
> these days,
> and see a drunken rat avert her eyes?
> Do I not feel the hunger so acutely
> that I would rather die than look
> into its face?
> I kneel once more,
> in case mercy should come
> in the nick of time.[15]

In an earlier essay on Sexton I maintained that poetry had saved her from suicide. It did, for the years in which she wrote and was the poet. But it is equally true that poetry could not prevent her death, "the exit," because it could not bring her to salvation, "the home."

For Sexton, salvation would have meant sanity: peace rather than perpetual conflict, integration rather than perpetual fragmentation. Sanity would have meant vanquishing at last her crazy bad evil gnawing self, the rat, the demon. Yet the rat was, at the same time, the source of her art. Its anxious visions needed to be nurtured so that she might be a poet. Sanity might bring peace to the woman, but it would destroy the poet. And it was not the woman, who made the peanut butter sandwiches and the marriage bed, whom Sexton liked. It was the poet. The discipline of her craft and the admiration, respect, and power that it brought allowed her to feel good about herself. That the woman and the poet were different "selves," and in conflict with each other, she was well aware. "I do not live a poet's life. I look and act like a housewife," she wrote. "I live the wrong life for the person I am."[16] Although this fragmentation of roles wrought conflict and confusion, it nonetheless made possible the kind of poetry that Sexton wrote. But more and more in her final years she seemed to have come to despise the balancing act itself, demanding all or, finally, nothing.

Perhaps the kind of salvation that Sexton sought was unattainable, because its very terms had become so contradictory. Certainly, her poetry could not offer it. In poetry she could make verbal and public what she knew about her private self; she could shape this knowledge, control it, give it a form that made it accessible to others. But she could not write what she did not know, so that while her poems document all the rat has seen, they never offer an alternative vision. They are always too "close" to herself for that. And they are at the same time too far from her. By creating through externalization and formalization yet another self with which to deal, her poetry increased her sense of self-fragmentation in the midst of her struggle toward wholeness.

Yet Sexton's poetry has offered salvation to others. Personal poetry of this kind, a genre that many women, in their search for self-understanding and that same elusive wholeness, have recently adopted, must be understood to have a different function for its readers and for its writers. Art as therapy appears less profitable for the artist, who gives the gift of herself, than for its recipients. I think that I can learn from Sexton's poems as she never could. They project a life that is like my own in important ways; I associate my feelings with hers, and the sense of a shared privacy is illuminating. At the same time, they are not my life; their distance from me permits a degree of objectivity, the ability to analyze as well as empathize. Possibly I can use the insights produced by such a process to further change in my own life. For the artist, however, because the distance between herself and the poem is at once much closer and much greater, it is more difficult, perhaps impossible, to use the poem in this way. Salvation for the artist must come, ultimately, from developing a life that operates out of tensions which are creative rather than destructive. Sexton's life, art, and death exemplify some of the difficulties faced by women artists in achieving this goal and also dramatically underline the necessity of overcoming them.

Notes

1. "Rowing," *The Awful Rowing Toward God* (Boston: Houghton Mifflin, 1975), p. 2.

2. Linda Gray Sexton and Lois Ames, eds., *Anne Sexton: A Self-Portrait in Letters* (Boston: Houghton Mifflin, 1977), pp. 266–67.

3. *Letters*, p. 144.

4. "Rats Live on No Evil Star," *The Death Notebooks* (Boston: Houghton Mifflin, 1974), p. 19.

5. Ibid.

6. " 'The Excitable Gift': The Poetry of Anne Sexton," *Naked and Fiery Forms: Modern American Poetry by Women, A New Tradition* (New York: Harper and Row, 1976), pp. 117–43.

7. *To Bedlam and Part Way Back* (Boston: Houghton Mifflin, 1960), pp. 51–52.

8. *Letters*, p. 105.

9. *Letters*, p. 110.

10. *The Awful Rowing*, p. 6.

11. *The Death Notebooks*, p. 97.

12. *Letters*, p. 267.

13. *45 Mercy Street*, Linda Gray Sexton, ed. (Boston: Houghton Mifflin, 1967), p. 106.

14. "The Big Boots of Pain," *45 Mercy Street*, p. 103.

15. Ibid., p. 89.

16. *Letters*, pp. 270, 271.

45 Mercy Street and Other Vacant Houses

Linda Wagner-Martin*

It would be a gross oversimplification to attempt to define the "New England tradition" in poetry as intellectual, instructive, patriarchal, British, and somewhat imitative. To use that sense of tradition would be to force such nineteenth-century poets as Emily Dickinson, Ralph Waldo Emerson, Henry David Thoreau, and—to stretch the boundaries a bit—Walt Whitman far outside the accepted patterns: too innovative, too American, too emotional, and certainly too personal, these poets were already working toward achieving a distinctly unique poetic voice, a concept we today regard as "modern." To illustrate, what a difference between the well-known lines of a poet who represents the formal New England poetic tradition, William Cullen Bryant, and those of Dickinson, Emerson, Whitman:

> To him who in the love of Nature holds
> Communion with her visible forms, she speaks
> A various language; for his gayer hours
> She has a voice of gladness, and a smile
> And eloquence of beauty, and she glides
> Into his darker musings, with a mild
> And gentle sympathy. . . .
>
>   "Thanatopsis"

*Reprinted with permission from *American Literature, The New England Heritage*, ed. James Nagel and Richard Astro (New York: Garland, 1981), 145–54, 162–65.

I celebrate myself, and sing myself,
And what I assume you shall assume,
For every atom belonging to me as good belongs
    to you
I loafe and invite my soul,
I lean and loafe at my ease observing a spear
    of summer grass.
My tongue, every atom of my blood, form'd from
    this soil, this air,
Born here of parents born here from parents the
    same, and their parents the same,
I, now thirty-seven years old in perfect
    health begin,
Hoping to cease not till death.[1]

When Whitman shares with us his biography (and nickname)—the fact that he is 37, a loafer, an American and expansive in his American confidence—we respond to that identity, that reaching out. "Camerado, this is no book," he writes in "So Long"; "Who touches this touches a man. . . . From behind the screen where I hid I advance personally solely to you" (p. 391). A new definition of the poem as a means of speaking intimately evolves here, not only with Whitman but with Emerson in "The Problem":

I like a church; I like a cowl;
I love a prophet of the soul;
And on my heart monastic aisles
Fall like sweet strains, or pensive smiles;
Yet for all his faith can see
Would I that cowled churchman be. . . .[2]

Simultaneously but very separately, in her timid yet strangely assertive voice, Emily Dickinson began the same process of using personal speech in poems that defied both classification and publication:

I tie my Hat—I crease my Shawl—
Life's little duties do—precisely. . . .[3]

I am alive—I guess
The branches on my Hand
Are full of Morning Glory—(pp. 225–26).

This is my letter to the World
that never wrote to Me—(p. 211).

I was the slightest in the House—
I took the smallest Room—
At night, my little Lamp, and Book—

And one Geranium—(p. 234).

These are hardly poems marked by any tones of imitation, any deference toward the Mother Country and its poetics, or any attempt to set forth large statements of intellectual weight. They are beginnings rather than culminations, forerunners of modern poetry rather than inheritors of an eighteenth-century mode. And they are strangely ungeographical, placed much more directly in the province of the heart than in any New England location. The conflict that must have existed between poetic convention—the use of place, landscape, to reveal larger ideas; the absence of the personal; the use of poetic diction rather than normal speech rhythms—and the interiority of these poems probably accounted for much of the poets' satisfaction with them.

From Dickinson's room in the family home in Amherst, Massachusetts, to Anne Sexton's lost family home on Mercy Street is only a brief walk. The wallpaper may be different, given the century that divides the houses, but the atmosphere is distressingly similar: both Sexton's and Dickinson's poems speak of the need for an identity as a writer and of their search for a male authority figure—father, brother, editor, analyst, husband, minister, critic, fellow writer—to support that writing process. The poems share a tone of apology for their emotional, feminine subject matter (as contrasted with supposedly "intellectual" themes) and an awareness on the part of each poet that this work is innovative, unconventional, and that it exists almost as a flight from accepted traditions. Both Sexton's and Dickinson's poems are marked with exuberance, anger, guilt, frustration, and finally, self-acceptance. The best account of these dichotomies between a woman's trying to come, aggressively, to art while simultaneously trying to survive in a social context that demands passivity is the recent *Madwoman in the Attic* by Susan Gubar and Sandra M. Gilbert. Their readings of Dickinson's poems explain full well her reclusive, questioning, unsure yet dramatic poetic persona; and the extensions one can make from Dickinson to some of the best-known New England poets of this century are clear.[4]

Without benefit of criticism or sociology, Anne Sexton captures these contradictions in the title poem from *45 Mercy Street*. Published posthumously in 1976, this collection creates a paradigm of the non-traditional poet's journey, the movement from the need for a place in the accepted mainstream to the strength to stand outside. The hegira that begins the book is, tellingly, a female hegira; and Sexton defines the journey as "a means of escaping from an undesirable or dangerous environment" as well as "a means of arriving at a highly desirable destination." Where are the models, in the canon of American literature, for a woman's initiation story? Where are the portraits of the young woman as artist? Here.

With "45 Mercy Street," Sexton creates that story, that portrait. She gives us Mercy and other subtle echoes of the "Twenty-third Psalm" throughout the collection: "Surely goodness and mercy shall / follow me all the days of my life; / and I will dwell in the house of the / Lord for ever." Sexton plays with *surely*, the female expectation of living a good, modest, loving life and being rewarded; with *goodness*, in both a social and sexual sense; and she sets those words against a recurring theme of *mercy*, the particularly female capacity for compassion that is non-judgmental. Inherent in Sexton's portrayal is the female ability to accept, to forgive; not surprisingly, the characters of these last Sexton poems are almost entirely female—her daughters Linda and Joy, her mother, grandmother, great aunt Nana, friends.

> In my dream,
> drilling into the marrow
> of my entire bone,
> my real dream,
> I'm walking up and down Beacon Hill
> searching for a street sign—
> namely MERCY STREET.
> Not there.
>
> I try the Back Bay.
> Not there.
> Not there.
> And yet I know the number.
> 45 Mercy Street.
> I know the stained-glass window
> of the foyer,
> the three flights of the house
> with its parquet floors.
> I know the furniture and
> mother, grandmother, great-grandmother,
> the servants.
> I know the cupboard of Spode,
> the boat of ice, solid silver,
> where the butter sits in neat squares
> like strange giant's teeth
> on the big mahogany table.
> I know it well.[5]

Sexton here accepts both the reality of dream, "real dream," and her need to find sources, home—and how maternal a home; she is also in her refrain affirming her own knowledge—"I know," "I know." Reality hits her with its contradictions, however, for no matter that she knows this house, knows it with the acute memories of the child, she cannot find it.

What she does find, in the next two stanzas, are the dichotomies inherent in being the female child: "When she was good, she was very, very good":

> Where did you go?
> 45 Mercy Street,
> with great-grandmother
> kneeling in her whale-bone corset
> and praying gently but fiercely

to the wash basin,
at five A.M.
at noon
dozing in her wiggy rocker,
grandfather taking a nip in the pantry,
grandmother pushing the bell for the downstairs
        maid,
and Nana rocking Mother with an oversized flower
on her forehead to cover the curl
of when she was good and when she was. . . .
And where she was begat
and in a generation
the third she will beget,
me,
with the stranger's seed blooming
into the flower called *Horrid*.

I walk in a yellow dress
and a white pocketbook stuffed with cigarettes,
enough pills, my wallet, my keys,
and being twenty-eight, or is it forty-five?
I walk. I walk.
I hold matches at the street signs
for it is dark,
as dark as the leathery dead
and I have lost my green Ford,
my house in the suburbs. . . .
and I am walking and looking
and this is no dream
just my oily life
where the people are alibis
and the street is unfindable for an
entire lifetime.

The significance of the poem's being titled "45 Mercy Street" instead of just "Mercy Street," as was her earlier play, now becomes clear. Sexton is 45. She will die at 45, just a scant month before turning 46. These chronological markings are as important to Sexton as is her astrological profile—Scorpios both, she and Plath, marked, she thought, by violence, unkindness, will.[6] Married at seventeen, Sexton found herself in her poetry at 28. That age, then, is important to her; it represents the myth that people *do* find themselves, do mature, do become independent. Even after divorce from the man who had husbanded her since she was 17, Sexton could not find that independence she seemed to prize so highly, and her anger, her disillusion, at this recognition leads to the stanza of withdrawal, denial, and finally a return to her own womanlinesss as her chief identity:

Pull the shades down—
I don't care!

> Bolt the door, mercy,
> erase the number,
> rip down my street sign,
> what can it matter,
> what can it matter to this cheapskate
> who wants to own the past. . . .
>
> Not there.
>
> I open my pocketbook,
> as women do. . . .
>
> Next I pull the dream off
> and slam into the cement wall
> of the clumsy calendar
> I live in,
>
> my life,
> and its hauled up
> notebooks.

Sexton as poet (Dickinson as poet, Plath as poet)—can we accept the persona as writer only, unmoored, lost, admittedly searching, unlocateable, certainly NOT New England bound. We can hear Sexton laugh as she writes to Jon Stallworthy in 1967, "I adore being called the Nefertiti of New England."[7] In 1963, to Robert Lowell, she had admitted, "One of these days, I will learn to bear to be myself."[8] The poems of *45 Mercy Street* show that bearing, that becoming, and the anger in having to remain outside an accepted tradition, both geographic and poetic.

Always "confessional," usually "hysterical," always maligned for poems written to menstruation, lovers, abortions, her uterus, Sexton turns to apology for that personal element, as in "Talking to Sheep," or to questioning her multiple roles, as in "The Falling Dolls":

> Dolls,
> by the thousands,
> are falling out of the sky
> and I look up in fear
> and wonder who will catch them?

Guilt—why are you a poet? Who's taking care of your children (daughters)?

> . . . I dream, awake, I dream of falling dolls
> who need cribs and blankets and pajamas
> with real feet in them.
> Why is there no mother?
> Why are all these dolls falling out of the sky?
> Was there a father?
> Or have the planets cut holes in their nets

> and let our childhood out,
> or are we the dolls themselves,
> born but never fed? (pp. 10–11).

As with her earlier collections, some of the best poems in *45 Mercy Street* are Sexton's poems to her children, but here the simple sense of love and responsibility—an awesome responsibility—is coupled with an anguish of lost identity, of lost place: *are we the dolls themselves?*

Parallel with that sense of loss, increasing because of that disorientation, runs a terrible, oppressive responsibility. Even the animal poems are marked with the maternal guilt, as when Sexton laments to a dead animal, "Mole dog, / I wish your mother would wake you up." The divorce poems carry similar guilt. Whether the wife is re-attaching her husband's severed hands and feet or worrying about her teenage daughters ("we, mothers, crumpled and flyspotted / with bringing them this far / can do nothing now but pray"), the female persona bears the responsibility. Not easily. Undeniably. She is born to it. As Sexton writes in "The Big Boots of Pain,"

> I would sell my life to avoid
> the pain that begins in the crib. . . .
> when the planets drill
> your future into you
> for better or worse
> as you marry life
> and the love that gets doled out
> or doesn't (p. 103).

The gamble of the traditional woman's life, be she Cinderella or Sexton, is her marriage, and that marriage is her primary responsibility. That such a single responsibility, carried singly, may wear into madness is the image of the poet's crucifixion in "The Passion of the Mad Rabbit":

> Next it was bad Friday and they nailed me up
> like a scarecrow and many gathered eating pop-
>   corn, carrying
> hymnals or balloons. There were three of us there,
> though *they* appeared normal. My ears, so pink like
>   powder
> were nailed. My paws, sweet as baby mittens, were
>   nailed.
> And my two fuzzy ankles. I said, "Pay no attention.
>   I am crazy."
> And some giggled and some knelt. My oxygen
>   became tiny
> and blood rang over and over in my head like a bell.
> The others died, the luck of it blurting through them.
> I could not. I was a silly broken umbrella
> and oblivion would not kiss me. For three days it
> was thus.

Then they took me down and had a conference.
It is Easter, they said, and you are the Easter
    Bunny.
Then they built a great pyre of kindling and laid me
    on top
and just before the match they handed me a pink
    basket
of eggs the color of the circus.
Fire lit, I tossed the eggs to them, *Hallelujah* I sang
    to the eggs,
singing as I burned to nothing in the tremor of the
    flames.
My blood came to a boil as I looked down the throat
    of madness,
but singing yellow egg, blue egg, pink egg, red egg,
    green egg,
Hallelujah, to each hard-boiled-colored egg . . .
                                            (pp. 90–91).

Poor lost Alice in Wonderland; poor mother, responsible for any ritual, tradition, food, spirit; poor woman lost in sexuality, fertility, the flames of lust and madness—here as in *Transformations* Sexton makes use of our common heritage of fairy tale, myth, archetype of sex goddess / mother, and poises it against that other set of opposites, sanity / insanity. She similarly uses the image of angel food in her poem about the virgin / whore identity, wishing to change her name from Anne to Mary (her mother's name); wishing for purity, for grace, and finally—pervasively—for mercy:

I kneel once more,
in case mercy should come . . . (p. 89).

finding my Mercy Street,
kissing it and tenderly gift-wrapping my love . . .
                                            (p. 105).

Much as she hopes for mercy, tired and resentful as she is of life's non-acceptance and its demands, still Sexton comes in these last poems to the confidence of her own self-possession. There is contentment of a sort in *45 Mercy Street*. There are images throughout the collection of houses, shelters gained through love, homes. The ultimate image of place occurs in her poem "Keeping the City." Lost from even that maternal ancestry, searching as she honestly recounts, Sexton yet finds her strength in her kinship with her maturing daughters, and through them, with herself as woman. Her strength is, however, but fragile, tentative, a veil of bright motion, a daisy, which some eyes might consider ineffectual:

The city
of my choice
that I guard

> like a butterfly, useless, useless
> in her yellow costume, swirling
> swirling around the gates.
> The city shifts, falls, rebuilds . . . (p. 24)

That place, unnamed as it is, that city, is, finally, of Sexton's *choice*—and her ability to make that choice is crucial. And while it is not a New England city but a much more interior and specifically female city, it does, finally, "rebuild."

[SECTION ON SYLVIA PLATH'S POEMS]

For all her emphasis on endurance, Plath's poems leave us rather with the anguish, the sense of displacement, the search for place, the terrible weight of responsibility. In Plath as in Sexton, in Dickinson as in Rich, the themes recur, pointing repeatedly to the double disenfranchisement, the double disorientation of being both writer and woman. I had intended to include two other poets, the vibrant and strangely androgynous E. E. Cummings and the divided but responsive Robert Lowell. Reminiscent as many of their poems are of the New England heritage, their poems differ greatly from those of Dickinson, Plath, and Sexton: the defiance against tradition is more often intellecutalized, controllable. The refusal to conform is itself a pose and, in that, more acceptable. As Richard Kennedy points out in his fine biography of Cummings,

> despite his hostilty to American culture, he is as American as Concord Bridge and the Statue of Liberty. "The tradition, after all, in this nation is bucking the tradition. . . ."[9]

Acceptance of attitudes, an intellectual understanding of defiance: our male writers feel secure enough in their roles as artists, and the cultural expectations of those roles, that they can deal with alienation and even with loss of place, parents, love. There is much less sense of torture, much less search imagery in the poems of Cummings and Lowell, and more of a tendency to offer wisdom, panacea, achieved knowledge. Just as in "Thanatopsis" Bryant's view of that final search, that final definition of place—death—is highly intellectualized:

> When thoughts
> Of the last bitter hour come like a blight
> Over thy spirit, and sad images
> Of the stern agony, and shroud, and pall,
> And breathless darkness, and the narrow house,
> Make thee to shudder, and grow sick at heart:—
> Go forth under the open sky, and list
> To Nature's teachings. . . .

Death as "pleasant dreams" in the Bryant poem has no echo in the work of Dickinson, Sexton, or Plath. The fact of actual death is the price we have all paid for their great alienation; the loss of place, the hostility of non-acceptance becomes the image throughout the poems so that Sexton may write, in *Words for Dr. Y.,*

> Home is my Bethlehem
> my succoring shelter[10]

but just as quickly admit "Houses haunt me. . . ."

> I am alone here in my own mind.
> There is no map
> and there is no road . . . (p. 63)

Lest we be tempted to read the pervasive images of Sexton's and Plath's poems as only contemporary, striking evidence of the interiority of the modern poetic focus, we must return to the poems of Emily Dickinson:

> One need not be a Chamber—to be Haunted—
> One need not be a House—
> The Brain has corridors—surpassing
> Material Place. . . .[11]

Isolation, loss of place, responsibility, guilt, the creation of a new world—alone, alone as both artist and woman. The New England tradition seems far removed from these poets, who are, perhaps, among our greatest. We should reach this recognition, I think, with less anger than with lament, for, as Dickinson wrote in 1863, one hundred years before Plath's suicide:

> Victory comes late—
> And is held low to freezing lips—
> Too rapt with frost
> To take it—
> How sweet it would have tasted—
> Just a drop. . . .
> Crumbs—fit such little mouths—[12]

Notes

1. Walt Whitman, *Leaves of Grass and Selected Prose,* ed. John Kouwenhoven (New York: Modern Library), pp. 23–24. Subsequent references are cited in the text.

2. Ralph Waldo Emerson, "The Problem" in *The Norton Anthology of American Literature,* I, eds. Gottesman, Holland, Kalstone, et al. (New York: W. W. Norton, 1979), p. 833.

3. *The Complete Poems of Emily Dickinson,* ed. Thomas H. Johnson (Boston: Little, Brown and Co., 1960), p. 212. Susequent references are cited in the text.

4. Sandra M. Gilbert and Susan Gubar, *The Madwoman in the Attic: The Woman Writer and the Nineteenth-Century Literary Imagination* (New Haven: Yale Univ. Press, 1979). That there still exists a sense of the modern "New England" poet seems clear from looking at the Table of Contents in Donald Hall's anthology *Contemporary American Poetry* (New York: Penguin Books, 1972). Nearly 75 percent of the 39 poets included are either from New England or were educated there. Of the 39 poets, only four—Sexton, Plath, Rich, and Denise

Levertov—are women; and of those four, Levertov is British and the other three are all New Englanders.

5. Anne Sexton, *45 Mercy Street*, ed. Linda Gray Sexton (Boston: Houghton Mifflin Co., 1976), p. 3. Hereafter cited in text.

6. Sexton's sequence of poems "Scorpio, Bad Spider, Die: The Horoscope Poems" was published in 1978 in the collection *Words for Dr. Y., Uncollected Poems with Three Stories*, ed. Linda Gray Sexton (Boston: Houghton Mifflin Co.) There are frequent references in both Sexton's and Plath's poetry and letters to astrology.

7. Included in *Anne Sexton, A Self-Portrait in Letters*, ed. Linda Gray Sexton and Lois Ames (Boston: Houghton Mifflin Co., 1977), p. 318.

8. *Anne Sexton*, p. 170.

9. Richard S. Kennedy, *Dreams in the Mirror: A Biography of E. E. Cummings* (New York: Liveright, 1980), p. 7.

10. *Words for Dr. Y.*, p. 61. Hereafter cited in text.

11. *Complete Poems*, p. 333.

12. *Complete Poems*, p. 340.

"This Is My Tale Which I Have Told": Anne Sexton as Storyteller
Steven E. Colburn*

In that portion of her work that is concerned with exploring the collective experience of women, the poetry of Anne Sexton tells a number of different stories about the fate of womankind in the world. This large body of work may be divided (for the sake of convenience) into three smaller groups, according to the central character that the plots of the poems focus upon. First there are the poems in which Sexton explores the fate of woman in her role as the outcast witch—a legendary woman of great power who, though she has the necessary confidence to assert herself in the face of societal disapproval and active opposition, does not ultimately succeed in escaping the reactionary forces that oppose her. Another of the roles into which Sexton's women characters are frequently cast is that of the temptress Eve— a conventional image of woman as the evil sinner—who is identified by tradition as the vehicle through which death, suffering, and injustice enter the world. The final role into which the woman is frequently cast in Sexton's work is that of the passive victim of man's aggression against his own kind—a role in which she shares the fate of all oppressed and defenseless groups in a world torn by war.

Sexton's poetry is shaped, to a significant degree, by a basic ontological condition: the fact of her womanhood. It is not surprising, therefore, to find that a woman such as Sexton—who is intensely conscious of the roles into which she is cast by her own status as a poet—should devote a substantial

*Previously unpublished excerpt from the author's "Anne Sexton: The Poet as Storyteller"; © 1987 by the author.

portion of her effort as a storyteller to portraying the experience of women in concrete, dramatic situations. Just as it is natural for the artist to reflect upon the nature of the creative enterprise, so it is natural that women should reflect upon the position of subordination in which they find themselves in the world, and seek to understand its causes, modes of operation, and consequences for their own lives. Sexton too explores these questions about the collective fate of womankind throughout her poems.

As with her portrayal of the artist, Sexton most often chooses to dramatize the experience of her female protagonists from the perspective of the woman herself who—presented with some challenge to her independence or threat to her security—reflects upon the reasons for her fate. The inside perspective for these stories about women's experience dominates Sexton's persuasive strategy. In having her woman characters tell their own stories, the poet allows their thought processes to dominate the reader's consciousness, creating an empathetic identification between reader and character. By using such a narrative perspective, Sexton is able to avoid didacticism while effectively challenging many of the conventional beliefs and prejudices about the nature of women and their experience of the world, which her readers already carry in their consciousness.

"HER KIND" (Sexton, 15)[1]

One of Sexton's best-known works that portrays the collective experience of women in dramatized form is "Her Kind," an early poem from *To Bedlam and Part Way Back* whose central character is the outcast witch, a figure who appears frequently in her work. In the three brief episodes that make up Sexton's story about the life of the witch in "Her Kind," this legendary figure of women's power is cast into a variety of situations by the storyteller that illustrate by turns the fortune of her character as rebel, servant, and victim.

The first stanza of the poem presents the witch in her role as rebel—a woman of freedom and power who, becoming "braver at night," goes out "haunting the black air." As she does her "hitch," soaring "over the plain houses," moving "light by light" during her nightly journey, she is "dreaming evil," planning her revenge against the society that rejects and oppresses her, making of the witch a "lonely thing," an isolated, "twelve-fingered" freak who is seen as being "possessed" and "out of mind." In this respect the fate of the witch and the madman at the hands of society is essentially the same, as Thomas Szasz argues in *The Manufacture of Madness*,[2] and the speaker's choice of language here reinforces the association between the two figures, inviting the reader to draw out the comparison. Thus, Sexton's storyteller observes, "A woman like that is not a woman, quite," but rather some fear-inspiring, inhuman "thing." Nevertheless, the speaker concludes: "I have been her kind." This nightly journey of the witch becomes, through his mediating role of the storyteller in Sexton's tale, a wish-fulfillment, a symbolic excursion out of the everyday, waking self, and by implication out of the oppressive roles that the dreaming witch's sisters must also play in "the plain houses" they occupy. In this respect, the experiences described by the witch, Sexton's storyteller reminds us, are part of every oppressed woman's life.

The second stanza of the poem presents us with a very different image of the witch, for here we are shown a character who—far from "dreaming evil"—is cast into the role of man's servant. In this role, the witch is a woman who uses her magical powers for "rearranging the disaligned" elements of the world. Yet despite this, she is not able to remedy her own situation. Images of domesticity predominate in this stanza, as the constructive activity of the witch is described in terms that suggest her connection with the chthonic powers of nature:

> I have found the warm caves in the woods,
> filled them with skillets, carvings, shelves,
> closets, silks, innumerable goods;
> fixed the suppers for the worms and the elves;
> whining, rearranging the disaligned.

Yet despite the positive effects of her power upon the world, this witch, too, seems to find her role dissatisfying—for it is an endless task never completed—as her "whining" complaint suggests. Thus, the storyteller concludes, "A woman like that is misunderstood. I have been her kind," as she once more asserts the representative nature of this character's experience in the world.

In the third stanza of the poem, yet another familiar image of the witch is presented; that of her fate as victim. In this final stanza, however, the character's testimony turns from an account of her own activities to a description of her treatment at the hands of her persecutors. This shift in perspective is signalled by the introduction of the second-person mode of address into the witch's account of her fate, as she turns and speaks directly to those who oppress her:

> I have ridden in your cart, driver,
> waved my nude arms at villages going by,
> learning the last bright routes, survivor
> where your flames still bite my thigh
> and my ribs crack where your wheels wind.

Here the reader becomes, by linguistic implication, the driver of this prison cart, as well as the executioner who lights the fire at the witch's feet as she stands at the stake. By this means the storyteller shifts the psychological burden of guilt for this woman's destruction squarely upon the reader's own shoulders—even though the reader has also shared, throughout the earlier part of the poem, the woman's own perspective. Sexton frequently uses the second-person point of view as she does here—to draw the reader into the action of her stories as a participant. In a dramatic poem such as "Her Kind," the emotive potential of this narrative device for moving and persuading her audience is effectively demonstrated. The storyteller completes this final episode in the troubled life of the witch by returning to the general terms of the refrain, and concludes the tale by once again equating her own personal situation with that of the character in her story: "A woman like that is not ashamed to die. / I have been her kind."

That Sexton's witch in "Her Kind" is a symbolic figure, whose experiences at the hands of a hostile, uncomprehending society are representative of the misfortunes of women in general, is strongly suggested to the reader by the handling of viewpoint in this poem. During the course of each stanza, the storyteller carefully shifts the focus of her viewpoint from an initial emphasis on the dramatized testimony of the witch herself, who speaks of her experience using the first-person (in the first five lines of each stanza), to that of a more generalized perspective in the penultimate line of each stanza—in which her exemplary character becomes merely "a woman"—as if the fate of the witch is that of any woman—to the narrative perspective of the concluding line of each stanza—where the storyteller equates her own experience as a woman with that of her character, asserting their identity. Sexton's handling of viewpoint in the poem leads the reader from one level of symbolic association to another within the story, which, as it moves from mere fiction, to moral fable, to personal confession, goes to the very heart of the storyteller's enterprise in the poem.

"RATS LIVE ON NO EVIL STAR" (Sexton, 359)

Besides the legendary figure of the witch, another of the roles in which Sexton portrays her women characters is that of the temptress Eve—an image of woman as sinner. Sexton's choice of Eve as symbolic of womankind's collective fate in the world is a particularly effective one, since the theological tradition that has associated Eve with the entry of evil, death, suffering, and injustice into the world is widely known and provides Sexton with a body of traditional beliefs and prejudices about the nature of women upon which to build her own contemporary account of man's exile from Eden.

In "Rats Live on No Evil Star," her most extended treatment of the figure of Eve, Sexton approaches her received material in a highly idiosyncratic fashion. Largely disregarding traditional interpretations of the biblical account of man's fall from perfection, Sexton constructs an imaginative account of the event, which expresses her own perceptions of the received story's implications for the collective experience of women in the world, shaping the material to her own purpose.

In focusing her attention on the biblical account of the Fall, Sexton's main efforts as a storyteller are directed toward a vindication of Eve's role in the process. Thus, her story consists, at least in part, of an effort to deny

Eve's culpability in man's fall from perfection, a role into which she has traditionally been cast by orthodox Christian theology. One of the most prominent features of Sexton's account of the Fall in "No Evil Star" is the storyteller's seeming rejection of the doctrine of original sin, a theological crux upon which the orthodox understanding of Eve's symbolic role as temptress in the Genesis narrative has largely depended.

Though "No Evil Star" follows the basic plot structure of the traditional account of man's creation, temptation, and fall as found in Genesis 2:3, Sexton chooses to retell the story from a feminine viewpoint, which subtly alters and undercuts this received material. In Sexton's account of the creation of man and woman in the first stanza, for example, she follows the same sequence of events. We see Adam created first, existing alone for a time in a state of isolation before the subsequent creation of Eve:

> After Adam broke his rib in two
> and ate it for supper,
> after Adam, from the waist up,
> an old mother,
> had begun to question the wonder
> Eve was brought forth.

Though Sexton's plot does not follow the same sequence of events found in the biblical account, a closer examination of the language and content here reveals some important departures from her source. In Sexton's version of the story, Adam had already "begun to question the wonder" of creation even before Eve is "brought forth." This is emphasized by the storyteller's twice-repeated assertion that her creation came "after" Adam had begun to act as an independent agent of his own fate. This is a significant departure from the biblical account of Adam's temptation, where Eve is identified as the questioner whose uncontrollable curiosity eventually precipitates man's fall. Though the storyteller's very language here appropriates the cultural authority of her source, she is subtly reshaping that material by reversing the traditional roles of the participants in the creation drama.

In the latter half of the first stanza, Sexton's storyteller turns her focus upon the separate creation of woman:

> Eve came out of that rib like an angry bird.
> She came forth like a bird that got loose
> suddenly from its cage.
> Out of the cage came Eve,
> escaping, escaping.
> She was clothed in her skin like the sun
> and her ankles were not for sale.

This description of Eve's creation, although it seems at first to follow the details of the received source, actually subverts it. The impatient anger that Sexton's Eve displays in her escape from the confining enclosure of her "cage" is a direct contradiction of the traditional account, where Eve's docile, submissive, and ingratiating behavior is emphasized. Here we see a good example of the degree to which the storyteller is reshaping the material to her own purpose. In Sexton's version of creation, Eve is a fully developed character, entirely different from the figure of Eve in Genesis—who exists only as a projection of man's sense of evil onto an alien Other. Sexton's Eve reacts in a plausible and understandable way to her unjust subjection to Adam in this separate creation, demonstrating the extent to which she has become, in Sexton's version of the story, a character whose fate is representative of the collective experience of women in the world. In Sexton's reworking of the biblical account of the creation, Eve's angry reaction to her fate is not essentially different from that of any woman who is subjected to an unasked-for, and undeserved, state of subjection.

Having concluded her account of Eve's creation, the storyteller draws back from her characters for an ironic aside on God's sense of pleasure in his creation of man and woman:

> God looked out through his tunnel
> and was pleased.

In the third stanza of the poem, the storyteller once again shifts the focus of her attention to the actions of Adam for the second episode in her version of man's fall from perfection. In this episode, he is captured in mid-action, sitting in the Garden of Eden "like a lawyer," reading "the book of life" like some sophistic *raisonneur*. Sexton's storyteller has carefully eliminated from her account the legalistic debate between the serpent and Eve in Genesis 3:15—which immediately precedes Eve's act of rebellion against God's prohibition—and here makes Adam the culpable party, transferring the guilt of rebellion to him alone. In Sexton's account of the Fall, it is Adam alone who—filled with pride in his reasoning abilities and his cleverness—ignores the spoken prohibition of God:

> Adam sat like a lawyer
> and read the book of life.
> Only his eyes were alive.
> They did the work of a blast furnace.

Lest her reader fail to comprehend the implication of this subversion of the traditional account of the Fall, the storyteller adds another parenthetical aside to her tale:

> Only later did Adam and Eve go galloping,
> galloping into the apple.
> They made the noise of the moon-chew
> and let the juice fall down like tears.

In the penultimate stanza of the poem, having playfully challenged and subverted the authority of her source, Sexton's storyteller returns at the end to focus on Eve who, despite her lack of culpability, is nevertheless seen suffering the terrible consequences of the Fall. Echoing the language of

God's curse upon mankind in Genesis 3:14–19, the storyteller focuses upon the act of generation, which has traditionally served as a symbol of the defective nature of the postlapsarian world:

> Because of this same apple
> Eve gave birth to the evilest of creatures
> with its bellyful of dirt
> and its hair seven inches long.
> It had two eyes full of poison
> and routine pointed teeth.
> Thus Eve gave birth.
> In this unnatural act
> she gave birth to a rat.
> It slid from her like a pearl.

In this episode of the story a new character—the rat—is introduced into the story of Adam and Eve. The figure of the rat is derived not from the received source, but from Sexton's own private symbolic repertoire, where it appears as a symbol for man's exile from God in a number of poems throughout the course of her career. In "No Evil Star," this direct descendant of Eve represents generated, postlapsarian mankind and carries the curse of exile God placed upon her own head and Adam's. This is illustrated in Eve's loving treatment of her unfortunate offspring after its birth, which is described with gentle, touching irony by Sexton's storyteller:

> It was ugly, of course,
> but Eve did not know that
> and when it died before its time
> she placed its tiny body
> on that piece of kindergarten called STAR.

In the final stanza of the poem, the storyteller makes a bold move to draw the reader into the story of the Fall, as she subtly shifts the focus of her narration from a description of her characters' fate to an assessment of the unfortunate state of the present world, in which she is constructing her contemporary version of the tale. As she moves from her retrospective account of man's mythic past to the present world of her reader—which includes such mundane trappings as watermelon, Asia, and the barbershop quartet—the verbs change from past to present tense, and the point of view shifts from third to first person:

> Now all us cursed ones falling out after
> with our evil mouths and our worried eyes
> die before our time
> but do not go to some heaven, some hell
> but are put on the RAT'S STAR
> which is as wide as Asia
> and as happy as a barbershop quartet.
> We are put there beside the three thieves

> for the lowest of us all
> deserve to smile in eternity
> like a watermelon.

Here the reader has become the direct descendant of this "cursed" woman, upon whom the blame for the fallen condition of world has been projected. Drawing out the all-too-obvious connections between the rat, "the evilest of creatures," and "all us cursed ones falling out after," the storyteller establishes a symbolic continuity between the mythic past, in which the story proper is set, and the historical present, in which it is being told. Like the rat, who "died before its time," we too "die before our time," but do not go to "some heaven, some hell / but are put on the RAT'S STAR," just like the rat whose "tiny body" Eve placed "on that piece of kindergarten called STAR." In the final lines of the poem the storyteller asserts, in a coy redaction of this twice-repeated phrase: "we are put there beside the three thieves." This final detail of her story seems to allude to the traditional account of the Crucifixion, according to which Christ was crucified between two thieves. Yet here there are, curiously, three thieves, not two.

Throughout the course of "Rats Live on No Evil Star," we have seen the various means by which Sexton's storyteller has shaped her source material to suit her own purposes. In following the basic narrative framework of Genesis 2–3, she has appropriated its cultural authority. By inverting, eliminating, and adding to the details of that framework, she not only vindicates Eve's role in that Fall, but manages to draw out its implications for the collective fate of women in the world.

"I'M DREAMING THE MY LAI SOLDIER AGAIN" (Sexton, 575)

In the final poem to be considered in this essay, "I'm Dreaming the My Lai Soldier Again," we see the third role in which womankind is frequently portrayed in Sexton's poetry—that of the passive victim of man's aggression against his own kind. In this poem Sexton's storyteller draws the material for her tale not from the legendary or mythical past, but from the historical events of contemporary life.

The connection made in "The My Lai Soldier" between the fate of women in the world and the destructive consequences of war is not by any means unique to Sexton's work. Many other contemporary women—both creative artists and theoreticians—have associated the objectification of woman, and her consequent misfortunes at the hands of society, with the political fate of all oppressed and defenseless groups.

The first thing one notices in "The My Lai Soldier" is that Sexton's storyteller has distanced or objectified the material from which her tale is constructed by presenting it in the form of a dream, much as the traditional Ashanti storyteller prefaces his tale by saying: "We do not really mean, we do not really mean, that what we are going to say is true."[3] By this act, Sexton's storyteller prepares her audience, placing her narrative in a specific fictional category about which her audience already holds many preconceptions and expectations.

"The My Lai Soldier" is part of an interrelated sequence of poems collectively entitled "Letters to Dr. Y.," which Sexton presents in the dramatic form of a series of letters from a female patient to her male analyst. In these poems the speaker presents an ongoing record of her fears, desires, and fantasies over an extended period of time, frequently appealing to the doctor to whom the letters are addressed for rational explanations of these psychic events that trouble her. In doing this she seeks emotional support from this figure of male objectivity and authority in the form of reassurances of her sanity. Of course, since this dramatic situation is a fictional premise devised by the author, we have only the testimony of the patient's letters here and—deprived of the doctor's learned interpretations—must consider the meaning of the patient's stories on our own.

Unlike many of the other poems in this sequence, "The My Lai Soldier" makes no direct reference to its intended auditor and exhibits more verselike qualities than many of the other "letters." It is presented in the form of a reported dream and has the general characteristics of a death-fantasy— whose disturbing content is expressed in the compressed, symbolic terms appropriate to this imaginative form of narrative.

In "The My Lai Soldier" the patient-speaker of the poem relates to her unnamed auditor a recurring dream she is having "night after night," in which she finds herself cast inexplicably into the role of war victim:

> I'm dreaming the My Lai soldier again,
> I'm dreaming the My Lai soldier night after night.
> He rings the doorbell like the Fuller Brush Man
> and wants to shake hands with me
> and I do because it would be rude to say no
> and I look at my hand and it is green
> with intestines.
> And they won't come off,
> they won't. He apologizes for this over and over.

The date assigned to this "letter" (17 December 1969) provides the reader with a useful explanation of the dream's reference to a contemporary war-atrocity, the My Lai massacre. Though the actual events to which the speaker's death-fantasy refer had occurred on 16 March 1968, more than a year before this date, it is not difficult to reconstruct in rough outline the precipitating occasion of the dream. The dreamer's memory of these events were, no doubt, recalled to consciousness when, on 2 December 1969, a U. S. Army board of inquiry began its investigation into the My Lai incident and its subsequent coverup—a highly publicized event that was prominent in world headlines during the entire month of December 1969.[4]

Though the American public reacted at first with disbelief to the revelation of what had really happened at My Lai, that feeling changed to one of revulsion as the atrocities committed by their own countrymen were brought to light and their truth confirmed by public testimony. The very substance and form of the speaker's dream about the My Lai massacre, however, suggests that the incident has—for this woman—more than a passing moral or national significance. The dreamer's fear, expressed in a fantasy about her own death at the hands of an American soldier, focuses on her perception of the interrelation between the personal and political realms of experience in the world and expresses her convictions about the relation of women's onto-logical position to the mechanisms of projection and scapegoating.

This intersection of the personal and the political is manifested by the shifting narrative perspective within the dream, as the speaker moves from describing an individual encounter with the My Lai soldier in the first stanza to the collective experiences of the massacre victims described in the latter half of the poem.

The soldier makes his appearance at the very outset of the poem, unex-pectedly intruding on the speaker's daily routine "like the Fuller Brush Man," whose arrival at first is not particularly threatening, merely annoying. Yet this innocuous-seeming figure has come to offer her not household prod-ucts but suffering and death, forcing his unwanted wares upon the harried but compliant housewife.

In the second part of her dream, the speaker is suddenly transported from her familiar domestic surroundings and cast into a setting whose details closely resemble those of the actual massacre at My Lai:[5]

> The My Lai soldier lifts me up again and again
> and lowers me down with the other dead women and babies
> saying, *It's my job. It's my job.*
>
> Then he gives me a bullet to swallow
> like a sleeping tablet.
> I am lying in this belly of dead babies
> each one belching up the yellow gasses of death
> and their mothers tumble, eyeballs, knees, upon me,
> each for the last time, each authentically dead.
> The soldier stands on a stepladder above us
> pointing his red penis right at me and saying,
> *Don't take this personally.*

In this latter portion of the poem, the first-person singular pronoun by which the speaker refers to herself in the dream is gradually replaced by the first-person plural pronoun as the speaker's identity merges with that of the massa-cre victims, drawing her auditor directly into the landscape of the dream.

The bitter irony of this latter episode is revealed by the verbal gestures the soldier makes in his attempt to justify the cruel victimization of the My Lai women and children. He refuses moral responsibility for his act, claim-ing: "*It's my job,*" denying any personal motive for his actions, or any guilt for the consequences. In doing this, the soldier echoes the strategy used by the actual My Lai defendants to deny legal responsibility for their acts, a subject that was discussed extensively in the media at the time.[6] Lest the soldier's appeal leave any room for doubt, however, the speaker's dream concludes by raising another important moral issue involved in the case—the matter of the rape—which is presented in her letter to the analyst through the synecdochic image of the red penis that the soldier brandishes, pointing it right at her. Though this act fixes, in a clear and undeniable way, the soldier's personal responsibility for his actions, he attempts to deny it verbally at the very moment he accomplishes the physical act. How else, one wonders, can such an act be taken except *"personally"*?

It is the paradoxical truth and falseness of the My Lai soldier's closing assertion about the impersonal nature of his aggressive act that indicates the speaker's inner conflict over the relation of her personal sense of identity to the collective experience of oppression which she shares with all women as a group. In the process of attempting an integration of these conflicting aspects of her fragmented self, she discovers the answer within her own unconscious. Sexton the storyteller, through the fictional premise of the patient's letters to her analyst, dramatizes the complex truth about the collective fate of women in the world, using the shifting perspective within her character's dream to draw us into the experience and to share her discovery.

As her work amply demonstrates, Sexton the poet is, above all else, a storyteller—who presents her observations about life in dramatized forms, creating characters and situations to suit her purposes, and transforming her received materials to reflect her own perceptions about reality. There is little doubt that the ontological fact of Sexton's womanhood exerts a strong influence upon the stories her poems tell—not only in her choice of subjects, but also in the particular methods by which she chooses to convey her material to the audience. Though the poems in which Sexton dramatizes the experience of women in the world are cast in the form of stories about the misfortunes of individual figures drawn from legend, myth, and history, her storyteller consistently moves, during the course of telling the tales, from the self-enclosed world of the story to a broader perspective—in which her characters are shown to be symbolic figures whose misfortunes are representative of the collective misfortunes of womankind. In "Her Kind," the repeated expansion and contraction of narrative focus within each stanza of the poem allows Sexton's storyteller to equate her own contemporary experience as a woman with the legendary fate of the witch. In "Rats Live on No Evil Star," the storyteller uses parallelism of detail during the course of her tale to establish a continuity of situation between man's mythical past in the biblical account of the Fall and the familiar, everyday world in which her contemporary reader lives. In "I'm Dreaming the My Lai Soldier," the storyteller uses the symbolic operations of the dreamer's unconscious mind to draw out the relation between her character's fantasy of victimization and the actual victimizing of women in the aggressive conflicts of warfare. These three poems offer examples of the recurring roles in which women appear in Sexton's poetry, as they take up by turns the figure of the outcast witch, the temptress Eve, and the helpless war-victim.

Notes

1. Anne Sexton, *The Complete Poems* (Boston: Houghton Mifflin, 1981), 15; subsequent references to this edition are cited in the text.

2. Thomas S. Szasz, "The Myths of Witchcraft and Mental Illness," in *The Manufacture of Madness* (New York: Harper, 1970), 111–34.

3. *African Folktales & Sculpture,* ed. Paul Radin (New York: Pantheon, 1952), 19.

4. See: Joseph Goldstein, Burke Marshall, and Jack Schwartz, *The My Lai Massacre and Its Cover-Up* (New York: Free Press, 1976); and Seymour Hersh, *Cover-Up* (New York: Random House, 1972).

5. Hersh, *Cover-Up,* 3.

6. Goldstein, Marshall, and Schwartz, *My Lai Massacre,* 192–206.

"I Dare to Live": The Transforming Art of Anne Sexton
Rise B. Axelrod*

> No longer in a merely physical universe, man lives in a symbolic universe. . . . Instead of dealing with the things themselves man is in a sense constantly conversing with himself [Ernst Cassirer, *An Essay on Man*].

> Where there is no vision, the people perish [*Proverbs,* 29:18].

As *animal symbolicum,* or symbol-maker, each person lives in a world of abstraction, or other-reality distinct from the world of multiplicity and sense experience. Civilization, that accumulation of symbolic constructs, forms a buffer between the individual, the internal self, and nature, the world without. "This capacity for living easily and familiarly at an extraordinary level of abstraction," is, as William Barret explains in *Irrational Man,* both the source of our immense technological power and the source of that "desolating sense of rootlessness, vacuity and the lack of concrete feeling that assails modern man in his moment of real anxiety."[1] The inevitable dead end of our epistemology is Nothingness: the tragedy of modern existence is that we are irrevocably alienated, cut off from our roots, imprisoned in the narrow cell of our own self-consciousness. Yet the poet in our time seeks to free the self from the deadly effect of symbolic entrapment. This quest for unification of self with other is the ultimate aim of Eros, the liberating and creative life

*Reprinted with permission of the author from *Concerning Poetry* 7 (Spring 1974): 6–13.

force. In her poetry, Anne Sexton plunges into the abyss of the isolated self and touches sources of regeneration. In her early books, *To Bedlam and Part Way Back*, *All My Pretty Ones*, and *Live or Die*, she explores the dark depths of her own consciousness. In the later three books, *Love Poems*, *Transformations*, and *The Book of Folly*, she experiments with mythopoeia providing possibilities of reconnection, and hence of rebirth.[2] Thus the movement of Sexton's poet is dual: centripetal as well as centrifugal. The inturning therapeutic mode analyzes the "cracked mirror" of the self in search of the origins of dissolution. The second, more visionary mode allows the resurrection of the true self and its reunification with others.

Anne Sexton's early poetry takes place in Bedlam, the realm of extremity and madness. She explained, in a *Paris Review* interview: "I was a victim of the American Dream. . . . The surface cracked when I was about twenty-eight. I had a psychotic break and tried to kill myself."[3] In the seminal poem, "For John, Who Begs Me Not to Enquire Further," that cracked surface of her brittle system of symbolic constructs is transformed into an image of "the cracked mirror," an image of her own and the world's insanity:

> Not that it was beautiful,
> but that, in the end, there was
> a certain sense of order there;
> a something worth learning
> in that narrow diary of my mind,
> in the commonplaces of the asylum
> where the cracked mirror
> or my own selfish death
> outstared me.

In this mirror, the poet comes face to face with her own disintegration, and with her ambivalent movement toward death. Evidences of the fragmentation of her psyche are scattered throughout the poetry in synecdochic images. Her very life is a burden: "lugging myself as if / I were a sawed-off body / in the trunk" (LD 87). Not only is her body irrevocably severed from her mind by a strictly enforced Cartesian dualism, but it is in revolt. In the madhouse, the poet tries to do therapy:

> I make
> moccasins all morning. At first my hands
> kept empty, unraveled for the lives
> they used to work. Now I learn to take
> them back, each angry finger that demands
> I mend what another will break
> tomorrow [B 3].

Those empty, death-embracing hands and those self-motivated, self-destructive fingers resist making a "mock of sin." They resist overturning the abstract system of guilt and repression, and so resist being cured, resist wholeness.

The "cracked mirror" also reflects the narcissistic self unable to perceive a world outside itself. According to Martin Heidegger, after Plato's Cave of Shadows each individual was trapped in solipsism.[4] In "The Double Image," Sexton has a corresponding "cave of the mirror," where two portraits, the dying mother and the suicidal daughter, face each other, mirroring each other's death and identity:

> my mocking mirror, my overthrown
> love, my first image. She eyes me from that face,
> that stony head of death
> I had outgrown.
>
> . . .
>
> And this was the cave of the mirror,
> that double woman who stares
> at herself, as if she were petrified
> in time. . . .

The portrait of the mother is a death mask, "petrified" in as well as by time and inevitably frightening to any witness. But to confront death in a double image of oneself forces one to view the abyss from a fragile precipice. For in the mother's death, the poet cannot escape the vision of "my mocking mirror"—her own failed suicides. Add guilt to that death and imagine the innumerable horrors the poet must suffer. The mother could not forgive her daughter's suicide attempts and held them responsible for her own death: "As if death were catching / . . . as if my dying had eaten inside of her / . . . [she] said I gave her cancer."

Traditionally, Western society offers two means of dealing with death: the economic institution of hereditary property and the religious promise of immortality. Sexton experiments with both of these systems, only to discover their ultimate inadequacy. In "The Division of Parts" and "All My Pretty Ones" she "shuffles" through "the love and legal verbiage" of both parents' wills. This ritual sorting and cataloguing of her inheritance is likened by Sexton to "piling stones one on top of the other."[5] These "gifts" are dead-weight which "settle on [her] like a debt"; but through the verbal piling process she is able to bury her parents, their deaths, and her guilt under an avalanche of physical material. Yet this escape from feeling into factuality ("Time, that rearranger / of estates, equips / me with your garments, but not with grief") proves unsuccessful, for even in her numbed sleep, nightmare visions violate her bed. The demon cannot be exorcized because the "brave ghost" is the mother, the double image, the self. Avoidance of death through materialism is really equivalent to a flight into schizophrenia and death itself.

The alternative religious solution is desperately sought by Sexton, but it too proves impossible, at least at this stage in her writing. Yearning to believe in the Resurrection and the mythology of eternal life, she is unbearably constrained by the physical reality of the Crucifixion. Christ's passion is too real, his human suffering too recognizable. Sexton's Protestantism prevents her from acceptance of the miracle: Christ is too much man to be God. She sadly states, "Need is not quite belief" (A 22). Worse still is her horrorific conclusion, for without a Heaven, without a God to rescue us from death, the fiction of Christ's resurrection becomes a cruel joke. His death, like our own, is a grotesquery. There is no escape from total annihilation: "Unto the bellies and jaws / of rats I commit my prophecy and fear. / Far below The Cross, I correct its flaws. / We have kept the miracle. I will not be here" (A 26). Thus, these imperfect systems rather than providing succor only aggravate the pain, forcing the poet to acknowledge the very truth she wishes to avoid.

"The only way to escape the abyss," Cesare Pavese claims, "is to look at it, measure it, sound its depths and go down into it."6 Through a suicidal leap into the void at the core of being, Anne Sexton finds the meaning of liberation. By taking death into oneself, she says, you "have possessed the enemy, eaten the enemy, / have taken on his craft, his magic" (LD 58). Suicide then is an attempt to conquer death, to master the existential dread, the fear that "in the end . . . drowns you" (LD 17). Besides this will to power over one's daily dying, the "suicide impulse" can be, as James Hillman explains in *Suicide and the Soul*, "a transformation drive."7 Oftentimes, the suicide finds it necessary to wrench herself violently out of one inadequate order of reality into another reality. In "Kind Sir: These Woods," Sexton describes this process in terms of a childhood game: "It was a trick / to turn around once and know you were lost; / . . . O Mademoiselle, / the rowboat rocked over. Then you were dead. / Turn around once, eyes tight, the thought in your head." This playing with dislocation, madness, and death becomes for the adult a terrifying but necessary experience. As the poem's epigraph from *Walden* advises: "Not till we are lost . . . do we begin to find ourselves." Like Thoreau, the poet in search of an authentic self realizes the therapeutic necessity of throwing off all the unnecessary surplusage of civilization and going naked into the woods of the psyche:

> And opening my eyes, I am afraid of course
> to look—this inward look that society scorns—
> Still, I search in these woods and find nothing worse
> than myself, caught between the grapes and the thorns.

This initial, self-analytical "inward look" into the "Heart of Darkness" leads Sexton to the wisdom of accepting her genuine self ("love your self's self where it lives" [B 54]). Only then is she enabled to escape solipsism and death through the emergent, coalescent poetic vision: "In a dark time, the eye begins to see."8 Imagery of the eye and seeing is, therefore, pervasive in Sexton's poetry. Blindness suggests death: it is a playful confrontation with the void ("eyes tight" shut in a childhood game [B 5]), or a desperate recognition of helplessness ("I come like the blind feeling for shelves" [LD 18]). This sense of extremity, of consciousness turned upon itself, adrift in Nothingness, is characteristic of existential anxiety: "They turned the light out / and the dark is moving in the corner" (B 8). In suicide, like schizophrenia, one "will enter death / like someone's lost optical lens" (LD 75); consciousness is divorced from being, the "eye" is estranged from the "I." But even at this radical moment of denial of life and vision ("my head in a death bowl / and my eyes shut up like clams" [F 36]) a vital counterforce is at work: "I have one glass eye. / My nerves push against its painted surface / but the other one / waiting for judgment / continues to see" (LD 22). Self-analysis is a re-education, a revision, a sharpening of one's latent vision ("eyes circling into my childhood, / eyes newly cut" [LD 7]). The process of freeing vision is regenerative: "I was the one / who opened the warm eyelid / like a surgeon" (LD 9). Not only is the self reborn, but others are "brought forth" also by means of this mystical caesarean section. For Sexton, poetic vision is true vision. Poetry liberates one from the "labyrinth" of inward existence, by soaring Icarus-like "into that hot eye," the sun, visionary source of life, seer and seen (A 8).

The only way to defeat death and abstraction, then, is through the liberation of vision, or true seeing. "Poetic creation," Carlyle observed, "What is this but *seeing* the thing sufficiently?" Poetry of this order reconnects the self with the roots of being. It "milks the unconscious," as Sexton explained to the *Paris Review* (p. 162), signifying a return to primal unity through the primordial model of wholeness and psychic comfort. A visionary poet like William Blake, Anne Sexton seeks to break through the "walls" of abstraction which enclose and pervert the creative life force, Eros, or the Blakean equivalent, Los. Mythology and ritual, which should ideally protect Eros, serving as a second womb for the emergent self, have now become repressive systems of moral, religious, and philosophical dogma. Therefore, instead of fulfilling the traditional role of witness and midwife of ritual rebirth, the modern seer must create new and viable myths of the self. The Confessional poetic is an attempt to extend the role of the visionary poet. By regarding the self as an archetype, the poet becomes a participant in, as well as herald of, rebirth. Sexton's early poetry creates a "mythology of the lost self";[9] her more recent volumes explore other archetypal realms of human experience: the myth of the body (*Love Poems*), the mythology of sexual maturation (*Transformations*), and the myth of the other (*The Book of Folly*). Her theme in these later books is not disunion but reunion, not loss but discovery.

In *Love Poems*, the Cartesian separation of mind and body is tentatively bridged by liberation of Eros, the uniting force of love. Sexton acknowledges the internal conflict between the death and love impulse, between Thanatos and Eros: "When I lie down to love, / old dwarf heart shakes her head" (A 10). "Old dwarf heart" signifies instinctual repression, the internalization of original sin and human mortality. Nevertheless, Sexton is affirmative in the midst of contradiction, advising acceptance of the self in all its multiplicity; she would assert with Blake, "Without Contraries is no progression. Attraction and Repulsion, Reason and Energy, Love and Hate, are necessary to Human existence." Countering "old dwarf heart," these love poems are a celebration of the body, so long disconnected and lifeless, like the synecdochic hand in the poem "The Touch." Through touch, connection with a lover, the hand is revitalized and the body is resurrected:

> Your hand found mine.
> Life rushed to my fingers like a blood clot.
> Oh, my carpenter,
> the fingers are rebuilt. . . .
>
> Nothing will stop it, for this is the kingdom
> and the kingdom come.

The lover is a "composer" (LP 3), a musician who performs his art upon the body, "the valley of my bones, / . . . / A xylophone maybe with skin / stretched over it awkwardly. / Only later did it become something real" (LP 4). Once awakened, the poet accepts her womanhood with ecstatic, Whitmanesque expansiveness:

> Sweet weight,
> in celebration of the woman I am
> and of the soul of the woman I am
> and of the central creature and its delight
> I sing for you. I dare to live [LP 12].

Through this joyful reintegration of the self, Sexton transcends the boundaries of time and space and individual separateness.

In love, wholeness has finally become realizable for Sexton. Yet she remains intensely aware of the difficulties inherent in sustaining love relationships. Many of the *Love Poems* are really "ironic love poems," as Robert Phillips claims, "speaking more of alienation than of conciliation."[10] Sexton emphasizes at times the predatory character of love affairs, each participant involved in a big game hunt for self-fulfillment; lovers "are a pair of scissors / who come together to cut," not complementary parts of John Donne's marriage compass (LP 57). But even if these poems present failures, they are consistently positive in their renunciation of destructive societal taboos. "The Ballad of the Lonely Masturbator," for example, breaks conventional silence upon a forbidden subject. But it is even more revolutionary in its assumption that sexual satisfaction can be achieved by a lone woman. Love affairs, as well as masturbation and its metaphorical equivalent, poetry writing, are all basically positive and creative experiences. These poems "come about," as Sexton explained, "as a result of new attitudes, an awareness of the possibly good as well as the possibly rotten. Inherent in the process is a rebirth of a sense of the self, each time stripping away a dead self."[11]

The cultural mechanism responsible for directing and easing the difficult rebirth into sexual selfhood is the rite of passage. In her book of adaptations of Grimm fairy tales, *Transformations,* Sexton makes explicit the mythology of maturation and satirically criticizes societal repressiveness. "Old dwarf heart" appears here in the guise of Rumpelstiltskin. In him Thanatos is victorious over Eros; he is the symbol of impotence, "a monster of despair. / . . . all decay" (T 17). The process of seduction is seen as an unnatural persecution and crucifixion of instinctual need by inhibitory institutions. In the Blakean tale "The Wonderful Musician," the symbols of sexuality are perversely transformed into mercantile and measuring systems. The female bird "lay as still / as a dollar bill" and the male "drowse-belly" snake "lay as still as a ruler." Not only is Eros murdered, but the wronged animals are prevented by legal restraint, in the person of the Woodcutter, from avenging themselves; revolution and rebirth are made impossible. Institutional repression exercised by the executioner, the Eichmann or repressive mother, is responsible for the degraded, balked state of our culture.

In Sexton's vision, neither the ending of the fairy tale nor the American Dream which the ending represents culminates in happiness. Rather, the maturation signalled in the completion of courtship—the institution of marriage—is really a deathly stasis:

> His tongue lay in her mouth
> as delicately as the white snake.
> They played house, little charmers,
> exceptionally well.
> So, of course,
> they were placed in a box
> and painted identically blue
> and thus passed their days
> living happily ever after—
> a kind of coffin,
> a kind of blue funk [T 14–15].

Marriage is an unconsummated image of consummation: when the man first ate the white snake he became magically attuned to nature and put into communication with universal truth ("he heard the animals / in all their voices speak"), but when he transfers this power to the woman, nothing happens, nothing at all.

Finally, Anne Sexton explodes the myth of the other-as-alien and successfully breaks free of the narrow prison of self-consciousness. Through the visionary medium of personae, the poet actually embodies another individual and in dramatic narrative re-enacts that person's life experience, which, though evocative of Sexton's own, remains unique. Similar to William Butler Yeats's use of mask, Sexton's assumption of personae is an expression of Eros, creative life that "is a re-birth as something not oneself, something which has no memory and is created in a moment and perpetually renewed."[12] This demonstration of poetic reincarnation in effect conquers human alienation and even death.

The protagonists of Sexton's dramatic poems fall into three categories: strangers whose suffering parallels the poet's (lonely women, soldiers facing death, mothers renouncing children); dead relatives, particularly a great-grandfather who symbolizes her New England Gothic origins and a great-aunt whose madness duplicates her own; and Jesus Christ, whom the poet is finally able to accept as a model. The most significant poems of the last-named kind are "The Jesus Papers" which appear in *The Book of Folly,* the title of which is adapted from Erasmus' *The Praise of Folly*. In his treatise, Erasmus called for the imitation of the life of Christ, a reunion of religion with the body, and the overthrow of institutional piety and dogma. In poems which celebrate the human experience of Christ, Sexton is able to balance her earlier despairing vision of the crucified Christ's grotesque suffering. She has learned to identify herself with Christ in his essential humanity. The Resurrection has finally become a realistic and viable concept for her, when seen through the visionary eye of poetry, that divine folly.

Beginning with the courage to seek the self's dark truth, however hidden away and horrible, Anne Sexton discovered a deep wellspring of poetic power. Her insight has made outsight possible; her poetry has become both an interior and exterior quest for meaning. Like a Phoenix, she rises out of the ashes of her own selves, in each successive book creating herself and her world anew. In this act of creative imagination—which ultimately aims to mend the "cracked mirror," to reunify the poet with her real inward and outward universes—Anne Sexton profoundly fulfills E. M. Forster's prescription for our modern Cartesian dilemma: "Only Connect."

AFTERWORD (1977)

When I heard of Anne Sexton's untimely death in fall of 1974, I felt a tinge of glad relief amid the sense of loss and sorrow. It seemed to me that in finally yielding to that necessity, Sexton had at least reached the end of her "hegira," her trip "undertaken as a means of escaping from an undesirable environment, or as a means of arriving at a highly desirable destination."[13] Sexton's *oeuvre* is her last will, her testament to the awful beauty of the world which offered her so much pain and joy.

In the three books published since my essay was originally written— *The Death Notebooks* (1974), *The Awful Rowing Toward God* (1975), and 45 *Mercy Street* (1976)—Anne Sexton continues her long and torturous journey from alienation to reconciliation. In the celebratory *Death Notebooks*, she rejoices in the possibility of rebirth through the power of art to transform "the abyss" into a "God Spot." The first posthumous volume, *The Awful Rowing Toward God,* shows even more clearly her deepening religious sensibility, her growing conviction of the interconnectedness and perhaps even the unity of imagination and God. Her voyage is, as it should be, both an inward journey and an arrival at a distant shore. Although she must exorcise the horror of herself by cutting out "the gnawing pestilential rat" within, Sexton will not deny the sanctity of her being. For this ugliness too is part of God's domain, and she knows that he is certain to "embrace it." In *45 Mercy Street*, edited with grace by her daughter Linda Gray Sexton, Anne Sexton embarks upon her final journey, a "hegira" simultaneously into past and future, seeking both self and communion with the other. Wanting desperately to "own the past," both to claim it and to confess it, Sexton imaginatively returns to the critical age ("twenty-eight, or is it forty-five?"), the time at which her poetic journey began. From this starting point, this reclaimed origin, she begins again for the last time the long journey home. In the volume's last poem, "The Consecrating Mother," she stands Whitman-like before the sea, committing herself to "its destiny":

> I am that clumsy human
> on the shore
> loving you, coming, coming,
> going. . . .

Notes

1. *Irrational Man* (Garden City, N. Y.: Doubleday Anchor, 1962), p. 31.

2. Quotations from Anne Sexton's poetry will be indicated parenthetically in the text by volume symbol and page reference. All volumes bear the same publisher imprint. *To Bedlam and Part Way Back* (Boston: Houghton Mifflin, 1960) (B); *All My Pretty Ones* (1962) (A); *Live or Die* (1966) (LD); *Love Poems* (1969) (LP); *Transformations* (1971) (T); *The Book of Folly* (1973) (F).

3. Barbara Kevles, "Anne Sexton: The Art of Poetry," *Paris Review*, 13 (August 1968), p. 160.

4. Barrett, pp. 225–26.

5. Charles F. Madden, ed., *Talking with Authors*, interview April 13, 1964 (Carbondale: Southern Illinois University Press, 1965), p. 161.

6. Quoted in A. Alvarez, *The Savage God* (New York: Bantam, 1972), p. 136.

7. *Suicide and the Soul* (New York: Harper-Colophon, 1964), Chapter 4.

8. Theodore Roethke, "In a Dark Time," *Collected Poems* (Garden City, N. Y.: Doubleday, 1966), p. 239.

9. Robert Phillips, *Confessional Poets* (Carbondale: Southern Illinois University Press, 1973), p. 8.

10. Phillips, p. 82.

11. *Paris Review* (note 3), p. 163.

12. Quoted in Richard Ellmann, *Yeats—The Man and the Masks* (New York: Dutton, 1948), p. 174.

13. *45 Mercy Street* (Boston: Houghton Mifflin, 1976), p. 1. The other two volumes discussed in this Afterword bear the same publisher imprint.

"What Are Patterns For?": Anger and Polarization in Women's Poetry [Excerpts]

Alicia S. Ostriker*

> The fire bites, the fire bites. Bites
> to the little death. Bites
>
> till she comes to nothing. Bites
> on her own sweet tongue. She goes on. Biting.
> Olga Broumas, "Circe," *Beginning With O*

For many readers, and for many writers, the overwhelming sensation to be gotten from contemporary women's poetry is the smell of camouflage burning, the crackle of anger, free at last, the whirl and rush of flamelike rage that has so often swept the soul, and as often been damped down, so that we never thought there could be words for it. A moment arrives when the volcano erupts, the simmering blood boils over, the fire breaks out. The imperative of this moment has become almost an axiom in feminist poetry and criticism. "It is always what is under pressure in us," remarks Adrienne Rich in an essay on Dickinson called "Vesuvius at Home," "especially under pressure of concealment—that explodes in poetry." "I still couldn't believe—I still can't—how angry I could become," writes Robin Morgan, describing "something like a five-thousand-year buried anger." "Strong women," writes Audre Lorde, "know the taste / of their own anger." Susan Griffin's "A Woman Defending Herself" chants a litany: "You are a woman who is angry. / You are a woman who is tired. / You are a woman clear in her rage. / And they are afraid of you."[1] The release of what we could call suppressed passion, were the passion not so thoroughly informed by astute analysis, becomes one of the most recognizable signs of the present movement in American women's poetry, a movement which begins in the early 1960s with volumes like Plath's *Ariel* and Rich's *Snapshots of a Daughter-in-Law*, and shows no indication of abating.[2]

The critic Jane Marcus, exploring the history of repression, disguise, and articulation of anger in women's writing, argues that "self-preservation is the source of anger and necessary for the artist." Marcus's conclusion expresses a common feminist faith: "When the fires of our rage have burnt out, think how clear the air will be for our daughters. They will write in joy and freedom only after we have written in anger."[3] But the story of female rage as a literary phenomenon is a more complex one than the expressive-purgative process implied by the quotes above. In the following essay I examine three extended poem sequences, written in the late 1960s and early 1970s, which suggest that anger is both necessary to the woman poet and inadequate as a solution to her predicament.

*Reprinted with permission from *Feminist Studies* 10, no. 3 (Fall 1984) and from Ostriker's *Stealing the Language* (Boston: Beacon Press, 1986), 126–27, 158–63.

Margaret Atwood's *Power Politics*, Diane Wakoski's *George Washington Poems*, and Anne Sexton's *The Jesus Papers* are major works, conceptually radical and formally experimental, each centering on the motif of female victimization within patriarchy. Depicting the patriarchal male as lover, hero, father, and God, the poems use a broad array of anger-generated devices to demystify, attack, and ridicule him, and the cultural script he embodies. In this script, male power, intrinsically violent, dominates the concentric worlds of personal life and society, supported by myths of superior male rationality and ultimately, male divinity. All three poets brilliantly employ gender-saturated metaphor, and all are profoundly subversive in their attack on our culture's systemic phallogocentricity, that potent combination of might and right ascribed to the deity and his Adamic sons. Yet, as I will try to show, far from offering literary catharsis or suggesting that dominance-submission structures can be dissolved by a purifying anger, the poems rather intensify our sense of a polarization in which the author is herself entrapped, and entraps her readers. Retaliatory strategies confirm rather than alter the unacceptable cruelty of the patterns by which we live: a reversed pattern remains a pattern. . . .

A further dimension appears, and the stakes are higher, when the antagonist is unveiled as that male who stands behind every lover, father and hero: God himself. Anne Sexton's *The Jesus Papers*, published in her 1972 collection *The Book of Folly*, is a mordantly comic dismantling of Christian myth from a female point of view, anticipating by several years the feminist critique of patriarchal religion triggered by Mary Daly's *Beyond God the Father*, and at the same time demonstrating the crucial distinction between critique and transformation.[4] The woman poet here can analytically penetrate, but cannot transcend—cannot imagine transcending—a patriarchal theology that swallows her alive. As in *Power Politics* and *The George Washington Poems*, an intellectually devastating subversion is equaled and canceled by an emotionally devastating submission.

The Jesus Papers begins with the most familiar and appealing image in Christian iconography, the Madonna and Child. "Jesus Suckles" places us within the consciousness of an infant who is at first engaged in a joyous and playful celebration of his connection with the mother whose "great white apples" make him "glad." This consciousness, exuberantly fertile in its metaphors, resembles Sexton's own in poems like "In Celebration of My Uterus," and for a similar reason. Sensuous bliss and abundance generate a blissfully abundant imagination:

> I'm a jelly-baby and you're my wife.
> You're a rock and I the fringy algae.
> You're a lily and I'm the bee that gets inside.
> I'm a kid in a rowboat and you're the sea,
> the salt, you're every fish of importance.

But the erotic extravaganza is followed by a correction:

> No. No.
> All lies.
> I am small
> and you hold me.
> You give me milk
> and we are the same
> and I am glad.

Then another correction, still briefer:

> No. No.
> All lies.
> I am a truck. I run everything.
> I own you.
>
> (Pp. 337–38)

"Jesus Suckles" recalls Sexton's earlier autobiographical poem "Those Times," where she recounts childhood humiliations inflicted by her mother and says she did not know "that my life, in the end, / Would run over my mother's like a truck." Unlike Sexton, however, "Jesus" is unapologetic. Thus we can see this infant as another variety of animus, a masculine self characterized by a guilt-free egoistic aggressiveness forbidden to the feminine Sexton, while at the same time he is precisely what Christian thought defines him as: a god who is also a boy child. To be a boy child, or to be a god, is to use the word "no." It is to deny, to divide. First metaphor, and then the blissful female connection that generates metaphor, must be sacrificed. To be a boy or a god means to seize power and possession, to reject nature, to embrace artifact, to transcend the erotic. Gospel accounts place this cruel moment—"Woman, what have I to do with thee"—in the god-man's adolescence. Sexton places it where psychoanalytic theory says it belongs, in infancy. "Jesus Suckles" records the differentiation of Jesus from Mary, and also from the poet. When attached to the female, his imagination lives; when detached, it dies. Jesus does not speak in the first person again until his crucifixion.

Succeeding poems illustrate the consequences of a dualism whereby God becomes superior to Nature, Logos to Eros, the reality principle to the pleasure principle, and boys to their mothers. Figures for Eros and Logos segregate themselves. The natural world remains voluptuous and orgiastic, a ripe melange of sex and food, where "Outdoors the kittens hung from their mother's tits / like sausages in a smokehouse," while Jesus stubbornly fasts and is celibate. "His sex," explains the narrator, "was sewn onto him like a medal" (p. 338). When asleep he still desires Mary, but using his penis as a chisel he carves a Pietà, and rehearses dying so that he can fuse with her at his death, when cross and woman are united "like a centerpiece."

Sexton's version of sexual sublimation—the subduing of libidinal energy and redirecting of it for socially valued ends—deviates from the gospel according to Freud. Her Jesus is motivated not by a forbidding father, but by an inner will to power which is incompatible with sensuous love. Because to repress love is to seek death, in Sexton's equation, sexual sublimation is the equivalent of the death wish, and results ironically in the most routine sort of domestic artifact, "a centerpiece," presumably on a wholesome bourgeois table. "Jesus Raises Up the Harlot," perhaps the most shocking poem in the sequence, gives us the gospel according to de Sade. In order to save the harlot from sin, the savior "lances" her breasts, "those two boils of whoredom," with his thumbs, until the milk runs out. Afterward, the poet's juxtaposition of biblical and contemporary diction is typical,

> The harlot followed Jesus around like a puppy
> for He had raised her up.
> Now she forsook her fornications
> and became His pet.
>
> (P. 340).

The relation of Son to Father is of junior to senior charlatan in "Jesus Cooks," where the miracle of the loaves and fishes involves opening "sardine cans on the sly." In "Jesus Dies," where Sexton again identifies with her protagonist, the poet's role as self-publicizing agonized performer comes into play. The crucifixion is presented as a sort of ultimate poetry reading, Jesus' first-person confession of his "sore need" for God is a half-infantile, half-competitive "man-to-man thing," and his attitude toward his audience is a mix of identification and contempt for its sensation seeking.[5]

Until this point, *The Jesus Papers* has been roughly if selectively chronological. Instead of a resurrection, however, the next poem returns to Mary at the moment of the Annunciation, where a reprise of sensuous imagery surrounding the Virgin is interrupted by a strange being who "lifts her chin firmly / and gazes at her with executioner's eyes." Consequently,

> Nine clocks spring open
> and smash themselves against the sun.
> The calendars of the world
> burn if you touch them.
> All this will be remembered.
> Now we will have a Christ.

Sexton's epilogue, "The Author of the Jesus Papers Speaks," confirms the defeat of a sensuous femaleness by manipulative masculine control. It is a brief dream poem beginning with a rich female drama between the poet and a cow-mother who gives blood instead of milk. God interrupts and asks for reassurance that people like Christmas, and the poet goes to the well and pulls up a baby. God then gives her a gingerbread lady to put in her oven, explaining:

> When the cow gives blood
> and the Christ is born
> we must all eat sacrifices.
> We must all eat beautiful women.

This conclusion reiterates the paternal demand for submission beneath the idiom of affection, and Sexton's psychological, theological, and rhetorical implications are all painful. Seemingly wishing for sympathy and communication, engaging in a gesture of apparent gift giving, God's "we must . . . we must" pretends to share with the poet a sense of fated necessity. But if "we" eat beautiful women, one of us thrives, one of us dies. To eat beautiful women is like the infant's suckling writ large and omnipotent, and the reader may wonder whether the notorious devouring mother is not a psychic screen for just such an unacceptable masculine wish, in the same way as we speculate that the concept of female penis envy was invented to screen male womb envy or breast envy.

Theologically, the substitution of a gingerbread lady for the eucharist reminds us that the central ritual of Christianity, and of the Passover feast from which it takes its symbolism, derives from earlier religions in which the object of worship was the fertile and nourishing mother. Far, however, from implying that we should return to goddess worship, the gingerbread offering means that we, and especially we women, must kill and suppress her anew. Rhetorically, God's authority extends to the language of the poem, as he successfully reduces a set of powerful female symbols to domesticity and powerlessness. What was a dream cow in the poet's frame becomes a cookie in his. The poet's tacit compliance with God's will is consistent with female passivity throughout *The Jesus Papers*. One's sense is that, although the poet has put up a brave analytical front, she is after all just another beautiful woman whom "we" can sacrifice, and who is all too ready to sacrifice herself. She has had many words, but God, who is Logos, has the last word.

What light do these three ambitious sequences cast on the theme of anger in women's poetry? Most obviously, of course, they represent anger as a psychic necessity, both emotionally and intellectually. To be conscious, as a woman, is to be conscious of hurt—and to demand reparation. If the best revenge is writing well, the demystifying power of these poems is primal triumph. Yet to represent these works as simply advocating a purifying female rage would be to misrepresent their view of gender antagonism, of the poet's role, and of the relation between poem and audience.

First, all three sequences present the war of the sexes as a power struggle insusceptible of resolution, into which participants of both sexes are inescapably locked. Gender polarity means hostility, and never more so than when it is disguised as love. This is the case whether we see the masculine figure in the poems as a genuine Other, a "real man," or as the poet's animus, her enemy within. It remains the case even when the roles of spirit and flesh, calculating mind and spontaneous feeling, authority and obedience, strength and weakness, reverse their usual gender attributions. When Atwood plays God, she remains as unable to rewrite a sadomasochistic script as when she plays victim. Wakoski's capacity for judgment and mockery does not reduce her hunger for love, nor does it cause the father-lover to satisfy her romantic longings. When Sexton dismantles the gentle Jesus of sentimental stereotype and reveals a sex-rejecting misogynist zealot, she increases rather than decreases our fear that there is no hiding place for women in religion.

Second, the authority of the poet in each of these sequences is employed as a weapon and is consequently self-defeating. The poet analyzes, categorizes, scrutinizes, superimposes female maps on male territory, and uses comedy and parody to reduce the foe to ridicule. As poet, she tries to win, rather than submit: a corrosive demystification is her mode of conquest. She becomes, in other words, precisely the phallic woman predicted by phallocentrism itself. What she does not do is synthesize opposites or imagine contexts larger than the ancient text of dualism. Like the smart fool in the tar baby story, the more she struggles against the rigid hierarchical scheme of patriarchy, the more she is trapped by it.

Third, these works are heavily surrealistic—absurd, bizarre, farcical, luridly nightmarish. In part they thereby demonstrate, and induce in the reader, an acute degree of psychic pain. The experience of reading *Power Politics*, *The George Washington Poems*, and *The Jesus Papers* is like walking barefoot on broken glass. But the surrealist mode subverts one's ability to accept suffering as ultimately necessary or ennobling. In contrast to tragic and lyric modes which persuade us that their visionary worlds are deeply true, and must be accepted, surrealism persuades us that its world is arbitrary and questionable. The confusion between "truth" and "lies" insisted on in each of these sequences reinforces this subversive effect, as do key formal devices designed to disorient the reader: absence of connectives, jumpcuts, shifting viewpoints; randomness of sequence and failure of closure in *Power Politics* and *The George Washington Poems;* progressive (but potholed) sequence followed by regression in *The Jesus Papers;* the collapse of past and present, the flaunted anachronisms. The polarized worlds these artists depict, and the polarized personalities they inhabit: are they not, finally, ridiculous?

If we compare these sequences with familiar masculine works exploring dissatisfaction and alienation in a modernist context, but without the seductive irrational sheen of surrealism—*Life Studies*, for example, or *The Dream Songs*—Robert Lowell and John Berryman appear relatively reconciled to their bruised destinies. No better can be had, they seem to imply. By contrast, the violence, the bitterness, the self-mockery, the sense of absurd entrapment, along with the smoldering nonresignation of Atwood, Wakoski, and Sexton, suggest that the desire encoded in women's anger poems is a desire to imagine precisely what cannot be imagined within the poems themselves. The stronger the poems, the more emphatically dualistic they are— and the more they convey to a reader that the pattern of dualism is intolerable.[6] When the tightly laced heroine in the formal garden of Amy Lowell's poem learns that her lover has died, significantly, "in a pattern called a war," she ends her poem with the exclamation "Christ! what are patterns for?" The poetry of women's anger in our time pursues that same question.

Notes

1. Adrienne Rich, "Vesuvius at Home: The Power of Emily Dickinson," in *On Lies, Secrets, and Silence: Selected Prose, 1966–1978* (New York: W. W. Norton & Co., 1979), 162; Robin Morgan, Introduction to *Sisterhood is Powerful: An Anthology of Writings from the Women's Liberation Movement* (New York: Vintage, 1970), xv; Audre Lorde, "Portrait," *The Black Unicorn* (New York: Norton, 1978), 51; Susan Griffin, "A Woman Defending Herself," *Like the Iris of an Eye* (New York: Harper & Row, 1978), 98.

2. An approximate point of departure for the women's movement in contemporary poetry is 1960. Among the breakthrough works appearing between 1959 and 1965 are Mona Van Duyn, *Valentines to the Wide World* (Boston: Houghton Mifflin, 1959), H. D., *Helen in Egypt* (New York: New Directions, 1961), Anne Sexton, *To Bedlam and Part Way Back* and *All My Pretty Ones* (Boston: Houghton Mifflin, 1960, 1962), Denise Levertov, *The Jacob's Ladder* and *O Taste and See* (New York: New Directions, 1961, 1964), Diane Wakoski, *Coins and Coffins* (Garden City, N.Y.: Doubleday, 1962), Adrienne Rich, *Snapshots of a Daughter-in-Law* (New York: W. W. Norton & Co., 1963), Carolyn Kizer, "Pro Femina," in *Knock upon Silence* (Garden City, N.Y.: Doubleday, 1963), Sylvia Plath, *Ariel* (New York: Harper & Row, 1965). The three works I discuss in this article are approximately contemporary with the slightly later development of the "second wave" of American feminism as a mass movement. The late 1960s saw the advent of women's consciousness-raising groups in which individuals—many of them already radicalized protestors against the Vietnam War, and / or refugees from the New Left— attempted to define the effects of male dominance in their private lives, and to connect personal with political oppression. In addition to Morgan's *Sisterhood is Powerful*, 1970 saw the publication of such volumes of radical feminist writing as Leslie Tanner, ed., *Voices from Women's Liberation* (New York: New American Library, Mentor Books), Shulamith Firestone, *The Dialectic of Sex: The Case for Feminist Revolution* (New York: Morrow), Vivian Gornick and Barbara K. Moran, eds., *Woman in Sexist Society: Studies in Power and Powerlessness* (New York: Basic Books), and Kate Millett, *Sexual Politics* (Garden City, N.Y.: Doubleday & Co.).

3. Jane Marcus, "Art and Anger," *Feminist Studies* 4 (February 1978): 69–98. This article concentrates on the feminist actress, novelist, and playwright Elizabeth Robins, and on Woolf's movement from *A Room of One's Own* to *Three Guineas*. Alex Zwerdling, in "Anger and Conciliation in Woolf's Feminism," *Representations* 3 (Summer 1983): 68–89, examines the conflict between overt expression and tactical repression of anger as a conscious one in Woolf, relating it historically to opposed ideas of strategy within the nineteenth- and early twentieth-century women's movements.

4. Anne Sexton's *The Jesus Papers* is included in its entirety in *Complete Poems* (Boston: Houghton Mifflin, 1981); page references (supplied in parentheses in the text) are to this edition. See also Mary Daly, *Beyond God the Father: Toward a Philosophy of Women's Liberation* (Boston: Beacon Press, 1973).

5. Sexton as a public performer is described in Maxine Kumin's introduction to the *Complete Poems*. That her audience was often composed of cultists "pruriently interested in her suicidal impulses, her psychotic breakdowns, her frequent hospitalizations" (xxxiv) both stimulated and aggrieved Sexton, as it does her "Jesus." See the autobiographical essay, "The Freak Show," *American Poetry Review* (1973): 38–40, describing Sexton's miseries as a performer.

6. For a discussion of poetic structures by women which attempts both to critique and to transform dualistic and polarized models of gender, see my article, "The Thieves of Language: Women Poets and Revisionist Mythmaking," *Signs* 8 (Fall 1982): 68–88. See especially 74–77, on images of the reunified female and the female as creatrix; and 78–88 on the revisionist myths in H.D.'s *Helen in Egypt*, Sexton's *Transformations*, and Susan Griffin's *Woman and Nature: The Roaring inside Her*, works which develop post-dualist models of female heterosexuality, asexuality, and lesbianism. For a theoretical elaboration of the antiauthoritarian, antihierarchical, depolarized "both / and vision . . . the end of the either-or, dichotomized universe"

which we can expect to characterize postmodern female writing, see Rachel DuPlessis et al., "For the Etruscans: Sexual Difference and Artistic Production—The Debate over a Female Aesthetic," in Hester Eisenstein and Alice Jardine, eds., *The Future of Difference* (Boston: G. K. Hall & Co., 1980).

Mysticism and Suicide: Anne Sexton's Last Poetry

William H. Shurr*

> Schweigen. Wer inniger schwieg rührt an die Wurzeln der Rede.
> —Rilke

> And Rilke, think of Rilke with his terrible pain.
> —Anne Sexton[1]

When Anne Sexton died in 1974, she had just produced what she intended to be her final book of poems, *The Awful Rowing toward God*.[2] Before that volume the direction of her work was unclear. There had been seven earlier books of poetry, beginning with the forceful and unsettling poems of *To Bedlam and Part Way Back* (1960). Her signature was the clear line of personal narrative; but it was frequently not clear whether the narratives were true biography or a kind of artistically manipulated pseudo-biography. She became famous, with the Pulitzer Prize in 1966, and the reader became familiar with such frequently anthologized poems as "Unknown Girl in the Maternity Ward," "The Truth the Dead Know," "The Farmer's Wife," and "The Abortion." We know her voice, but each poem seemed an unrelated victory. Her early classification among the "confessional poets" never seemed to confer the insights it had promised.[3] One fellow poet dismissed her work as garbage[4]; at the other pole, Sandra Gilbert canonized her divine madness in an essay entitled "Jubilate Anne."[5]

The reader's reward was finally *The Awful Rowing toward God*, the book of a mature poet whose dedication to art was single-minded and supreme, who could finally declare with utter simplicity "I am in love with words" (71). Sexton had prepared and intended *The Awful Rowing toward God* as a posthumous publication. A year before she died she told an interviewer that she had written the first drafts of these poems in two and a half weeks, that she would continue to polish them, but that she would allow publication only after her death.[6] Her published letters add the chilling information that she had then sent the manuscript to her publisher and was actually reading the galley proofs on the day she took her own life.

The volume gains authority as Anne Sexton's intended final work. The shape and direction of her poetic career finally becomes clear. Clear also is the grim fact that the suicide is a consciously intended part of the book. We

*Reprinted with permission from *Soundings: An Interdisciplinary Journal* 68 (Fall 1985): 335–56.

miss her meaning, the total program she provided for her reader to experience, without this stark fact.

As the "Rowing" of the title suggests, the image of the Sea pervades this
collection; and it soon becomes obvious that this metaphorical Sea is the
carrier for one of the most profound and pervasive ideas of western culture.

One of Sexton's earliest reviewers noticed the prominence of the Sea in
her work,[8] and when a later interviewer asked her about it she affirmed its
personal importance to her. She was a New Englander: the sea was in her
history and in her daily experience.[9] The imagery aligns her, also, with some
of the most prominent American writers. Emily Dickinson was another virtually land-locked lady in whose poetry the Sea is pervasive. The New England
tradition was remembered as having begun with a dangerous adventure
across the unknown ocean; the culture was supported throughout its history
by commerce on the sea. For Sexton personally, the sea was escape and
renewal, where the family had vacationed since her childhood. It is both a
danger and life-support system. In most of her poetry it is also the setting for
the journey of the soul. The phrase most often quoted by the reviewers from
her early books was the one she retrieved from Kafka and used as epigraph
for *All My Pretty Ones*: ". . . a book should serve as the axe for the frozen sea
within us."[10]

In her final volume this Sea becomes warm with swarming life. The two
poems which begin and end the collection, "Rowing" and "The Rowing
Endeth," set up a framework of sea-exploration, and there are overt references to the Sea in two-thirds of the poems. The Sea is quite literally the
fluid medium in which the mental life of this poetry takes place. The first
poem begins with the emergence of the Self from non-being; the child is
gradually able to do more human things but feels itself still "undersea all the
time." We are only seven pages into the collection when the perception
becomes clear that the Sea is the source of all life:

> From the sea came up a hand,
> ignorant as a penny,
> troubled with the salt of its mother,
> mute with the silence of the fishes,
> quick with the altars of the tides,
> and God reached out of His mouth
> and called it man.
> Up came the other hand
> and God called it woman.
> The hands applauded.
> And this was no sin.
> It was as it was meant to be. (7)

There is a calm rightness carrying this statement along, a sense of order,
and—new for Sexton—an untroubled account of the invention of sexuality.
The poem achieves dignity and authority by its imitation of Biblical diction.

But the Sea is not only origin; it is also metaphor for the continuing flow of life within the human being. Sexton, for example, perceives the pulse that beats in her arteries as "the sea that bangs in my throat" (10). The figure is extended a few pages later, where "the heart / . . . swallows the tides / and spits them out cleansed" (25). The Sea is simultaneously within and without. Even the ears are "conch shells," fashioned to bring in the sound of the Sea constantly to human consciousness. This seems to intimate that human beings live in a Sea of Life, but if one knows that the conch shell really amplifies the rush of the blood within the hearer, then this line also indicates that the Sea of Life is within.

There are negative elements in this massive symbolic Seaworld. On the margin between sea and land, between spirit and matter, are the crab who causes painful cancer (28), the sand flea who might enter the ear and cause madness in the brain (34–35), the turtle who furnishes an image of human sloth and insensitivity (36). There is also the land itself which supports human iniquity (44) and furnishes images for spiritual dryness and desolation (42, 44, 62). But in this world the margin between sea and land is also creative; it is the area where "the sea places its many fingers on the shore" and opposites can interact. The sea is necessary "mother," as the earth is necessary "father," and without interaction between the two there is no life (56).

Still another perception unfolds as Sexton explores her sea-subject: "Perhaps the earth is floating" on the Sea (28). The world of matter floats on the Sea of spirit and life; and so that Sea is never far off from any of us. Even the earth-bound can dig wells in the middle of the desert, and tap into that Sea, as the Sphinx advises the poet to do in another poem:

> I found the well [of God]
> . . . and there was water,
> and I drank,
> . . . Then the well spoke to me.
> It said: Abundance is scooped from abundance,
> Yet abundance remains. (64–65)

The appreciative reader has now arrived, at this point in the book, at the ancient literary perception of a metaphoric Sea that surrounds and animates all life with a creative vitality, the fluid medium in which things live and more and have their being, a creative "Abundance" prodigal of its forms. This is the same perception that is behind much literature that can be described as "Romantic," "Enthusiastic," or in any way "Mystical."

These figures and tropes carry us to one of Sexton's most moving poems, the only poem in the collection in which the obvious and awaited word "Logos" appears:

> When man
> enters woman,
> like the surf biting the shore,

again and again,
and the woman opens her mouth in pleasure
and her teeth gleam
like the alphabet,

Logos appears milking a star,
and the man
inside of woman
ties a knot
so that they will
never again be separate
and the woman
climbs into a flower
and swallows its stem
and Logos appears
and unleashes their rivers. (19)

Sexton recapitulates twenty-five centuries of western erotic mysticism here, where the imagery of the *Song of Solomon* merged early with the worship of the *Torah*, and then developed through the writings of St. John the Divine into the Logos Christology of the Greek Fathers, who were themselves influenced by Plato's lovely idea, in the *Timaeus*, of the world as divine creative Body. Divine creative energy, which unleashes itself in permanent joyous activity, has—according to the poem—its momentary analogue in human ecstasy: the human being can, at least briefly during intercourse, "reach through / the curtain of God" to participate by immediate contact in the creative flow of life.

Image carries idea. The most important function of the Sea images in *The Awful Rowing toward God* is to carry the items that produce this Logos mysticism as Sexton's final achievement, the final life-conferring idea her work came to embody.

One of the most important poems in this personal synthesis then becomes the strange one called "The Fish that Walked" (20–21). The title introduces the scenario: a fish enters the human element for a period, finds the place "awkward" and "without grace": "There is no rhythm / in this country of dirt" he says. But the experiment stimulates deep memories in the poet-observer, of her own vague pre-existence in the Sea, floating in "the salt of God's belly," with deep longings "for your country, fish." In view of the Logos poem which immediately precedes it, this poem is not so strange. With its allusions to grace and to the traditional symbol of fish as Christ, this is Anne Sexton's highly personal version of the Logos made flesh and dwelling among men. Sexton asserts that she herself has enjoyed the mystical experience of living in the flowing life of the Divine: the poem ends with the conversation between the lady-poet and the fish-Logos.

Sexton's Logos-intuition is itself creative, generating further imaginative work. More developments follow, and more connections are made. God is incomplete without a body, for example: according to a poem called "The Earth,"

> God owns heaven,
> but He craves the earth
> . . . but most of all He envies the bodies,
> He who has no body. (24)

And in a later poem in the collection, the Logos would like to be incarnated more than once:

> I have been born many times, a false Messiah,
> but let me be born again
> into something true. (61)

Such a world, in which the Logos is the Sea where the poet lives, is charged with Personality or Personhood. Near the end of the collection a poem begins

> I cannot walk an inch
> without trying to walk to God.
> I cannot move a finger
> without trying to touch God. (83)

The grounds here are those of mystics and theologians who have perceived the Logos as eternally existing, responsible for the creation of the physical world, and responsible also for preventing its lapse back into non-being.[11]

The image of the Sea, as it merges into the idea of the Logos, is thus the underlying metaphor that gives *The Awful Rowing toward God* its largest meaning and its undeniable power: the Sea-Logos gives life initially, sustains and supports it, and finally receives it back. The Sea-Logos is the personalized arena for the struggle of the human mind; it is as well the goal of the human mind and affections. And the poet's consciousness is at the center of this world. Her genius comes alive in this vital connection with its source. With this collection Anne Sexton's work creates a highly personal synthesis of the mystical potential in Western civilization.

It is startling to find such traditional piety in the sophisticated lady whose conversation was sprinkled with conventional obscenities, whose trademark was the ever-present pack of Salems. In the photographs that accompany her works she is immaculately groomed, expensively dressed, posing against a glassed-in sunporch amid wicker furniture and potted plants. If this is the setting of anguish, it seems mockingly ironic. On the evidence of the photographs one might almost accuse Anne Sexton of self-indulgence; we might almost agree with one of her early critics that she is "a poet without mystical inclinations."[12] But her voice is deeply formed from layers of authentic experience. Style in this last volume has grown lean and precise, the presentation of a personal idiom.

It is surprising also to find the lady so learned in the tradition. She despised her formal education: "I'm not an intellectual of any sort I know of. . . . I had never gone to college, I absolutely was a flunk-out in any schooling I had, I laughed my way through exams. . . . And until I started at twenty-seven, hadn't done much reading."[13] Her comments led one sympathetic friend to write (mistakenly, I think): "Nor was Sexton a particularly reflective or intellectual person. She came to poetry late, to learning even later, and though she worked hard to educate herself, she never acquired a vocabulary to discuss her ideas on a level of enduring interest or value."[14] But the reader emerges from *The Awful Rowing toward God* with the sense of having been put deeply in touch with the tradition of letters and religious sensibility; she embodies both the length and the richness of that tradition.

For example, the title, *The Awful Rowing toward God,* seems to arrest with its overtones from Emily Dickinson, some of whose love poems feature images of rowing to safe harbor.[15] And, indeed, one of the first impressions that the book makes is that it recapitulates the American experience in literature. The myth from Poe's *Eureka* is reflected in these lines: "I will take a crowbar / and pry out the broken / pieces of God in me" (3). She repeats Whitman in calling her poems "a song of myself" (4). The later voice of T. S. Eliot can surely be heard in these lines:

> Listen.
> We must all stop dying in the little ways,
> in the craters of hate,
> in the potholes of indifference—
> a murder in the temple.
> The place I live in
> is a kind of maze
> and I keep seeking
> the exit or the home.
> Yet if I could listen
> to the bulldog courage of those children
> and turn inward into the plague of my soul
> with more eyes than the stars
> I could melt the darkness. . . .(6)

There must be a nod to Thoreau's personified pond as she notices "the pond wearing its mustache of frost" (13). There is direct engagement with one of Emily Dickinson's poems when she says "Perhaps I am no one" (28). The American Indian legacy is briefly regarded as she imagines a reservation with "their plastic feathers, / the dead dream" (44) and tries herself to revitalize those Indian dreams of fire, vulture, coyote, and wren (66). The great American writers are also apparent in the sea imagery on almost every page of *The Awful Rowing toward God*. She extends as well an American writer's interest in evolution: the two themes emerge in one poem, where "the sea . . . is the kitchen of God" (46).

But she can be found even more intensely among the Modernist concerns of the century. She sounds like Yeats early in her collection: "[the children] are writing down their life / on a century fallen to ruin": (5). She has learned the modern temper from Kierkegaard and in one poem gives her own personal version of "The Sickness Unto Death" (40). She has learned from Beckett to construct scenarios of the Absurd with her own life as the text (38). She has learned the metaphysical seriousness of *The Seventh Seal* of Ingmar Bergman: the last poem of this collection imagines Sexton playing her royal flush against the lyrically wild cards of God (86). She has learned from Lowell, Berryman, and Snodgrass so to liberate her writing as to match the tones and concerns of modern inner speech. The language taboos are broken through: the banal reductions of ordinary speech are as telling, in context, as were the flights of fancy in former times. Formal structures of versification in her final work are valid only for the individual poem—each poem has its own form.

The Awful Rowing toward God embodies a stratum of even deeper and longer historical traditions. What will make the poetry of Anne Sexton permanently valid is her modernization of the perennial meditative wisdom of the West. C. S. Lewis said many years ago that "Humanity does not pass through phases as a train passes through stations: being alive, it has the privilege of ever moving yet never leaving anything behind."[16] Heaven and hell remain useful for the mind to locate itself, even for a population without the "faith" to regard them as actual places. Anne Sexton's last volume presents a very personalized compendium of the permanent wisdom of the West, of those questions that frame our enquiry, those values that are constantly meditated on in our solitude. She has written her own psalm sequences, her own proverbs of wisdom. She can look at traces of evil within and strike a playful explanation from the first text of Western Literature: "Not meaning to be [evil], you understand, / just something I ate" (49). The fabric is densely woven by a woman of "little education."

The Awful Rowing toward God describes not only perception of the Logos, but also the traditional journey of the ascetic soul towards encounter. A voice present from the earliest volumes reiterates the neurotic intensity of her perceptions, the hypersensitivity produced by inner disorder. But in this final book the voice that had earlier spoken her madness now seems cultivated for insight. The room where she writes has become sacred and magical: the electric wall sockets are perhaps "a cave of bees" (9), the phone takes root and flowers (9), "birds explode" outside the window (10); her typewriter is at the center, with forty-eight eyeballs that never shut (9); it holds carols for the dance of Joy, songs that come from God (80–81). This room of the writer becomes the geographical center of her poems, as her writing becomes the one passion that has mercilessly excluded all others—the lover who had been celebrated in *Love Poems*, the recently divorced husband, the growing daughters, the friends who have been alienated or abandoned, have all dropped beneath the mental horizon of this collection. Perhaps there is the ruthless egotism that Perry Miller believed he saw in Thoreau, the violent simplification to gain her writer's solitude. But perhaps it is the last instinct of the ascetic, ruthlessly to exclude everything from one's life that suggests this world, that does not furnish essential baggage for the next.

The journey within this room begins with savage emptying. Sexton imagines herself as the Witch, a figure from earlier poems now assumed as a personal identity. She goes to her window only to shout "Get out of my life" (11). She imagines herself as old and ridiculous to look at.

> I am shovelling the children out,
> scoop after scoop. . . .
> Maybe I am becoming a hermit,
> opening the door for only
> a few special animals. . . .
> Maybe I have plugged up my sockets
> to keep the gods in. . . .

But it is all required, she says in a magnificent phrase, for "climbing the primordial climb" (11–12).

In the earliest stages of the climb, the power of evil intrudes and impedes. She senses "the bomb of an alien God":

> The children are all crying in their pens. . . .
> They are old men who have seen too much,
> their mouths full of dirty clothes,
> the tongues poverty, tears like pus. (5)

She takes this evil upon herself and sings the lament of the ancient psalmist:

> God went out of me
> as if the sea had dried up like sandpaper,
> as if the sun had become a latrine.
> God went out of my fingers.
> They became stone.
> My body became a side of mutton
> and despair roamed the slaughterhouse. (40)

As a sufferer herself her compassion expands to all of humanity caught in the hell of a bad dream:

> They are mute.
> They do not cry help
> except inside
> where their hearts are covered with grubs. (42–43)

And insight arrives with compassion. She senses that her heart is dead, but only because she called it Evil (36–37). And further light appears when she sees that physical isolation is an aspect of human misery; in a poem called

"Locked Doors" she looks into the human hell: "The people inside have no water / and are never allowed to touch" (42). In the earliest poem in this collection she had already started this theme of isolation:

> Then there was life
> with its cruel houses
> and people who seldom touched—
> though touch is all. (1)

Three poems which appear near the center of the collection recapitulate aspects of the journey towards perception of the Logos. The most historically based poem of the collection is called "The Sickness unto Death," and it is a Kierkegaardian meditation on the human sense of loss and isolation, of estrangement from the Sea of Life. What is left is evil, excremental; it must be eaten slowly and bitterly. The poem stands as a pivot at the center of the book and it ends with a turn upwards, with a catharsis:

> tears washed me
> wave after cowardly wave. . . .
> and Jesus stood over me looking down
> and He laughed to find me gone,
> and put His mouth to mine
> and gave me His air. (41)

The next poem in this series follows a few pages later and continues this upward development. "The Wall" begins with the paradox that over the millions of years of evolution the only thing that has not changed in nature is the phenomenon of change; mutability is the only constant. It is a part of wisdom to participate consciously in this reality. At the end the poet's voice assumes great authority and formality. She is now the seer who has lived close enough to her experience to emerge with wisdom worth imparting:

> For all you who are going,
> and there are many who are climbing their pain,
> many who will be painted out with a black ink
> suddenly and before it is time,
> for these many I say,
> awkwardly, clumsily,
> take off your life like trousers,
> your shoes, your underwear,
> then take off your flesh,
> unpick the lock of your bones.
> In other words take off the wall
> that separates you from God. (47)

The road upwards, the journey of affirmation, contains moments of joy and vision. The grounding insight, which regulates the rest of the ascent, comes in a third poem called "Is It True?" the longest poem in the collection and also located near the book's center. It is a poem of occupations and blessings for ordinary things, which become transparent and holy. But in the midst of these the poet still senses herself "in this country of black mud" (51) and can see herself as animal, filled with excrement, living in a country which still prosecuted the Vietnam War. The poem begins with the natural instinct of the human to stop his work and look up at the sun occasionally; it ends with looking up to find Christ in the figure of the wounded seagull:

> For I look up,
> and in a blaze of butter is
> Christ,
> soiled with my sour tears,
> Christ,
> a lamb that has been slain,
> his guts drooping like a sea worm,
> but who lives on, lives on
> like the wings of an Atlantic seagull.
> Though he has stopped flying,
> the wings go on flapping
> despite it all,
> despite it all. (57)

The next poem records moments of pure ecstasy, where daily chores and ordinary occupations are permeated with the presence of the divine: "There is joy / in all" (58). She is transported by the impulse "to faint down by the kitchen table / in a prayer of rejoicing" (58). She expands in a poem called "The Big Heart" a few pages later, accepting a new repose at a higher level of reconciliation:

> And God is filling me,
> though there are times of doubt
> as hollow as the Grand Canyon,
> still God is filling me.
> He is giving me the thoughts of dogs,
> the spider in its intricate web,
> the sun
> in all its amazement,
> and the slain ram
> that is the glory,
> the mystery of great cost,
> and my heart,
> which is very big,
> I promise it is very large,
> a monster of sorts,
> takes it all in—
> and in comes the fury of love. (70)

This leads, in the poems that follow, to multiple reconciliations. Friends are gathered around her, valued for their "abundance" (69). Words sometimes fail the poet, but they are "miraculous" nevertheless,

> I am in love with words.
> They are the doves falling out of the ceiling.
> They are six holy oranges sitting in my lap.
> They are the trees, the legs of summer,
> and the sun, its passionate face. (71)

She becomes reconciled with the Mother who had been a harsh presence in earlier volumes; she relives life at the breast, life at the knee, and now feels the strength necessary to face what she calls "the big people's world" (73). The whole of the mystical tradition now becomes her personal domain, and she can speak of the Jesus of Christianity as "the Christ who walked for me" (76).

We must, then, come down to Anne Sexton as a *religious* poet; critics have found this aspect of her poetry more difficult than her shocking language or her revelation of family secrets. It is quite obvious in the later collections that she becomes progressively more interested in exploring aspects of the western religious tradition. Barbara Kevles was the interviewer who was able to probe most deeply into this aspect of Sexton's experience. In the *Paris Review* interview of 1971 her gently persistent questions led Sexton to reveal a great deal about her religious experiences. She protested initially that she was not "a lapsed Catholic" as some had conjectured; she was religious on her own Protestant terms. The most startling revelation of this interview was her experience with visions: "I have visions—sometimes ritualized visions—that come to me of God, or of Christ, or of the Saints, and I feel that I can touch them almost . . . that they are a part of me. . . . If you want to know the truth, the leaves talk to me every June. . . . I feel very much in touch with things after I've had a vision. It's somewhat like the beginning of writing a poem; the whole world is very sharp and well defined, and I'm intensely alive. . . ." One recalls the story that Hilda Doolittle told on herself—it was only after she mentioned to Sigmund Freud that she had religious visions that Freud felt she was sufficiently interesting, and sufficiently sick, for him to take her on as a patient. But in this interview Sexton was able to keep religion and mental illness separated at least to her own satisfaction: "When you're mad, [the visions are] silly and out of place, whereas if it's so-called mystical experience, you've put everything in its proper place." She protested that speaking of these things to the interviewer caused her some discomfort and she would prefer to move on to other subjects. But the line of questioning produced this final insight: "I think in time to come people will be more shocked by my mystical poetry than by my so-called confessional poetry."[17]

The mystical poetry has not been universally appreciated. For one hostile critic, the religious poems read like "verbal comicstrips . . . the pathetic figure of 'Mrs. Sexton' reminds one less of St. Theresa than of Charlie Brown."[18] Another critic, though, could recognize in her the "sacerdotal . . . a priestess celebrating mysteries," and could use such words as "hieratic . . . sibyl . . . vatic."[19]

It may be that Sexton herself was somewhat surprised or even embarrassed by this turn of her interests, this direction of her own growth. At least this seems a possible explanation for her decision to leave the poems for posthumous publication—though the careful reader can already discern seeds of this book, hints of this evolution, in her earlier collections.

We come then finally to deal with Saint Anne, who found the western tradition of spirituality anything but bankrupt. Towards the end of this collection we find that she has been reading the lives of the saints (79), and that she even has meditations on the three theological virtues of faith, hope, and charity. Faith is initially described as a great weight of information hung on a small wire. The small wire then becomes a thin vein with love pulsing back and forth through it, sustaining the believer with a higher life. The relation is life-giving and life-sustaining, as the twig feeds life to the grape, from another figure in the poem. The ending is dramatically modern, with one of Sexton's reductive banalizing similes: the pulsing vein of faith is man's contract with God, who "will enter your hands / as easily as ten cents used to / bring forth a Coke" (78). The poem is remarkable for its intelligence and its compactness, as well as for its historical sweep.

Two rowing poems bracket this collection and give its title. The two poems are the only ones to use the rowing metaphor. The first is a poem of beginnings: recollections of the crib, dolls, early schoolyears, the gradual recognition of inner pain and loneliness. Consciousness emerges from all of these experiences as if rising from under a sea, gradually discerning God as an island goal. The rower as in a dream fights absurd obstacles, but has the hope of possible calm and resolution at journey's end.

The last poem is full of joy. The rowing has ended, the struggle is over. The surprise in the poem is the game of poker which God requires of the newcomer. He deals her a royal flush, the complete family of cards. But he has tricked her—with a wild card he holds five aces. The game and the trickery serve to release the final tensions of the volume. Laughter spills out and the hoop of his laughter rolls into her mouth, joining God and the Rower in intimate union.

> Then I laugh, the fishy dock laughs,
> the sea laughs. The Island laughs.
> The Absurd laughs. (86)

The poem and the volume end with love for the wild card, the "Dearest dealer," the "eternal . . . and lucky love."

The Awful Rowing toward God seems a complex harmonium, a radical simplification achieved at great personal expense. Anaïs Nin once described her own work as a writer in the following way: "Why one writes is a question I can answer easily, having so often asked it of myself. I believe one writes because one has to create a world in which one can live. I could not live in any of the worlds offered to me—the world of my parents, the world of war, the world of politics. I had to create a world of my own, like a climate, a country, an atmosphere in which I could breathe, reign, and recreate myself when destroyed by living. That, I believe, is the reason for every work of art."[20]

The Awful Rowing toward God is a polished and completed "alternative world," inevitable like every great work of art. It is the personal embodiment of one of the oldest and most invigorating ideas in the Western tradition, the idea of the Logos. She does not die as does Henry James's character Dencombe, in *The Middle Years,* feeling that he had never completed the artistic work for which his whole life had been a preparation. But her achievement in this book of poems is penultimate; the final action, the suicide, remains to be pondered.

There is a body of scientific theory on the nature of suicide. One socio-psychological theorist begins with questions such as: "Why does man induce so fearful a thing as death when nothing so terrifying as death is imminent?"[21] His assumption is that death is always and in every case "fearful" and "terrifying." Sexton's final work is contrary evidence. "Exhilaration" would be a more appropriate word.

It may be that we are closer to the reality with A. Alvarez. In his extraordinary study of literature and suicide Alvarez writes that "each suicide is a closed world with its own irresistible logic."[22] Each suicide is special, wrapped in its own individual mystery. We must then build a theory for each case, and for a start we may cull a brief anthology of Sexton's comments on death, from her letters to friends:

> "Killing yourself is merely a way to avoid pain."
> "Suicide is the opposite of a poem."
> "Once I thought God didn't want me up there in the sky. Now I'm convinced he does."
> "In my opinion Hemingway did the right thing."
> "One writes to forestall being blotted out."
> "I'm so God damned sure I'm going to die soon."[23]

The list is chronological, and though the statements are in ragged prose, unsupported by the framework of a poem, they show progression, from a conventional and guilt-ridden attitude toward suicide to a more open understanding of it. Sexton's ideas on suicide obviously changed as she came closer to her own death.

Much of Sexton's artistic speculation on suicide she herself gathered in her third book of poems, *Live or Die* (1966), and a full account of the genesis of her thought would have to deal extensively with these explorations. A brief tour through that book produces several direct statements about "the almost unnameable lust" for self-destruction:

> But suicides have a special language.
> Like carpenters they want to know *which tools*.
> They never ask *why build*. (59)

Her voyage has already set in that direction. But so in a more general sense has everyone's:

> But surely you know that everyone has a death,
> his own death,
> waiting for him.
> So I will go now without old age or disease. . . .(77)

The last poem of *Live or Die* was actually called a "hokey" ending to the collection by an unsympathetic reader.[24] But it can be seen as strongly defining the collection. The decision not to take one's life is "a sort of human statement" (87), a celebration

> of the sun
> the dream, the excitable gift. (90)

It was about this time that Sexton recorded her psychiatrist's plea, "Don't kill yourself. Your poems might mean something to someone some day."[25] It was as if she sensed a mission still to be completed.

But what may be the most powerful poem in the 1966 volume comes in the center, "To Lose the Earth." The reader is arrested by the epigraph, from Thomas Wolfe:

> To lose the earth you know, for greater knowing;
> to lose the life you have, for greater life;
> to leave the friends you loved for greater loving;
> to find a land more kind than home, more large
> than earth. . . .(35)

The poem itself goes on to conduct the reader's entry into a work of art, and it is a remarkably moving experience. It is an entry into the world of timeless beauty which is elevating and utterly mind-altering. But introduced as it is by the quotation from Wolfe, the poem is ambivalent: it is, equally, the experience of death into which she conducts us. The poem is Sexton's "Ode on a Grecian Urn" and "Ode to a Nightingale" stated simultaneously: the lure of death merges with the idea of timeless beauty. It is escape of the Ego, with its Imagination, into the eternal stasis of beauty and truth. Joyce Carol Oates wrote, much more sympathetically, that "Sexton yearned for that larger experience, that rush of near divine certainty that the self *is* immortal."[26] Freud had already generalized on this phenomenon: "Our unconscious . . .

does not believe in its own death; it behaves as if it were immortal."[27] We need, then, a broader set of categories for suicide.

As a young man Ralph Waldo Emerson speculated quite generously on the variety of motivations leading to suicide, and provided this listing:

> It is wrong to say generally that the suicide is a hero or that he is a coward. . . . The merit of the action must obviously depend in all cases upon the particular condition of the individual. It may be in one the effect of despair, in one of madness, in one of fear, in one of magnanimity, in one of ardent curiosity to know the wonders of the other world.[28]

Emerson's last two categories, startling for a young clergyman, carry us farther towards meanings latent in *The Awful Rowing toward God*.

One accomplishment of the collection is an enormous expansion of awareness, of consciousness. As Sexton grows from inner disorder to inner harmony, from madness to poetry, the themes and images of the mystical tradition provide rungs for that "primordial climb." A vast inwardness develops: silence and introspection sculpt the inner world until it matches the larger lineaments of the common tradition of western mysticism. The journey is the dangerous work of solitude:

> One must listen hard to the animal within,
> one must walk like a sleepwalker
> on the edge of the roof,
> one must throw some part of her body
> into the devil's mouth. (44)

The flight from multiplicity, in the search for "the pure, the everlasting, the immortal and unchanging," which Plato described in *The Phaedo*, results in a sense of accomplishment, of self control and rest, of "being in communion with the unchanging."[29] Sexton comes to embody one form of the long tradition of liberal inquiry and inward search for concepts and values which, as Socrates observed, make human life worth living. There results a sense, as in Poe's *Eureka*, of the return from fragmentation to unity, to the primordial Paradise, the home of Life, Beauty, Intelligence. The preliminary report of this world can now be tendered by one "in love with words," but the reality itself is fully experienced only when one takes the final step into the Great Silence which climaxes Thoreau's journey in *A Week on the Concord and Merrimack Rivers*. To borrow a phrase from Rilke, Sexton "steps, festively clothed, out of the great darkness" of her solitude. She has achieved, in her climactic work, exactly what Emerson called "magnanimity."

It is not enough to say that literature is an imitation of life. It is rather an abstract of life and a forced patterning of life. Time, in art, is stopped, repeatable, arranged, enriched, reversible—as it is not in life. The events that befall a person in a drama or a narrative may be the experiences of a real person in real life. But there is an important difference. In real life the experience is part of a flow; significant experiences are merged with experiences of entirely different meaning or of no apparent meaning at all. The pattern of significance is clouded over by other events. Even the profoundest introspection may not uncover the exact beginning or the final end of the reverberations of an experience. In art, on the other hand, even the most abstract art, there is selectivity and conscious pattern. Art and the life-experience are rarely identical. There are cases where life becomes signifi-cant when it tries to imitate art, as closely as possible, as when one might try to live up to a code or an ideal.

Sexton became totally an artist, to the exclusion of any other role, an artist whose medium, in the final event, was her own life. The major actions of her final months seem deliberate attempts at *denouement:* the final book was shaped to its final order; the final task was to act the *finis.* How else guarantee the permanence of the accomplishment; how else act authentically on the present state of insight?

The most famous twentieth-century comment on suicide was Albert Camus's, in *The Myth of Sisyphus:* "There is only one philosophical problem which is truly serious; it is suicide. To judge whether life itself is or is not worth the trouble of being lived—that is the basic question of philosophy." It is generally assumed, in the context of Camus's thought, that suicide would be a negative judgement of the "worth" of life. In Sexton's case the contrary is true.

In Sexton's case, one can see suicide as grounded in "magnanimity," as the result of "ardent curiosity," the self-chosen final capstone to a structure of life and art now satisfactorily completed. Suicide becomes a version of Kierke-gaard's leap of faith, a step into what the imagination had seemed, by its harmonizings, to authenticate. Should there be no light beyond, at least the adventurer has left behind a vision of sublime light. Sexton's way is not everyone's, but it has its own rationale and, as artistic vision, its own extraor-dinary beauty.

Notes

1. Patricia Marx, "Interview with Anne Sexton," *Hudson Review*, 18 (Winter, 1965–66):562.

2. Anne Sexton, *The Awful Rowing toward God* (Boston: Houghton Mifflin Co., 1975). At the time of her death Sexton was working on still more poems, but she does not seem to have prized them as highly; they appear to be more of a miscellany. They were edited by her daughter, Linda Grey Sexton, and published as *45 Mercy Street* (Boston: Houghton Mifflin, 1976).

3. M.L. Rosenthal, who invented the phrase, says "The term 'confessional poetry' natu-rally came to mind when I reviewed Robert Lowell's *Life Studies* in 1959"; see *The New Poets: American and British Poetry since World War II* (New York: Oxford University Press, 1967) 25. Robert Phillips' book, *The Confessional Poets* (Carbondale: Southern Illinois University Press, 1973), places Anne Sexton as a member of this "school" and discusses the themes of her early poetry at some length. Sexton showed herself to be interested in the designation: in an inter-view with Patricia Berg in the *New York Times* for November 9, 1969, she said "About a year ago I decided I was about the only confessional poet around. Well . . . Allen Ginsberg too. He holds

back nothing and I hold back nothing." But such a statement puts the reader off balance for at least two reasons: Ginsberg has never been suggested as belonging to the "Confessional" school of poetry, nor has any one else ever thought to compare Ginsberg with Sexton.

4. James Dickey, in a review of Sexton's volume *All My Pretty Ones,* in the *New York Times* Book Review Section, April 28, 1963. Dickey reprinted the remarks, thus appearing to re-confirm them, in *Babel to Byzantium: Poets and Poetry* (New York: Grosset and Dunlap, 1971) 133–34. Other early reviewers also showed considerable animus in their initial responses to Sexton. Peggy Rizza, for example, felt Sexton to be "excessively personal," a devotee of "the feminine stereotype of Hysteria," "obsessive"; for Rizza, "we feel like voyeurs, as though we have read something we hadn't quite intended to read, something which is revealing or embarrassing but in no way instructive." See "Another Side of This Life: Women as Poets," in *American Poetry since 1960,* edited by Robert B. Shaw (Cheshire, England: Carcanet Press, 1973) 169–74, passim. Such snarling from reviewers is almost always a sign that something new and significant is happening in literature.

5. Sandra Gilbert, a review of *The Death Notebooks,* in *The Nation,* 219 (September 14, 1974): 214–16. Margaret Ferrari, though somewhat uneasy about the theological orthodoxy of the poems, also concentrated on Sexton's religious intensity throughout her poetic career. See "Anne Sexton: Between Death and God," in *America,* 131 (November 9, 1974): 281–84.

6. "From 1928 to Whenever: A Conversation with Anne Sexton," in *The American Poets in 1976,* by William Heyen (Indianapolis: Bobbs-Merrill, 1976) 316–17.

7. *Anne Sexton: A Self-Portrait in Letters,* ed. Linda Grey Sexton and Lois Ames (Boston: Houghton Mifflin, 1977) 423.

8. Melvin Maddocks, in a review of *To Bedlam and Part Way Back,* in the *Christian Science Monitor,* September 1, 1960, 1.

9. An interview with Anne Sexton, April 13, 1964, in *Talks with Authors,* ed. Charles F. Madden (Carbondale: Southern Illinois University Press, 1968) 178: "I . . . live right near the sea and love it. Your region becomes embedded in you."

10. Anne Sexton, *All My Pretty Ones* (Boston: Houghton Mifflin, 1962), vii.

11. A few samples from the tradition may suffice. Origin, in his commentary on Psalm 36, writes of the Logos "of whom all human kind and, maybe, the whole universe of creation, is the body." Maximus the Confessor, one of the major sources of western mysticism, wrote that "the mystery of the Incarnation of the Logos contains in itself the meaning of the whole of creation." An Easter sermon attributed to a disciple of St. Hippolytus, speaks of the cross of Jesus, after the Resurrection, as "strong bulwark of the universe, bond that holds all things together, foundation of the world we live upon, framework of the cosmos. . . . It maintains that which exists, preserves that which lives, animates that which feels, enlightens that which thinks." St. Gregory of Nyssa, in his first homily on the Resurrection, stated that the Logos "unites firmly and fits to himself the whole universe, bringing back into one single concord and one single harmony, through his own person, the different natures of the world." More expansively, St. Bonaventura wrote at the end of chapter five of his famous treatise, *The Mind's Road to God,*

> Because, then, Being is most pure and absolute, that which is Being simply is first and last and, therefore, the origin and the final cause of all. Because eternal and most present, therefore it encompasses and penetrates all duration, existing at once as their center and circumference. Because most simple and greatest, therefore it is entirely within and entirely without all things and, therefore, is an intelligible sphere whose center is everywhere and whose circumference nowhere. Because most actual and most immutable, then 'remaining stable it causes the universe to move,' as Boethius says. Because most perfect and immense, therefore within all, though not included in them; beyond all, but not excluded from them; above all, but not transported beyond them; below all, yet not cast down beneath them. Because most highly one and all-inclusive, therefore all in all, although all things are many and it is only one. And this is

so since through most simple unity, clearest truth, and most sincere goodness there is in it all power, all exemplary causality, and all communicability. And therefore from it and by it and in it are all things. And this is so since it is omnipotent, omniscient, and all-good. And to see this perfectly is to be blessed.

For the notion of the personification and divinization of the Torah, see for example the *Pirke Aboth* (3,23), "There was given to [Israel] a precious instrument [i.e., Torah] whereby the world was created." I do not wish to suggest, by any means, that Sexton knew all of these texts, but rather to assert that she did have a full intuitive grasp of the meaning of "Logos" in the mystical and theological tradition.

12. Ralph J. Mills, Jr., *Contemporary American Poetry* (New York: Random House, 1966) 232.

13. Heyen 315. On her lack of formal education see also Barbara Kevles's interview with Anne Sexton in *Writers at Work: The Paris Review Interviews,* ed. George Plimpton, fourth series (New York: Viking, 1976) 399–400; the interview was originally published in the *Paris Review,* 13 (Summer, 1971).

14. This remark was published in a review of *Anne Sexton: A Portrait in Letters,* and perhaps was intended to apply only to the diction of the letters and to the writer's recollection of conversations with Sexton. The topic of Sexton's lack of education also finds a place in the mystical tradition in which I have been placing her. Richard Rolle, for example, in the *Incendium Amoris* (Book 2, Chapter 3) says, "those taught by wisdom acquired, not inshed, and those swollen with folded arguments, will disdain him [the humble contemplative] saying, 'Where did he learn? Under what doctor did he sit?' For they do not admit that the lovers of eternity are taught by a doctor from within to speak more eloquently than they themselves, who have learned from men, and studied all the time for empty honors."

15. See for example #249 ("Wild Nights") and #368 ("How sick . . . to wait . . .") in *The Complete Poems of Emily Dickinson,* ed. Thomas H. Johnson (Boston: Little Brown and Co., 1960) 114 and 175.

16. C.S. Lewis, *The Allegory of Love: A Study in Medieval Tradition* (London: Oxford University Press, 1936) 1.

17. Interview with Barbara Kevles, in *Writers at Work,* 418–21.

18. Ben Howard, in a review of *The Book of Folly, The Death Notebooks,* and *The Awful Rowing Toward God,* in *Poetry,* 127 (February, 1976): 286–92.

19. Richard Howard, *Alone with America: Essays on the Art of Poetry in the United States Since 1950* (New York: Atheneum, 1969) 442, 450.

20. Anaïs Nin, *In Favor of the Sensitive Man and Other Essays* (New York: Harcourt, Brace, Jovanovich, 1976) 12.

21. Maurice L. Farber, *Theory of Suicide* (New York: Funk and Wagnalls, 1968) 3.

22. A. Alvarez, *The Savage God: A Study of Suicide* (New York: Random House, 1972) 120. Alvarez remarks, and I think his narrative poem proves it, that the suicide of Sylvia Plath "adds nothing at all to the poetry" (40); Sexton's case, I feel, is quite different.

23. *Anne Sexton: A Portrait in Letters* 209, 246, 257, 282, 326, 336.

24. Rizza, 175.

25. Interview with Barbara Kevles, in *Writers at Work* 400.

26. Joyce Carol Oates, a review of *The Awful Rowing Toward God,* in the *New York Times* Book Review Section, March 23, 1975, 3–4.

27. Quoted in A. Alvarez, *The Savage God* 210.

28. Ralph Waldo Emerson, *Journals and Miscellaneous Notebooks,* ed. William H. Gilman, *et al.* (Cambridge: The Belknap Press of Harvard University Press, 1960) II, 257 (1824).

29. The Jowett Translation, #79c.

Anne Sexton's Suicide Poems   Diana Hume George*

> Anne, I don't want to live. . . . Now listen, life is lovely, but *I Can't Live It*. I can't even explain. I know how silly it sounds . . . but if you knew how it *Felt*. To be alive, yes, alive, but not be able to live it. Ay that's the rub. I am like a stone that lives . . . locked outside of all that's real. . . . Anne, do you know of such things, can you hear???? I wish, or think I wish, that *I* were dying of something for then I could be brave, but to be not dying, and yet . . . and yet to [be] behind a wall, watching everyone fit in where I can't, to talk behind a gray foggy wall, to live but to not reach or to reach wrong . . . to do it all wrong . . . believe me, (can you?) . . . what's wrong. I want to belong. I'm like a jew who ends up in the wrong country. I'm not a part. I'm not a member. I'm frozen.
>
> —Anne Sexton, from a letter to Anne Clark, October 13, 1964

"THE VIOLENT AGAINST THEMSELVES:"
CONTEMPORARY ATTITUDES TOWARD SUICIDE

> To start with what is most important: we have no conception of the inner torture which precedes suicide.
> —Boris Pasternak

Dante places the "Violent against Themselves" in Circle Seven of *The Inferno,* where their souls are encased in thorny trees and the Harpies feed upon their leaves, opening wounds from which come "words and blood together." Only as long as the blood flows may the souls speak, so that this tortuous feeding gives them "pain and pain's outlet simultaneously." Because they have thrown away their bodies—"betrayed the body," as Anne Sexton writes in "Wanting to Die"—they will not be permitted to regain them even at Judgment:

> Like the rest, we shall go for our husks on Judgment Day,
> but not that we may wear them, for it is not just
> that a man be given what he throws away.
>
> Here shall we drag them and in this mournful glade
> our bodies will dangle to the end of time,
> each on the thorns of its tormented shade.[1]

Even though Dante himself cannot speak upon hearing the fate of his suicides—"such compassion chokes my heart"—there is no room in his theology for extenuating circumstances, wrinkles in the DNA, chemical imbalances, the overthrow of justice by love. Is there such room in our "theology," our eccentric amalgam of psychology, social science, humanism, codes of

*Reprinted with permission from *Journal of Popular Culture* 18 (Fall 1984): 17–31.

ethics? I sometimes think that there is not. For what other deaths do we reserve such a pietistic, bastard mixture of pity, contempt, disapproval, fear?

In a culture that dedicates itself aggressively, even if not successfully, to the sanctity of life, we do not like to deal with the fact that some people want to die. Despite all the alterations that the last decade may have brought about in humane attitudes toward suicide, a hard-jawed resistance persists toward accepting the wish to die, an unwillingness to permit that wish to anyone. Such resistance and unwillingness may be born of tenderly humanistic impulses; even so, those impulses undergo a mean transformation when they are codified in culture. The euthanasia and living will movements may have altered American attitudes toward the desire to die under some circumstances; but those circumstances—the only ones which sufficiently compel social, moral and sometimes legal compassion—are always extreme and always physical. That is, arguments for changing attitudes toward the voluntary ending of one's life are still restricted to cases involving terminal physical disease and / or unendurable physical agony. For all the theoretical efforts to establish the legitimacy of mental agony comparable to physical agony—efforts, in other words, to banish simplistic mind / body dichotomies that are nearly definitive of Western culture—fear and disapproval of the desire to end emotional pain by means of suicide still seem utterly undisturbed. Perhaps this is as it should be, in many respects. Any culture which begins tampering with boundaries between life and death must proceed cautiously. But even if such conservatism is well advised, one may regret the cruelly anti-humanistic face often worn by the human need to protect its own.

Antipathy toward suicide is not as deep as it once was, but most people still think of suicide as ethically and morally reprehensible—even sinful, although many of us are not comfortable with the word. Perhaps we no longer bury suicides separately, or hang their already dead bodies, or say that they are going to hell; at least those of us who consider ourselves enlightened do not say such things. But our compassion and sympathy are inflected with reprobation at the very least, and with repulsion in many instances, especially when the suicide occurs for other than "legitimate" reasons. The collective societal definition of legitimacy for suicide is fuzzy at best, but we can identify its components more clearly, though indirectly and partially, through attitudes toward euthanasia.

In the past several decades, euthanasia societies have formed in many European countries as well as in America. Britain's controversial Voluntary Euthanasia Society (formerly EXIT) lists 26 such societies worldwide, including chapters in India, Japan, South Africa, and Zimbabwe. Most are located in western Europe. Given the size of our country and its population, America has surprisingly few: Hemlock in California, and Concern for Dying and the Society for the Right to Die in New York. There's something to be learned from the rhetoric of euthanasia advocates, who are very aware that their cause is sensitive and controversial. Both the British VES and the American group Hemlock publish Guides to Self Deliverance, and from them one can measure how conservative are the aims even of these most radical organizations.

VES's Guide to Self Deliverance, the first of its kind, is under constant attack. VES Newsletters in 1982 and 1983 carried continuing coverage of the society's struggle to keep their Guide in print. As recently as 1983, Britain's Attorney General was still seeking to have the high court of Britain declare the booklet illegal on the ground that it violates a law that forbids assisting would-be suicides. (Suicide itself is no longer a crime in Britain or in America; assisting suicide is.) Although VES has now won its case, the organization expects to encounter further difficulties.

The limitations on VES's purposes and intentions are very clear in the Introduction to the Guide, which is available to members of the organization over 25:

> The main objectives of the Society are to secure the enactment of the 1969 Voluntary Euthanasia Bill by Parliament. This would authorize doctors to give patients euthanasia when they wish it, provided:
>
> (A) the patient has signed an appropriate declaration at least 30 days previously;
>
> (B) two doctors, one of consultant status, have certified in writing that the patient is suffering from an incurable condition likely to cause her or him severe distress or render her or him incapable of rational existence.[2]

The lines of demarcation are clear. Euthanasia for terminally ill patients only, and only for terminal *physical* illness. The legally necessary limitations on assisted suicide inherent in the current definition of euthanasia extend as well to VES's advice on who should and should not make private use of their Guide to Self Deliverance—which, by its nature, implies but does not require the assistance of a second party.

> The advice that follows is intended for self-deliverance, and if it comes into the hands of people who are merely unhappy, we hope they will heed the Society's motto: "Live well, Die well." People should die happy; and we hope that people whose troubles are emotional and temporary, rather than physical and incurable, will look for reasons to live rather than ways to die.[3]

Note the equation of emotional and temporary, and of physical and incurable. I do not disagree with VES's caution, by any means; nor do I wish to imply that its writer is unaware that emotional disease can be excruciating, even "incurable." But the rhetoric of VES is permeated with just such assumptions. The repeated formula, in VES's newsletters and other publications, is that only in cases of incurable physical conditions are people "justified" in the desire to die.

Hemlock's listing of "General Principles" emphasizes the same approach. The first two are of particular interest:

> 1. *Hemlock* will seek to provide a climate of public opinion which is tolerant of the right of people who are terminally ill to end their own lives in a planned manner.

2. *Hemlock* does not encourage suicide for any primary emotional, traumatic, or financial reasons in the absence of terminal illness. It approves the work of those involved in suicide prevention.[4]

Among Hemlock's listed "objectives" is "clarifying existing laws on suicide and assisted suicide," but it's clear that they do not mean suicide outside of the euthanasia context, as euthanasia has come to be defined. In fact, it is of course in the interests of all such societies to declare themselves against suicide for "primary emotional" reasons. Much of the rhetoric of both VES and Hemlock repeats that people should be able to get out of life when and how they want to; one could at first mistake their motives, and it is exactly such a mistake that these organizations must prevent in the public mind. If public resistance, even governmental resistance, to euthanasia is so strong, such societies must utterly divorce themselves from concern for and understanding of any suicide *not* undertaken in the presence of physical suffering.

Mary Stott, Vice President of VES, presented a talk at the 1981 VES general meeting which began: "I believe as profoundly in the right to death as I believe in the right to life." Perhaps Mrs. Stott privately holds that conviction for all people, including those who want to die because they have been emotionally miserable for most of their lives; if so, she cannot afford to have us think so. The rest of her talk simply presupposes terminal illness or intolerable physical pain. She asks: "Why should we persist in this extraordinary idea that it is better in all circumstances to be alive than dead?"[5] Stott is referring exclusively to circumstances arising from terminal illness or intolerable physical pain. But the question strikes me as a legitimate one for other reasons. In the case of people whose emotional or mental illness has remained intractable to medication and to human love for years, even decades, for whom the mental agony of staying alive is indeed intolerable and unendurable, for whom the best that can be said of their mental state is that their dis-ease with life is subject to occasional remission, even of considerable duration—why do we so automatically assume that they should endure, stick it out, to the bitter and "natural" end?

The question is only partly ingenuous. Certainly we all know the answers, or some of them. Our bias in favor of life is to some extent self-explanatory, and needs no justification. This places the burden of justification on the potential suicide, who, according to Allen Alvarez, may always have felt he or she was born to die as soon as possible. And when the living of life is itself a nearly unendurable burden, this extra burden, of disapproval or uncomprehending sympathy, of the need to explain and justify to people who cannot understand why one would not want to live, who assume that "it is better in all circumstances to be alive than dead," who assume this so utterly that even their deepest sympathy is threaded with repulsion and disapproval, this extra burden, I think, must be heavy beyond endurance. If even the death-radicals among us, those courageous individuals responsible for the formation of euthanasia societies, must show such insensitivity for strategic or other reasons to the legitimacy of motivation and cause for suicide due to emotional agony or depression, then the potential suicide must feel intolerably alone.

The *60 Minutes* segment on euthanasia aired for the third time in July of 1983 begins, "Rational suicide. It sounds like a contradiction in terms." The segment goes on to present both sides of the euthanasia debate, never mentioning the assumption that underlies the rhetoric of that opening statement. From the assumption that we all share in this society—that any suicide is by definition irrational—the program moves toward sympathetic examination of this one form of suicide, self-deliverance for the terminally ill. The implication that *only* such a suicide could qualify as "rational" is so deeply shared that we do not think to question it. How lonely the potential suicides who watched that program must have felt, knowing that even suicide for the terminally ill faced with constant physical pain is so sensitive an issue, knowing that their own plight would receive even less genuine understanding from a public biased fiercely in favor of life under all circumstances and at all costs. Such a person will find counseling to prevent him or her from committing the final act—and that is just as it should be. But if decades of treatment or medication do not alleviate the suffering sufficiently, it is probably not possible for the potential suicide to end his or her life without a tremendous burden of guilt.

Contrary to our shared assumption that suicide is never rational unless it takes place in the presence of racking physical pain or terminal physical illness, Alvarez in *The Savage God* presents what is still the clearest recent explanation in prose of the suicidal stance toward life. Speaking of the majority of suicides, he says:

> For them, the act is neither rash nor operatic nor, in any obvious way, unbalanced. Instead it is, insidiously, a vocation. Once inside the closed world, there seems never to have been a time when one was not suicidal. Just as a writer feels himself never to have been anything except a writer, even if he can remember with embarrassment his first doggerel, even if he has spent years, like Conrad, disguised as a sea dog, so the suicide feels he has always been preparing in secret for this last act.[6]

To such a one, whose "memory is stored with long black afternoons of childhood, with taste of pleasures that gave no pleasure, with sour losses and failures, all repeated endlessly like a scratched phonograph record,"[7] admonitions to live courageously for an indefinite period of time must seem absurd. Most terminally ill people, in the restricted sense in which we have come to use the term, have at least the comfort of an end in sight, which they wish legitimately to hasten. The suicide Alvarez describes, and which he considers to represent most achieved and potential suicides, has no such comfort if he or she is in decent bodily condition—using "bodily" in the further and similarly restricted way we do. Few people would consider saying to the lucid person afflicted with terminal throat and jaw cancer, "Well, at least you have your mental health. Be thankful for that." But we say the reverse equivalent to the seriously and chronically depressed person whose condition may be just as beyond her control, and just as "terminal."

"WANTING TO DIE"

In the interim between Anne Sexton's first suicide attempt and her final and successful one, an interval of some seventeen years, she wrote at least twenty poems primarily dedicated to explaining what it feels like to want, or need, to die. These poems translate into understandable idiom the language, so foreign to most people, of the suicide. As poems, I find them various in their degree of successful achievement. I find them similarly various—and more than incidentally, identically various—in their degree of success in being persuasive, in rendering understandable the suicidal impulse. By "identically various," I mean that those poems which are what I'd call excellent poetically are also those which are polemically persuasive—if this can be called a polemic, and I think it can. The least successful, ironically, is the one she wrote for "Sylvia's Death" in her third collection, *Live or Die*. Reading this poem, and this one only, I feel I am overhearing a pathetic competition between suicides, one accomplished and one potential, full of petty jealousy and envy masquerading as eulogy. (It is the masquerade I find unsuccessful, even offensive, not the open admission of envy that Sylvia got "that ride home with *our* boy" before Sexton did.) But in the same collection is her finest single poem on the subject, "Wanting to Die" which I want to explicate with the attention to detail I think it, and the issue, deserve.[8]

> Since you ask, most days I cannot remember.
> I walk in my clothing, unmarked by that voyage.
> Then the almost unnameable lust returns.

The speaker answers a question asked outside the poem's frame. It's not possible to know exactly what that question was, but a reasonable inference is that the questioner has inquired about her feelings toward life. She has been asked, in other words, to explain herself. The reader should not lose sight of the implicit audience whose question is the occasion of the poem; that outsider *is* the reader, who comes to such a poem with predictable assumptions and resistances. The first two lines are distant, detached, calm, as well as open and frank. The speaker is answering the question as directly as she can. But the lines are end-stopped, clipped, flat, almost tired. Each day is a trip, a voyage, but one the speaker moves through rather than participates in. The third line shifts abruptly from the weary business of life to the desire for death. The diction suggests intense, passionate, almost sexual involvement, but even this line is still explanatory in tone. The speaker explains the sequence of emotional events:

> Even then I have nothing against life.
> I know well the grass blades you mention,
> the furniture you have placed under the sun.

This could be an institutional lawn where the speaker might be talking to her doctor. But the questioner could as well be any person who cares about the speaker: a husband, a friend, a lover. In any case, an attitude has been conveyed from outside the frame of reference in the poem, and that attitude says, "see how good life is." The simple diction points to the forces of fertility and evokes the comfort of manmade things as well. The furniture under the sun recalls warmth, human company, even perhaps domesticity, things that ordinarily make life worthwhile. Again, the tone of her response is detached and assessive:

> But suicides have a special language.
> Like carpenters, they want to know *which tools*.
> They never ask *why build*.

The speaker has shifted here from acknowledging the argument for life, to asserting the desire for death. To effect this, she is forced to use a metaphorical language, an analogy with something ordinary that the hearer will understand. Now the speaker must begin the arduous task of translating from a foreign language. This job becomes the central work of the poem, the subtle and controlling metaphor on which the poem stands—or falls. The effectiveness and precision of the translation, the communication of nuance and idiom into the words the hearer will understand through his or her own language, are measures of the poem's success. The "language" of the suicide, to make the matter conceptually and practically tougher, is essentially non-verbal, and has to do with act rather than word. The speaker is trapped doubly: not only must she translate into words the hearer can understand; she must deal with the problem that the only words at her disposal are in a language whose structure emphatically asserts life. The connotations of the words she must press to her service are all loaded against her: life is good, death is bad. The moral imperatives of this language censure her position from the outset, for its values are as foreign to her as are the values of her speechless language to the hearer. She will be forced literally to overturn the structure of the hearer's language.

The speaker begins with an elementary analogy, a concrete simile easy enough to understand. In order to explain this "lust" of hers to someone who does not feel it, she chooses a dry, uncharged, explicit image to convey a state of mind whose essence is passionate. The carpenter comparison implies an unmentioned third element, the architect or planner who *does* ask "why build," as contrasted with the carpenter whose job it is to arrive at the site and begin to work. Suicides are like this, says the speaker. There is no word for them that translates into "why;" there is only "how," because it is definitive of a carpenter that he find the way to build, and just as definitive of the suicide that she find a way to die. The irony is effective, and underscores the reversal of connotative value that the poem has begun: carpenters are creators and builders. Suicides, as normal perception sees them, are destroyed. The hearer, if he is to enter into the linguistic universe of the suicide, must begin to see that for the suicide, killing oneself is a kind of building, a kind of creating. A final advantage of the simile is that its detached, apparently logical construction will mark the suicidal speaker as reasonable, capable of explaining irrationality in a rational, credible manner.

> Twice I have so simply declared myself,
> have possessed the enemy, eaten the enemy,
> have taken on his craft, his magic.

The speaker characterizes her two previous suicide attempts as totally integrated declarations of self. But who is the "enemy?" Is it death, or the means to death, perhaps some kind of drug? If she is using language in an ordinary sense, the enemy is obviously death. But consider the speaker's linguistic dilemma; in the special language of the suicide, everything has duplicitous and paradoxical meaning. The enemy may, then, be life itself. When she takes the drug she mentions later, she finally possesses life completely, eats it up, burns it out, ends it. The ambiguity of the grammatical and thematic referent is a problem only if the reader demands that the language of the poem be irreducible. That ambiguity represents the central problem of the poem, the attempt to balance between two paradoxical versions of linguistic and intellectual reality.

From this point on, the "double language" of the poem becomes increasingly important; words and images are always both double and connotatively contradictory. With this stanza, Sexton introduces another mediator between the two languages. Ritual and magic are invoked, just at the moment when the reader is asked to make the leap that abandons logic. The suicide has already made that leap. The poem has gently led to this, carefully remaining within the realm of the rational until now; it is time to listen to the suicide talking as much in her own terms as in the listener's. We have been well prepared by the poem for this reversal of values.

> In this way, heavy and thoughtful,
> warmer than oil or water,
> I have rested, drooling at the mouthhole.

The tone here is subtly but decidedly positive. The speaker might be talking about taking a good nap. But "warm" and "thoughtful" are yoked to other words not easily understood in a positive way. She is "heavy," and she "drools," not from the mouth, but from "the mouthhole." That phrase manages to objectify the self and the body, making both a vacancy, an absence, a hole. On my first reading of this poem, I reacted negatively to this stanza. If the speaker was trying to convince me that dying isn't so bad, "drooling at the mouthhole" was hardly the way to win my approval, or even my understanding. But after a close and careful reading during which I was persuaded to enter the linguistic world of the poem, my reaction was different. I understand now how such a repellant image could be appealing *for the suicide*. Even if the suicide's language is never to be my own, I have come to understand that uneasy, careful translation of images.

> I did not think of my body at needlepoint.
> Even the cornea and the leftover urine was gone.
> Suicides have already betrayed the body.

The speaker grows bolder and less apologetic, more trusting of the hearer's understanding. She remains direct and unwavering in the presentation of details, but now they are unmitigated by helpful analogy. Instead, the speaker shifts to a cryptic explanatory line with the statement that suicides have always already betrayed the body, even, by implication, before they try to leave it. This kind of assertion is considerably distant from the language and the tone of the first stanzas of the poem, a long way from the sun and grass and lawn furniture and reasonable explanations.

> Still-born, they don't always die,
> but dazzled, they can't forget a drug so sweet
> that even children would look on and smile.

The image of a child in happy contemplation of the sweetness of death is difficult to stomach; somehow, it is especially objectionable to think of children half in love with easeful death. Why does this poem insist on the complicity of children? Why would the poet risk arousing our passionate defense of innocence? According to the speaker, her particular kind of suicide is figuratively still-born, always close to that thin line between life and death first differentiated in the womb. The implication is that such people should have been born dead, and since they were not, they naturally spend their lives trying to return to the security of the womb, nexus of the boundary between life and death. The use of "children" attempts to communicate the purity and innocence of that feeling, from the suicide's perspective.

As the speaker moves further into the experience and language of the suicide, she maintains minimal but vital contact with the listener:

> To thrust all that life under your tongue!—
> that, all by itself, becomes a passion.

"Life" is perhaps the drug, the agent of death; this stanza presents the same kind of ambiguity as in stanza four. The issue of control versus loss of it is the paradox: the speaker does the "thrusting" in an act of will. To gain control over life and death becomes a passion. But that passion is also the desire utterly to lose control.

> Death's a sad bone; bruised, you'd say,
> and yet she waits for me, year after year,

> to so delicately undo an old wound,
> to empty my breath from its bad prison.

Death is a sad bone and it is, by implication, in her bones—bones can signify both the skeletal outside and the very core or essence. "You'd say" that death is a sad bone, "bruised" in the sense that the desire for it results from a wound that can be healed. "You" refers directly back to the listener. For the last several stanzas, the poem has involved itself so totally in rendering the suicidal experience that the reader, if the poem has achieved the proper effect, is taken far away from the sun, the lawn chair, and the sympathetic questioner of the first stanza, even if the reader began by identifying with that questioner. "You'd" say—you, who do not want to admit that death waits from the beginning, that a person can be born sad. If the "old wound" is life, death undoes that by emptying the breath from her body and releasing her. But the poem has taught its readers to expect ambiguity; the old wound may be the unsuccessful suicide attempts the speaker mentioned earlier. In that case, death is still there, waiting to open the wound again, break open the scars, pull out the stitches, and let her die.

> Balanced there, suicides sometimes meet,
> raging at the fruit, a pumped-up moon,
> leaving the bread they mistook for a kiss

This use of language is bewildering no matter what you do with it. The poem has now progressed almost entirely into that "special language," and it is here that it will leave behind any reader who has not listened closely to the suicidal idiom. This stanza speaks of the suicide's nearly complete isolation from the comforting world of human touch, the total breakdown of predictable relationship between the human and the natural, the alienation from all people and objects, with the exception of the accidental "meeting" that can occur between one suicide and another. All the moorings of ordinary life are gone when the suicides are "balanced there," in a limbo of distortion and hallucination, on the boundary between life and death. To reflect this state of spirit, the poet "balances" the poem "there," on the boundary between intelligibility and incoherence. It's exactly at this point that "reading" the poem in the formal sense stops working; the process of translation fails. This is purely the suicide's language. The speaker has turned inward to other suicides, and away from her listener,

> leaving the page of the book carelessly open,
> something unsaid, the phone off the hook,
> and the love, whatever it was, an infection.

The speaker has become part of the recollected experience, and it is now through her disappearance from the world of the listener that the poem persuades. True to its subject, the poem has become a kind of suicide attempt.

In my experience, college students are rigorously normal in their response to suicide. In a discussion before we looked at this poem, the class in which I first taught it asserted positively that wanting to die because you are suffering physically is understandable; wanting to die without what they called "a real reason," by which they meant a physical one attached to disease, is sad. Not merely sad, but bad, reprehensible, morally irresponsible, ethically debased. Depression, unlike cancer, said my students, must be reasoned with and always cured. One may never simply give over the struggle. My students also uniformly denied the legitimacy—even the credibility—of an attitude that says from the beginning, "I would rather not live." (I think of Bartleby, who would always prefer not to, and who, by god, does not.)

I did not discuss these issues with my students as they relate to Anne Sexton's personal agony. Whether or not Sexton's own desire to die could be traced to situational factors or to chemical imbalances in the DNA is irrelevant to the assumptions and commitments of this poem. We concentrated on the poem as poem, and in the world created by this poem, it's useless to say that the speaker "shouldn't" feel like dying. My class, full of good students who were also good people, wanted to engage in humane and helpful and therapeutic argument with the absent speaker.

But through an explication of the kind I have reconstructed here, my students came to an uneasy, genuine understanding of the suicide's "special language." When we reached the final two stanzas, and came up against the limitations of explication, I still felt obliged to "finish the poem" by examining the remaining imagery and anatomizing the language. That had proved, after all, to be the right way into the poem, a poem that concerns itself with translation of language. To end here would be, I thought, to "leave the page of the book carelessly open, something unsaid." I was met with blank faces, but not the kind a teacher meets with when students are uninterested, bored, or even confused. This was the silence of compassionate insight. Finally, one student said, "It's idiomatic." Another said, "It doesn't translate." A third said, "There's nothing left to say." Class simply ended with a fourth comment: "The phone is off the hook." "Wanting to Die" ends in the silence of suicide because, for me and for the students to whom I taught it, the poem is a successful attempt. As one of my students said, "The poem self-destructs."

Perhaps successful suicide attempts, figurative or otherwise, are strange things to celebrate. I do not mean to suggest that there were any converts to suicide in my class. That was not the intention of the poem, and it certainly wasn't the purpose of my class discussion. The speaker of this poem asks only to be understood, to explain herself; she does not recruit company for her agony. Clearly, I did and do find something here to celebrate. "Wanting to Die" taught my students more about poetic process than any other single poem. It is one thing to learn that language is a powerful tool. It is another but related thing to know that language can be a mediator of this kind, that it can work either to alienate people or to bring them together in an understanding of their disparate and painfully separated selves.

"SUICIDE NOTE"

"Suicide Note" is the only death poem Anne Sexton cast in this form, and the decision creates formal peculiarities of expectation and response. In many respects it is like the other suicide poems, all of which are written from slightly differing perspectives, all of which tell this suicide's story from a new narrative angle, all of which provide new images for understanding this state of mind. But the carefully constructed multistanza "note" is alone among the poems in that it purports to be a communication left to a "dear friend" prior to the speaker's suicide.

Situated as it is in *Live or Die*, a collection shaped by the decision implied in the title, "Suicide Note" is part of the group of "Die" poems that includes "Wanting to Die," "Sylvia's Death," and "The Addict," among others. These poems anatomize the desire to die, the ways of doing it slowly, the post-attempt explanations, but no other poem is situated in time *before* a planned attempt, whether that attempt is fictive, or really about to take place, or real but remembered.

It is an odd experience to read an artfully constructed, cool, restrained note to one the speaker assumes will have survived her, one who will want to know why. It would feel peculiar even if the poet were not now dead. But the actual ironies are denser than that: this is a 1965 poem, published in a collection which concludes with the decision to "Live," the title of its final poem. Anne Sexton, the poet and *perhaps* the speaker—I insist on the separation at this moment for specific reasons—killed herself nearly ten years after this poem was written. Reading it nearly ten years after her death and almost twenty after its composition, I find it difficult to refrain from experiencing it as what it purports to be and yet is not: a suicide note.

Having been content to collapse speaker and poet in many other poems, I am wary of the ease with which I might do so in this case. Aside from the fact that to equate speaker and poet in a poem with this title is to invite scorn, I find this among her most aloof and "literary" productions, entirely different in tenor from, say, "Sylvia's Death," in which Anne Sexton the potential suicide nearly overwhelms Anne Sexton the poet and crafts-person. To call this speaker "Anne Sexton" is to risk minimizing the impact of poetic technique and tight control. For this poem which presents itself as "note" before killing oneslf is actually a highly formalized poetic epistle, written to a constructed self as much as to another addressee.

> Better,
> despite the worms talking to
> the mare's hoof in the field;

> better,
> despite the season of young girls
> dropping their blood,
> better somehow
> to drop myself quickly
> into an old room.

The beginning is presented as a conclusion reached after consideration. It is "despite" the worms and the young girls' blood that the speaker finds it "better" to die. The worms and the girls' blood are both ambiguous in their emotional content and their relation to life and death: while one seems primarily death-directed and the other life-directed, both are at the intersection of fertility and decay. The worms "talking to the mare's hoof" are the rich yeast of the soil on which the horse walks and from which it gains sustenance; yet the worms will ultimately speak not only of nurture but of decay. The season of menarche is the season of greatest potential for life, but blood-letting is also symbolic of destruction. "Despite" the mares and the girls, whose being at this time of year (it is June) affirm life as well as death, the speaker wants to escape into the "old room" of her death. For she has decided that it is better "not to be born" at all; and far better not to be "born twice," as women are (See, "String Bean," *Live or Die*).

Now, having already presented her conclusion, the speaker introduces the "dear friend" to whom she speaks, telling him or her that "I will enter death / like someone's lost optical lens." In contrast to her own sense of smallness—"I will be a light thing"—she says that "life is half enlarged." Describing her own distorted vision, she speaks of life tilting "backward and forward." Close to the natural world of mares and blood, she feels the fierceness of fish and owls on this portentous day. Having made her decision to die, she observes these portents unaffected: "Even the wasps cannot find my eyes." Nothing can sting her now, for she is immune, and her sight has turned to vision by means of distortion and reduction. Once those eyes were "immediate," and "truly awake"; now they have been "pierced."

Recalling her old "hunger" for Jesus, whom she has loved as suffering man more than as God, she thinks of him as a fellow suicide, who "rode calmly into Jerusalem / in search of death" *before* he grew old. She has tried this herself before, but failed. This time, she does not ask for understanding,

> and yet I hope everyone else
> will turn their heads when an unrehearsed fish jumps
> on the surface of Echo Lake;
> when moonlight,
> its bass note turned up loud,
> hurts some building in Boston,
> when the truly beautiful lie together.

These rich lines begin with a disclaimer that the ensuing lines seem to renege on: "I do not ask for understanding, and yet . . ." what is it that she "hopes?" That everyone will be sorry she has died? That the natural and man-made world—fish, moon, buildings, people—will take note of the moment of her death? Perhaps. But the lines are larger than that; they may mean almost the opposite; that everyone who has not "dropped quickly into an old room" because of the inability to stand the pain and beauty of life, will respond to that beauty and pain. This is the "understanding" she solicits: that she cannot deal with an "unrehearsed" fish breaking the surface of still water in a surge of lifeforce; that she cannot bear the "bass note" of moonlight bursting on walls; that she is unable to be, or to see, the "truly beautiful" who lie together. Like the images with which the poem begins, these are tonally poised, tilting "backward and forward" as life does for the speaker, refusing a readerly desire for definitive emotional form and statement. (Were her eyes "pierced" so that she could see "the whole story?" Or does that piercing render them unable to see at all?) Ambiguous as this series of images is, the weight of the lines that follow presses toward the more generous appraisal of motives and meaning:

> I think of this, surely,
> and would think of it far longer
> if I were not . . . if I were not
> at that old fire.

She has reminded herself of the painful beauty of life, and the memory might make her hesitate, if she were not "at that old fire," needing death. She knows, she says, that she is "only a coward," but she feels compelled to this death as moths are forced to "suck on the electric bulb." (See interviews and letters, on Sexton and Plath at Boston workshops). She offers what defense she can. Now that defense takes a form similar to "The Death Baby," a poem Sexton was to write years after "Suicide Note:"

> But surely you know that everyone has a death,
> his own death,
> waiting for him.
> So I will go now
> without old age or disease,
> wildly but accurately,
> knowing my best route,
> carried by that toy donkey I rode all these years,
> never asking, "Where are we going?"
> We were riding (if I'd only known)
> to this.

If everyone has his own death waiting anyway, if we are all only riding "to this," the speaker will choose her own moment, without the infirmities of old age or disease, just as she earlier suggests Christ did when he rode into Jerusalem "in search of death." And like Christ, she will ride on a donkey. Three years before the composition of "Suicide Note," Sexton had ridden her donkey out of madness and out of "this sad hotel," the mental hospital, in "Flee on Your Donkey," the third poem in *Live or Die*.

> Anne, Anne,
> flee on your donkey
> flee this sad hotel,
> ride out on some hairy beast,
> gallop backward pressing
> your buttocks to his withers. . . .

Now she rides the same beast out of life, into a madness that has much method: "wildly but accurately / knowing my best route. . . ." That she has never asked "where are we going" has the same content as never asking "Why build?" in "Wanting to Die."

The final stanza is an attempt to assure the addressee that the speaker has no illusions about the effect of her death on either the world she leaves behind or the one she goes to. No guitars playing, no kiss from her mother's mouth, no major disturbance in the natural world ("The snakes will certainly not notice") or in the man-made world ("New York City will not mind"). She will die in June, "so concrete with its green breasts and bellies;" the "note" ends where it began, with the abundance of life that the speaker cannot endure. Only the bats will take notice, beating on the trees, "knowing it all, / seeing what they sensed all day."

In "Suicide Note," we are given the formal framework that is all artifice, the pretense of suicide note which is *not* suicide note, but rather a deliberate re-creation of a state of mind that the speaker could hardly be in at the moment of composition, else she could not compose. The very form is artful ruse, the kind of lie we may need to hold in check such intensely emotional content.

Worksheets of "Suicide Note" published in *NYQ* give us a clearer than usual indication of the composition process, and address the very problem at issue here.[9] Sexton took the poem through at least five drafts before the final one, in late May and June of 1965. The revision, expansion and cuts are extensive—the first draft is a mere twenty lines, written in crayon. Says Sexton: "I never heard of anyone committing suicide with a crayon in their hand, but then I wasn't committing suicide, was I, I was only writing about it." Whatever ironies she may have intended with this comment—perhaps she means us to realize that the poem grew out of a real attempt, and perhaps she means to say that it didn't—she speaks wryly here of the misconceptions that can arise in a gullible or, one must conclude from critical comments about Sexton's poetry, even a sophisticated poetic audience. In three drafts, the poem ends with, "I am only Anne, / coward, Anne," or variations on that. I consider it important that these lines appear nowhere in the finished draft. In several Sexton poems, "Anne" remains, but here she is deleted. The effect is not so much a de-personalized excision of self, but the creation of a larger space for us to envision the speaker, who *might* be Anne, and might also be someone else, not only this woman, but any suicide with fantasies of identification with Christ, a catalogue of justifications, a need to be understood.

As I prepare this article for press, Marsha Norman's *'night, Mother* is playing to full houses on Broadway. Norman's two-character play about a young woman named Jessie Cates, who kills herself at the end of the play, may well be changing the attitudes of large numbers of people toward suicide committed in the absence of terminal illness. Jessie doesn't want to live anymore, and she spends the final evening of her life trying to explain to her mother why she wants to "get off the bus." Jessie's need to be understood is not nearly as strong as her mother's need to understand. Jessie tries to make her point of view accessible to Thelma in images of simplicity and poignance.

> . . . It's somebody I lost, all right, it's my own self. Who I never was. Or who I tried to be and never got there. Somebody I waited for who never came. And never will. So, see, it doesn't matter what else happens in the world or in this house, even. I'm what was worth waiting for and I didn't make it. Me . . . who might have made a difference to me . . . I'm not going to show up, so there's no reason to stay . . .[10]

Perhaps the reception of American audiences to *'night, Mother* indicates a newly awakened willingness to extend our sympathies toward this alien state of mind and heart.

A friend whose daughter recently killed herself writes to me: "I don't know that you can understand this, but I feel more love for her than ever, and beyond that a tremendous respect for what I would almost call the silent heroism and sacred mystery of the dark glory of her dreadful end." I don't know if I can fully understand that. I can try.

Notes

1. Dante, *The Inferno*, Canto XIII, 11.103–108, (New American Library, 1954), p. 122.

2. *EXIT: A Guide to Self Deliverance* (London: Executive Committee of Exit, 1981), p. 4. EXIT, now the Voluntary Euthanasia Society, makes the *Guide* available only to members of the society over twenty-five who have belonged to the society for over three months. The address of VES is: 13 Prince of Wales Terrace, Kensington, London W8 5 PG.

3. *EXIT: Guide*, p. 64.

4. Derek Humphrey, *Let Me Die Before I Wake* (Los Angeles: Hemlock, 1982), forematter.

5. Mary Stott, "The Right to Die," Voluntary Euthanasia Society *Newsletter*, No. 14, January 1982, pp. 6–7.

6. A. Alvarez, *The Savage God: A Study of Suicide* (New York: Bantam Books, 1973), p. 119.

7. Alvarez, *The Savage God*, p. 119.

8. Kim Carpenter discussed "Wanting to Die" from a similar standpoint in "Four Positions on Suicide," *The Journal of Popular Culture* XIV:4, Spring 1981, pp. 732–739. The "Indepth

Section" of *JPC* XIV:4 on "American Attitudes Toward Death" was co-edited by me and by Malcolm Nelson; Ms. Carpenter's reading of "Wanting to Die" was the result of extended conversations among the three of us, and in that respect, the current reading is an extension of Carpenter's work with us.

9. "Worksheets: Anne Sexton's 'Suicide Note,' " *New York Quarterly*, No. 4, Fall 1970, pp. 81–94.

10. Marsha Norman, *'night, Mother* (New York: Hill and Wang, 1983), p. 76. *'night, Mother* stars Kathy Bates and Anne Pitoniak, is directed by Tom Moore, and is currently (Spring 1984) playing at the John Golden Theater in Manhattan.

What Is Confessional Poetry?
[Excerpts]
Laurence Lerner*

[Lerner's essay asks the important and leading questions: How does confessional poetry differ from confession, and how does it differ from other poetry? Through historical survey, Lerner concludes that "confessional poetry," as illustrated through the writing of Anne Sexton and John Berryman, is distinctive and essential. These sections show his use of Sexton's work to illustrate his thesis.]

Confessional poetry being a practice, not just the subject of individual poems, we ought to turn now to a body of work, and the choice of poet almost makes itself. No poet was more consistently and uniformly confessional than Anne Sexton, and her name has almost become identified with the genre.

Take, for instance, "The double image." This poem in seven parts is addressed to her daughter Joyce, who was taken from her and brought up by her mother-in-law, because of her mental illness and her inability to look after the child herself. The title refers to the portrait of Anne which was painted "instead" and the portrait of her mother, angry and unforgiving. ("On the first of September she looked at me / and said I gave her cancer"), which hung opposite each other at the top of the stairs ("She eyes me from that face, / that stony head of death"). The poem is filled with facts about the poet's life and mental history: her age and her daughter's, specific locations ("I came to my mother's house in Gloucester, Massachusetts"), specific incidents ("once I mailed you a picture of a rabbit / and a post card of Motif number one, / as if it were normal / to be a mother and be gone"), facts about her illness, often tersely stated (I . . . tried a second suicide" . . . "I checked out for the last time / on the first of May"); it is also filled with images of her mental distress:

*Reprinted with permission from *Critical Quarterly* 29 (Summer 1987), and from Lerner's *The Frontiers of Literature* (New York: Basil Blackwell, 1988).

> —Ugly angels spoke to me. The blame
> I heard them say, was mine. They tattled
> Like green witches in my head, letting doom
> leak like a broken faucet—

and with images for her love for her daughter and the joy of reunion; and along with that, analyses of her own motives in wanting the child back:

> I, who was never quite sure
> about being a girl, needed another
> life, another image to remind me.
> And this was my worst guilt; you could not cure
> nor soothe it. I made you to find me.

The poem was modelled on W. D. Snodgrass's *Heart's Needle*, about his separation from his daughter because of divorce, which Anne Sexton was deeply influenced by, and which, she claimed, made her write this poem about her own similar experience, and even led her to demand her daughter back (so poetry does influence life, after all! But perhaps only the life of poets). "The double image" is certainly representative of her first three volumes, which contain her best and her most clearly confessional work. The world which these volumes establish is easily described; it is a world of mental illness, with details of admission into hospital, suicide attempts, medical treatment, and also images for the terrifying experiences themselves:

> This August I began to dream of drowning. The dying went on and on in water as white and clear as the gin I drank each day at half-past five. Going down for the last time, the last breath lying. I grapple with eels like ropes—it's ether, it's queer and then, at last, it's done. Now the scavengers arrive the hard crawlers who come to clean up the ocean floor. And death, that old butcher, will bother me no more.
>
> ("Imitations of drowning")

It is a world of family love and conflict, describing her childhood, her often hostile feelings toward her mother (and her insistence on her mother's hostility to her), and her love for her own daughters, her re-enactment of their pain. When her trip to Europe is described, her crossing of the Atlantic reminds her of her mother's similar voyage, her time in Paris reminds her of "Nana" (a beloved great-aunt):

> I read your Paris letters of 1890.
> Each night I take them to my thin bed
> and learn them as an actress learns her lines.

Also prominent in this world is an intermittent religious concern, which leads her to compare herself with Jesus Christ (this became much more prominent in her later work), not as a way of finding redemption and consolation, but as a way of suggesting that Jesus too was crazy and suffered ("I sat in a tunnel when I was five . . . Maybe Jesus knew my tunnel / and I crawled right through to the river / so he could wash all the blood off"), even of seeing herself as exceptional ("I'm no more a woman / than Christ was a man"). And, finally, there is a concern (also intermittent, also intense) with the physiology of being a woman: she writes about sex, menstruation, childbirth with total openness.

It is not difficult to see why this material is called "confessional," but when we try to say why we can notice that there are two, possibly three, reasons not necessarily connected with each other. First, there is the factual element: she provides plenty of biographical detail, identifies the members of her family, states the time and place of many of the episodes, not attempting to disguise the fact that all these things happened to the poet-outside-the-poems. That is one meaning of "confessional." Second, there is the sordid, often degrading nature of the experiences: she confesses to pain as well as joy and (more difficult) to experiences that deprive her of dignity in her suffering—precisely what one is normally most ashamed to own up to. That is another meaning of "confessional." And then there is a peculiar and disturbing intensity in the language, an attempt to render raw and disturbing experience through ugly and disturbing images that do not always seem to be under control ("grapple with eels like ropes"); and along with this, a deliberate jokiness, a shrugging off of her own suffering as something melodramatic:

> Sleepmonger,
> deathmonger,
> with capsules in my palm each night,
> eight at a time from sweet pharmaceutical bottles
> I make arrangements for a pint-sized journey.

This is the quality that makes Sexton most like Plath, and it too could be called confessional (or even, because of the self-dramatising, "confessional").

Anne Sexton's poetry aroused intense responses. Reviewers disliked the thrusting upon them of such intimate details: "These are not poems at all," writes Charles Gullans, "and I feel that I have, without right or desire, been made a third party to her conversations with her psychiatrist. It is painful, embarrassing and irritating." "Art requires more than emotional indulgence," writes Patricia Meyer Spacks. At the same time audiences (supported by some enthusiastic reviewers) gave her standing ovations at readings, judges showered literary prizes on her and psychiatrists (though some might hold that this confirms Spacks's point) used her poems as therapeutic material with their own patients. Clearly all this brouhaha was set off by the confessional element.

But on the other hand, Sexton herself sometimes insisted that confession is not art, and that a poem needs to depart from factual truth and raw emotion. "I'll often confess to things that never happened," she writes, and she did on occasion alter the facts when writing. Thus "The double image" makes no mention of her elder daughter "because the dramatic point was I had one child and was writing to her," and also takes liberties with the facts of how often she went into hospital. More striking is the fact that there are a few fictitious poems in the volumes that do not sound very different from the confessions. "Two sons," for instance, is a bitter resentful poem spoken by a woman to the two sons who have married without telling her beforehand, sending home "silly postcards" to announce the fact,

> one of them written in grease
> as you undid her dress
> in Mexico, the other airmailed to Boston from Rome.

Almost every reader of Anne Sexton knows that she had daughters not sons, but if we can postulate a reader who was ignorant of the biography, he would not, surely, perceive this poem as any different from the others.

Fiction is only the most obvious, and not necessarily the most complete, way of detaching oneself from one's own experience. Anne Sexton's ambivalence on the need for such detachment is clear. On the one hand, she claims "if you could just document the imagination, experiences, everything, even some wit, whatever, of one life, one life, however long it may last, it might be of some value," and says of her work "It was not a planned thing . . . I was just writing, and what I was writing was what I was feeling, and that's what I needed to write." On the other hand, when she sent Snodgrass the as yet unpublished "Double image," she asked anxiously "if you think this works, if it has a reason for its violence, a reason for being written (or rather read) aside from my own need to make form from chaos. . . ."

Reminiscences

In Memory of Anne Sexton
Kathleen Spivack*

Anne Sexton died this October. She was nearly forty six years old. Anne had visited death as a tourist many times. Now that she has gone the feelings are complicated. All her adult life she had flirted with, tried out, written about, loved and feared death. Most immediate is the loss, that particular energy spent and the gift stopped.

Anne Sexton was ten years older than myself, already traveling the women-roles when I was starting to take writing seriously. We shared work and life issues for the past fifteen years. She was for me a fixed star, a friend, a colleague, a more experienced poet, a supportive woman and at the same time a generous critic and advisor. She was honest, she loved the sun and swimming, she loved to laugh, and though suffering frequent intense mental anguish she was always, in a strange contradictory way, an outrageous life force. She wore a necklace upon which was engraved: "Don't let the bastards win."

That she lived an inner life of tumult must be said. But what must be celebrated is her outstanding gift as a poet, her ability to transmute that private struggle into compressed felt moving human utterance, poetry.

Anne Sexton and Sylvia Plath were in the writing seminar taught by Robert Lowell at Boston University in the late '50's, a seminar to which I came as a young student. Anne was soft and romantic in, I seem to remember, polka-dot chiffon. No matter that she was overwhelmed with the care of two young children, or that she had just driven in, terrified, from the suburbs for the class. Her deep eyes and hoarse and thrilling voice resonated feeling. She was eager to learn. Her beautiful green eyes reflected each shade of thought. Sylvia, on the other hand, was angular and angry, tightly buttoned and proper and held in. She was shy, her voice stuck in her throat. She was at the time writing the quietly controlled poems which formed part of *The Colossus*. Anne electrified the class by her moving reading of her poem "The Double Image," which was to be part of her first book, *To Bedlam and Part Way Back*. It illuminated, for all of us, the possibility of writing about intense personal and painful experience, while still keeping the tension of form. "The Double Image" is a formal poem. But the autobiography and anguish it encompassed

*Reprinted with permission from *American Poetry Review* (May–June 1975): 18–19.

still amaze. While it may be said that there were parallels in the lives of Plath and Sexton—Anne herself thought so—to me the personalities and talents of the two women were quite different. Sylvia had a literary education, Anne did not. Sylvia had to write through that education to get to the scorching poems in *Ariel*. Anne had no such barriers; she began at Sylvia's end-point: "repression" was not part of her handicap. On the other hand, a literary education was something she was to acquire later, and with it, control.

Anne was one of the most "naturally gifted" poets I have known. By this I mean that she had a natural gift for metaphor: the use of the exact image to compress feeling-states. It is the essence of poetry. Combined with this was the fact of her material, deep, human, universal. She did not fritter her poetic imagination on trivia; she articulated what most of us did not dare say. Her themes are love, death, madness, blood, time, sex, religion and relation, and she had the courage to write them in a time when "women poets" were still amputated males.

In some of her work, her image-making gift took over; she stretched too much for them and they dominate some of the poems. But in much of it the gift is pure, unflawed, with images that make one shiver and gasp as if in cold water. Anne kept the poems she was working on in notebooks, the drafts typed, crisscrossed with lines and pencilled corrections. I was privileged to read most of her work in draft, and she read much of mine. Sitting in her study, occasionally accosted by Anne's thoughtful green eyes, pouring over the work, I was struck again and again by the profundity of her vision, and the richness of her imagistic mind.

Anne Sexton was both a prolific poet and a hard worker. She worked on several books at once, according to the themes each dealt with. An astounding book might be followed by a slightly less remarkable one, but the lesser would turn out to be a way station to a more ambitious book yet. For instance, *Transformations* was a highly innovative attempt to break out of the preoccupation with self that, Anne felt, had dominated her earlier books. She wanted to expand and she did. Using Grimm's Fairy Tales as her starting point, she retold, in both mythic and ironic terms, their larger scope, her larger worldview. She enjoyed writing this book tremendously, and the poems leap with humor, life and feeling. A beautiful reader of her own work, the book was a release for her. To hear Anne read from *Transformations* was to have one's senses tickled, stirred, and stroked by her deep dramatic voice. *Transformations* was followed by *The Book of Folly*, to my mind a less interesting, certainly a less "total" conception. However, this in turn was followed by *The Death Notebooks*, the volume of her poems which I consider the most daring. Anne Sexton originally intended the book to be published posthumously. Curiosity, interest in the poems, a sense of completion, led her to publish it while she was still very much alive.

The cycle of poems, "The Fury" poems, is a tour de force. They were written in a white heat. Anne made a list, before she began on the series, of the Furies she wanted to write about. The list itself, the titles, read like a poem. The poems deal with "Beautiful Bones," "Abandonment," "Flowers and Worms," "God's Good-bye,"—symbols of her own preoccupations. My particular favorites are "The Fury of Sunsets," "The Fury of Cocks," "The Fury of Overshoes," and "The Fury of Sunrises."

"The Fury of Sunrises," a great poem, unfolds slowly; the pace is exquisite, like sunrise itself. Day opens quietly; the poet celebrates the miracle of still-being-alive; of the beauty of light. In this poem, Anne combined all her best: her imagery, her acute visual sensibility, her sense of rhythm and music, a sense of the concrete world contrasted with the utmost human yearnings; all allowed with a discipline, and delicacy and control that intensify still further the poem's sense of the preciousness of life.

Also included in *The Death Notebooks*, however, was a poem called "Hurry Up Please It's Time." In that poem Anne Sexton deals with her own fascination with death, its inevitability, and her situation in life. More ragged than the "Fury" poems, it moves in and out of a loose stream-of-consciousness, and uses much private imagery. The poem struck me when I first read it, as a fairly realistic appraisal of mortality, and a map of the poet's questions and despair.

Anne worried that readers would not understand the "Psalms" section of *The Death Notebooks*, and, worse still, that they would not like them. I had to confess to her that, though moved by the power and sweep of the "Psalms," I did not completely understand them. What I also did not understand, in reading them, was the importance they were to play in the development of her next book (unpublished) tentatively entitled *The Awful Rowing toward God. The Awful Rowing toward God* was to deal with Anne's religious feelings, her sense of abandonment by and longing for God. The poems, when I last heard her read them, were still unfinished. She was also working simultaneously on several other collections of poetry, and no doubt we shall all see them eventually.

Anne Sexton was amazing in her gift, in her hard work and follow-through on the gift. Her output was prodigous, but even more so was her reach. She continued to grow, to question and explore as a poet. She had an immense curiosity, matched only by her ambition. Her inventiveness was our encouragement. I wish for myself, for all of us, that she had stayed alive. The pity of her death is that we shall not know where she would have grown to. For death—and Anne was a persistent student—is an inquiry that ends with the first serious question.

A Friendship Remembered   Maxine Kumin*

As the world knows, we were intimate friends and professional allies. Early on in our friendship, indeed almost as soon as we began to share

*Reprinted with permission from *To Make a Prairie, Essays on Poets, Poetry, and Country Living* (Ann Arbor: University of Michigan Press, 1979), 83–92.

poems, we began to share them on the telephone. Since we lived initially in the same Boston suburb and later in contiguous ones (Ma Bell's unlimited contiguous service be praised!), there were no message units to reckon with, which surely would have inhibited me, though probably not Annie, whose long-distance phone bills were monumental down the years. It was her habit, when alone at night (and alone at night meant depressed always, sometimes anxious to the point of pain as well) to call on old friends. But that's a digression. What I wanted to say was I don't know what year, but fairly early on, we both installed second phone lines in our houses so that the rest of each of our families—the two husbands, the five children—could have equal access to a phone and we could talk privately for as long as we wanted. I confess we sometimes connected with a phone call and kept that line linked for hours at a stretch, interrupting poem-talk to stir the spaghetti sauce, switch the laundry, or try out a new image on the typewriter; we whistled into the receiver for each other when we were ready to resume. It worked wonders. And to think that it only cost seven or eight bucks a month!

How different from January and February of 1973, when I went to Centre College in Danville, Kentucky, as a writer-in-residence. We agreed ahead of time to divide the phone bills we would incur. Anne called me every afternoon at five; she was then writing *The Awful Rowing toward God* at white heat—two, three, even four poems a day. I tried hard to retard the process for I felt it was all happening too fast and it scared me. It was too much like Plath spewing out those last poems. Nevertheless, I listened, commented, helped, tried to provide some sort of organizational focus. We averaged one hour a day on the phone, only because I was too cheap to talk longer. My share of the bill came to about three hundred dollars, which was pretty liberated for me. I am descended from a lineage that panics as soon as the three-minute mark is passed.

Writing poems and bouncing them off each other by phone does develop the ear. You learn to hear line breaks, to pick up and be critical of unintended internal rhyme, or intended slant rhyme or whatever. We did this so comfortably and over such an extended period of time that indeed when we met—usually over lunch at my house, for Anne almost always stopped off to lunch with me after seeing whichever of her infamously inept psychiatrists—we were somewhat shy of each other's poems there on the page. I can remember so often saying, "oh, so *that's* what it looks like" of a poem I had heard and visualized through half a dozen revisions.

Over the years, her lines shortened and the line breaks grew, I think, more unexpected. In the early days we were both working quite strictly in form. We measured and cut and pasted and reworked arduously, with an intense sense of purpose, both of us believing in the rigors of form as a forcing agent, that the hardest truths would come right if they were hammered to fit (see the title poem in *All My Pretty Ones*). I confess we both had rhyming dictionaries and we both used them. Typically, we had totally different kinds. Anne's grouped rhyme-words according to their common endings—all the one-syllable words, for example, followed by the two-syllable ones, and so on—whereas mine worked by orthography, which made it quirkier because it went not by sound but by spelling. It was Anne's aim to use rhyme unexpectedly, brilliantly, but aptly. Even the most unusual rhyme, she felt, must never obtrude on the sense of the line, nor must the normal word order, the easy tone of natural vernacular usage, be wrenched to save a rhyme. She would willingly push a poem through twenty or more drafts; she had an unparalleled tenacity and only abandoned a "failed" poem with regret if not downright anger after dozens of sessions.

Nevertheless, I would say that Anne's poems were frequently "given" ones. "Riding the Elevator into the Sky" (in *The Awful Rowing toward God*) is an example. The newspaper article mentioned in its first stanza gave rise to the poem and the poem itself came quite easily and cleanly, as if written out beforehand in the clear air and then transcribed onto the page with very few alterations. "Letter Written on a Ferry while Crossing Long Island Sound" (in *All My Pretty Ones*) was a "given" poem, too; given by the fortuitous sight of the nuns. As I remember it, the poem was written much as it now appears on the printed page, except for the minor skirmishes required to effect that marvelous closure in each stanza where the fourth line from the last and the last lines rhyme (save for the first stanza, and "cup" and "up" in the middle of the last stanza). Also, it was originally called "Letter Written on the Long Island Ferry" and was made more specific on the advice of Howard Moss. "Young" and "I Remember" (both also in *All My Pretty Ones*) required very little revision, as my memory serves, whereas "The Truth the Dead Know" went through innumerable workings to arrive at its final form. In this poem, the poet is locked into an *a b a b* rhyme scheme with little room for pyrotechnics. The language is purified to an amazing degree, I think, reflecting Anne's wish to open *All My Pretty Ones* with a spare, terse, tough elegy for her parents, one without biographical detail, the very detail she would get into later, in the title poem or in "The House." That title poem was one which underwent many revisions to force it into the exigency of an *abab cdcd ee* stanza. We both admired the multisyllabic rhymes of "slumber" / "disencumber" and "navigator" / "later," to say nothing of the *tour de force* final couplet.

The initial impetus for her poems usually came as a direct visitation to the cave of her desk. She invoked the muse by reading other poets and playing her favorite records over and over. The background of music acted in some way to free her to create, which always astonished me, for whom it is an intrusion. Often with the volume turned up loud, loud enough to drown out all other sounds, she could pull an intricate rhyme scheme out of the air. Is it worth noting that massed orchestral strings, full volume, served too as a device for her to cover and block out the bad voices? (The time before the time she killed herself, it was with music at crescendo: a scream, I thought when I got there. I don't know if the radio was playing that last time; I think so.) As for her subject matter, we all know it came for the most part directly out of her own life and times, with little if any psychic distance on the trauma or pleasure that gave rise to the poem. Still, she transmuted the events. She was able to take the rawest facts—her mother's agonizingly slow death from cancer, her father's stroke, her entire wretched childhood experience as what was undoubtedly an undiagnosed hyperkinetic youngster, kept behind a gate in her own room—and to make of them a whole.

Someone once said that we have art in order not to die of the truth. Sexton's confessional poems most vividly and truly not only kept her alive, but they sustained and spoke to a vast audience. I would say that she drew greater sustenance and comfort from the knowledge that her work reached out to and beyond the normal sensitive reader of poetry (though, for God's sake, what is "normal" or "sensitive"?) and touched the minds of many deeply troubled people. For a while it seemed that psychiatrists all over the country were referring their patients to Anne's work, as if it were the balm in Gilead. At the same time that it comforted and fed her to know that she mattered as a poet beyond the usual sphere of self-congratulating, self-adulating bards, she had considerable ambivalence about her work. Accused of exhibitionism, she was determined only to be more flamboyant; nevertheless, the large Puritan hiding inside suffered and grieved over the label "confessional" poet. For instance, when she wrote "Cripples and Other Stories" (in *Live or Die*), a poem that almost totally "occurred" on the page, she crumpled it up, as if in embarrassment, and tossed it into the wastebasket. We fished it out and saved it; I thought it then and think it now a remarkable document.

The "saving" of that poem was to make the tone consistent and to smooth out some of the cruder rhythmical spots. This was the sort of mechanical task Anne could fling herself into gladly. The results were often doubly effective. In "The Operation" (a key poem in *All My Pretty Ones*), for example, the experience—awesome and painful—is hammered into art by way of form and rhyme. Both squeeze the raw event until the juice runs into the reader, I think. I do not mean to downplay the force of metaphor in the poem—the "historic thief," the 'Humpty-Dumpty," etc.—but it is the impact of rhyme and the shape of the poem's three parts (i.e., its form) that bring it off. For instance, the retardation of the rhyming sounds at the end of the first section—"leaf" / "straw" / "lawn" / "car" / "thief" / "house" / "upon"—in those short, fairly sharply end-stopped lines, build to the impact. Or, to take yet another poem, I remember "Faustus and I" (in *The Death Notebooks*) was headed for the discard pile; it was then a free-verse poem and as such had, for me, an evilly flippant tone. I seem to remember that I often helplessly suggested, "why don't you pound it into form?" and often it worked. In the case of "Faustus and I" the suggestion worked because the rhyme scheme gave the poem a dignity and nobility it deserved. It worked because the pounding elicited a level of language, a level of metaphor, she hadn't quite reached in the early versions.

Anne also had an almost mystical faith in the "found" word or image, as well as in metaphor by mistake, by typo or misapprehension. She would fight hard to keep an image, a line, a word usage, but if you were just as dogged in your conviction that the line didn't work, was sentimental or mawkish, that the word usage was ill suited or trite, she would capitulate—unless she was totally convinced of her own rightness. Then there was no shaking her. We learned somehow, from each other and from trusting each other's critical sense, not to go past the unshakable core, not to trespass on style or voice. Perhaps we learned this in the early years of our student workshops, first at the Boston Center in classes with John Holmes, and later in our own house by house workshops with John Holmes and George Starbuck and Sam Albert. These were often real encounters, real square-offs, but we all respected and admired one another—an idea that seems terribly old-fashioned somehow today, that poets could be competitive and full of ego but genuinely care for one another's well-being. That was a good group, now that I think back on it; we all wrote at white heat and many of the best poems any of us ever wrote were tested in that crucible. Anne, in fact, as a result of this experience, came to believe in the value of work-shops. She loved growing this way herself, and she urged the technique on her students. Her whole *Bedlam* book grew during her workshop years and virtually every one of those poems was scrutinized across the table. We were still at it when *All My Pretty Ones* was in process. It was awesome the way Anne could come into the workshop biweekly with three, four, five new and complicated poems. She was never meek about it, but she did listen and she did care. She gave generous help and she required, de-manded, insisted on generous response.

We might talk for a moment about *Transformations*. Anne was fasci-nated by fairy tales. They were for her what the Greek myths had been, perhaps, for others. Since she had not had—and she was grim about this—the advantage of a higher education (by which she meant Beowulf, the Norse eddas, Homer, Milton, etc.—all denied her), she lapsed back to what must have been a halcyon time in her life, the time when her great aunt, the colossal mother figure of her past, had read German fairy tales to her. Now she reread them all and scoured the libraries for more, even asking my daughter Judy to translate and retranslate some tales from the German so that she could be sure she had gotten every final variant on the story. The wonderful self-mocking, society-mocking wit of *Transformations* is entirely her own; she was a very funny person, quick to satirize a given situation. The book more or less evolved; she had no thought of a collection at first, and I must immodestly state that I urged and bullied her to go on after the first few poems to think in terms of a whole book of them. I also take outright credit for the title. We had been talking about the way many contemporary poets translated from languages they did not themselves read, but used trots or had these poems filtered through an interpreter, and that these poems were *adaptations*. It struck me then that Anne's poems about the fairy tales went one step further and were *transformations*. And for the record let me state that in the same conversation Annie was urging me to collect the "pastoral" poems I'd written, and I said, "but what will I call it?" and she said, "*Up Country*, of course."

The Book of Folly gives further evidence of Anne's interest in myth making. Whether or not they succeed, she has written three myths of her own and she labored strenuously in the vineyard of prose, finding it foreign and harsh work. But it is true that the storyteller inside the poet sometimes yearns desperately to be let out. Anne's storyteller burst out in these tales, and in the Daisy play she wrote early in her career on a Ford grant. (*Tell Me Your Answer True* was its original title, though it ended up as *Mercy Street*—an image that turned up in a dream, the dream a plea for mercy from somewhere, anywhere, from Life.) It wasn't the first verbalization of her Christ fascination, nor was it destined to be the last. Christ as Prime Sufferer, and God (any kind of god who'd be there) became her final obsessions, perhaps because as her life deteriorated, people were less dependable. But Jesus figured prominently from the very beginning.

What I chiefly remember is how much fun Anne had working on the play, how richly she enjoyed working in dialogue, for which she had a considerable talent. Her ear was quick and true; I always trusted implicitly her criticism of the dialogue in my fiction, and could point to dozens of lines—responses, usually—in my own work which came pure out of Sexton's mouth. She also loved the excitement of being in the theater and being in New York and staying at the Algonquin. She adored her leading actress Marian Seldes (as who would not!), and loved most of all the late nights after a rehearsal when she would sit up till dawn reworking a speech here, a phrase there, loving the tinkering even more than the glamor of actually having her play produced.

Anne's way of working, whether with a poem or the play or an attempted story, was to try out the draft on as many listeners as she could amass. I felt sometimes that she was putting the matter to a vote, and indeed in her classes at Boston University she fell into the always amusing pattern of inviting the students to vote for or against an image, a line break, an ending. But she invited and needed the interchange of ideas and attitudes, something that is anathema to most writers, who cannot brook outside interference or involvement in an unfinished piece. Anne took strength from outside reactions, as much strength from the negative as from the positive remarks (I am not now speaking of reviewers!), and genuinely felt that there was always something to be gained in this sharing process. It was her conviction that the least experienced student could bring something to bear on a work sheet; she weighed and evaluated opinions, keeping some, discarding others, but using them all as a kind of emotional ballast for going on with her work. And she was equally willing to bring her own energy to bear on the meanest poem. She was generous, yes; but it transcends generosity, really. It was evangelical, it was for Poetry, the Higher Good. She lived her poetry, poetry was her life. It had saved her life in a real sense when, in the mid-1950s she began to write poems as a therapeutic act urged on her by her then psychiatrist. The clear thread that runs through all the books of poems is how tenuous that life was. She was on loan to poetry, as it were. We always knew it would end. We just didn't know when or exactly how.

1957: Anne Sexton's Bedlam   Diane Wood Middlebrook*

It took Anne Sexton three years to master the writing skills that brought her national attention and local fame in 1960 when her first book was published with the title *To Bedlam and Part Way Back*. The poems are in fact very skillful, but that is not why they were noticed. Their strength is the arrowy candor with which they move to the emotional targets suggested in the title and captured in *Bedlam*'s first poem:

> You, Dr. Martin, walk
> from breakfast to madness. Late August,
> I speed through the antiseptic tunnel
> where the moving dead still talk
> of pushing their bones aginst the thrust
> of cure. And I am queen of this summer hotel . . .

The candor of Anne Sexton's early poems had two sources. One was her literary naivete. Since she had never studied literature (or anything else) systematically, she was unschooled in the practices, and the literary values, that made the honored poetry of the late 1950s so abstract. In the poetry world, but especially in Sexton's literary circle in Boston, the highest accolades went to poems that were ironic, learned, allusive, and intellectually agile, whereas Sexton's most striking poems were directly autobiographical and dealt with cancer, mental illness, suicide, death: bedlam. Like other admired poetry of its time, Sexton's lyrics were brief and formal, but they were not "academic."

What Sexton learned when she began studying poetry in 1957 were the "tricks" (her word) of making complex stanzas. But the imagery that so arrested the attention of readers came from her education in psychotherapy. It was not that Sexton's early poems were reports from therapy sessions; they were not. But in therapy Sexton had practiced subverting her own capacities to avoid and falsify painful truths; and the habit of seeking truth—a habit, really, of both relaxing the mind for uncensored association and alerting the mind to its deflections—carried over in her poetry. A painfully acquired honesty, together with the craft that made possible its compelling artistic expression, are signified in the "Part Way Back" of her title. And the acquisi-

*An excerpt from Professor Middlebrook's biography of Anne Sexton, in progress. Reprinted with permission from *Pequod*, 1988, 23–24.

tion of both honesty and poetic craft began in earnest shortly after Sexton's second release from bedlam, in 1957.

A way of life built on accepting Anne's depression as chronic began shaping in her family during the winter and spring in 1957. Returning home to the Boston suburbs from her second hospitalization following a suicide attempt, Sexton was caught between two worried observers as she tried to return to normal life. One was her mother, Mary Gray Harvey, a phone call away in nearby Annisquam on Boston's North Shore. Mary Gray and Anne talked frequently on the phone, and a neighbor who often witnessed those calls thought they had a bad influence on Anne's confidence. Anne knew that Mary Gray was anxious and untrusting and felt she was under surveillance— though Anne was grateful for the help her mother sent twice a week from her own staff of housekeepers. Anne's mother did not visit her very often in person.

Anne's other watchdog was her mother-in-law, Billie. Ever since the first year of marriage, when Anne and her new husband (Alfred Muller Sexton II, always called "Kayo") had lived with Kayo's parents, Anne had been intimidated by Kayo's mother. Billie was the model of the self-sacrificing wife and mother. As a girl, Wilhelmine Muller had lived in the lap of luxury, and when she married George Sexton she married into a family as wealthy as her own. The stock market crash of 1929 had wiped them out: they lost almost everything but their house, and Billie turned her considerable energy to its upkeep. It was a house meant to be staffed upstairs and downstairs by servants, but Billie managed it entirely by herself. When Anne and Kayo moved into their own house, Billie made frequent visits. Anne, indifferent to housekeeping, relied on Billie's willingness to take over mundane tasks, but being Anne, smoldered at the criticism Billie's ready help implied.

The birth of Anne's daughter Linda in 1953 delighted Billie. Linda was her first grandchild; she loved babies and had now only a grown-up, divorced daughter living in her house. Anne maybe overstated the case in an interview, when she claimed that after Linda's birth her mother-in-law spent all her time with Anne and Kayo, wanting to be with the baby every minute. Billie was so attached to Linda that Anne felt a certain relief when her second child arrived two years later: another girl, Joy.

Both grandmothers had reached out to help in the family crisis at the time of Anne's first hospitalization in July of 1956, and again after her suicide attempt that November. When Anne's doctor gave consent for Linda's return at Christmastime, Billie was alarmed, and persuaded Anne that Joy should *not* return. Overt rivalry over Joy sprang up between the two mothers that winter. Billie always invited the Kayo Sextons to dinner each Sunday, and when Kayo was away on his long trips as a traveling salesman, Anne came to Billie's with Linda. Anne's journal notes for a week in mid-February suggest that these occasions aroused bitter emotions in both women. Sunday: "Went to Billie's—made me angry interfering with Linda." Monday:

"Told Billie wanted Joy back soon—she is fighting me right down the line—I hate her—" Tuesday: "Am ready to take Joy back but not ready to face Billie's anger."[1]

Billie, of course, saw the situation from another angle, resurrected in an interview many years later. She recalled that Anne had been thoroughly disabled emotionally by depression—that she took no interest in baby Joy. On these occasions Anne always seemed withdrawn and aloof. The family would tense up around her, never knowing when or how she would blow up. Toward Joy, Anne seemed indifferent. If Billie suggested Anne get Joy ready for bed, Anne would refuse stiffly; Billie remembered that Anne wouldn't even kiss Joy goodnight.

Living with Anne that winter of 1957 was hard on everybody. Kayo remembers the grim sense of uncertainty with which he set off for work in the mornings, leaving Anne groggy from the aftereffects of sleeping medications, afraid he would find her sitting apathetically, incapable of any effort, on his return. When she was "in one of her downers" Anne tended to be either very quiet or very sarcastic. "She'd feel terribly sorry for herself and cry at the drop of a hat"—that was how it looked to Kayo. Anne's own view from inside a depression survives in a couple of sets of notes she made for her doctor. One is dated 16 January:

> I don't know what is wrong with me today but something certainly is. I feel as if I were going to jump right out of my skin. I would like to scream until it blotted every other sound out of existence.—I am so alone—nothing seems worth while—I walk from room to room trying to think of something to do—for a while I will do something, make cookies or clean the bathroom—make beds—answer the telephone—but all along I have this almost terrible energy in me and nothing seems to help—I sit in a chair and try to read a magazine and twirl my hair until it is a mass of snarls—then as I pass a mirror I see myself and comb it again—Then I walk up and down the room—back and forth—and I feel like a caged tiger and I hate everyone and I know that if I could kill someone that I would get over this. . . .
>
> Now Kayo is gone—his absence absolutely removes all reason for a day to begin or end.—I am rudderless with no direction. I thought I could try writing more poetry when he had gone—Now I can't even write. I just shuffle back and forth in the little cage of my mind and wait.

These notes go on for six typed pages. Another set of notes, handwritten, is dated "Feb 16th or so" and carries the same burdens:

> I am unhappy, I am depressed—nothing seems to matter because too much matters and I would rather die. Everything seems to derail me. All the crutches seem to be falling away and here I am—the same, the horrible same I have always been. . . . I had Joy for the weekend and she has gone back today—I love her, she is adorable and winning—but it seems to take so much patience and energy and I was glad to see her go . . . I guess I don't love anyone—that is a terrible statement and now I am crying . . .

> Take the whole picture—no cigarettes, food is repulsive and I feel as if I were going to throw up every minute—I am not happy in this house but there is no where I want to go—all the poems are terrible—my heart pounds and it's all I can hear—my feeling for my children does not surpass my desire to be free of their demands upon my emotions . . . What have I got? Who would want to live feeling that way? (Restricted collection, Anne Sexton Archives, Humanities Research Center)

The contrast between Kayo's memory and Anne's journal is arresting. Kayo emphasizes the unfair division of labor Anne's illness created in the family. Anne's depressed view is that the work to be done is not so much physical as emotional, and she formulates her problems in terms of an economy of scarcity. An emotional investment in others simply costs too much; she is needy and undernourished herself. She has a surplus of sexual feelings, but they cannot be spent on Kayo; equally, her emotions toward her children are measured by their power to gratify herself: affection for her children feels good but not so good as the feeling of freedom from their demands. It is the poet in Sexton who finds a metaphor to connect this defeating, anxious self-love with illness. The overwrought heart obliterates everything but its own painful beating: "my heart pounds and it's all I can hear."

Sexton's depression presented everyone close to her with a dilemma of interpretation. She was really ill, but was her illness real—biologically based, like an infection—that is, not her fault? Or was it a cunning psychosomatic evasion of responsibility, a solution of the problem of growing into adulthood, into motherhood? And what was the remedy? Did she need hospitalization, shock treatment, drugs? Or did she only need some rest and a change of attitude? Anne's parents and her mother-in-law concurred in the latter view. "When you think of Linda, Kayo, me you are happy—when you think of yourself, you are unhappy," her mother scolded. Sexton shared this bewilderment. As she told an interviewer, Alice Ryerson, at the Radcliffe Institute in 1962,

> I was all my life striving for something; it was just that I never knew what it was I wanted. I thought, before I had children, that the answer was to have a home and children. I was married, but I hadn't really established a real home.—I wanted to get married from the age of thirteen on. I wanted nothing else. I thought that having children was some kind of answer, then, and that the feeling of frustration, or whatever it is, would be gone.—I mean, I knew I wanted to do *something*, but I didn't have anyone to take me by the hand.—But I was much happier than I had ever been as a child. You see, marriage . . . I was happier. Only I was getting older and things weren't quite getting answered, but . . . I mean I was loved, you know, and this made quite a difference.[2]

Depression swiped at this happiness like a big paw, exposing the incompleteness, for Anne Sexton, in the idea that "having a home and children was the answer." It was probably only half the answer. Psychologically, Sexton needed a strong home base, a secure attachment to a protective and caretaking person. Kayo was such a person, dependable, assertive, but also very tender: married to Kayo, she affirmed, she was happier than she had ever been as a child. The same need made her exquisitely sensitive to loss or separation. That Kayo started taking long business trips shortly after Linda's birth built into Anne's life a routine of losses that periodically battered her sense of security.

The timing of Anne Sexton's breakdown eight months after Joy's birth tends to underscore the crucial role played by separations in Anne's depressive illness.[3] She was surely depleted by the hardship of being alone with two very young children: Linda an exploring and inquiring toddler, into everything; Joy an infant requiring almost constant attention; both were constantly cluttering the house and dirtying a lot of laundry. But Sexton's breakdown was not merely the consequence of physical exhaustion; it exposed a psychological fissure formed, probably, in her own infancy, in her disturbed relationship with her mother.

Attachments form between babies and their caretakers in a fairly predictable sequence. Extreme dependency on the mother loosens as a baby grows; by eight months a baby has begun to reach out with an air of recognition, and to show emphatic desires and dislikes. A minimal but distinctive autonomy emerges. The child grows less physically dependent but more emotionally attached to the mother, requiring more interaction. Strangers begin to be frightening, too. Now the mother must not only supply physical care; she must respond to the alternating currents of the baby's emotional outreach and withdrawal. She must be prepared to be pushed away; she must welcome a snuggling return. Most people suited to taking care of young children respond comfortably, rather unconsciously, to the struggling and squirming and investigation that encodes this important early behavior in infants, and it is thought to be extremely important to the child's emotional development that their caretakers *do* so respond, and continue to respond with approving reciprocity, as the baby, then the toddler, ventures farther away and for longer periods of time, returning sometimes in panic to the familiar lap. As a child grows up, the need for acceptance of both going forth and coming back grows more subtle, but endures in the dynamics of later relationships.

Some parents, of course, are not very well suited to caring for babies, or for children of any age. Nor do parents take the same kind of care of each of their children. When the caretakers are unresponsive or unavailable, anxieties develop in the child; and when these are severe anxieties, they are likely to last well into adult life and distort the adult's experience of the comings and goings of those they care about. Throughout the rest of a person's life the attachment behavior formed in early infancy is never far beneath the surface, and conditions of stress can trigger very old, but still raw, feelings of insecurity. Neurotic symptoms, depression and phobias are very common in adults whose parents were actively disparaging or rejecting,

or persistently unresponsive to the child's appeals for care, or—a more subtle transaction—encouraged clinginess and timidness; such adults themslves
are often seen as overdependent, immature, insecure.

The Yankee eye of Anne's neighbor and best friend, Sandy Robart,
witnessed Anne taking just such a neurotic role in relation to both mother
and mother-in-law, becoming "a helpless, dependent, goody-goody" as she
stood at the phone talking to Mary Gray, or stepped aside while Billie shaped
things around the house. It was an insight into herself that Anne eventually
grasped too: that toward mothers—including the motherly Kayo—she would
frequently turn into a child begging for love. But at the time Sexton's depression developed into suicidal impulses, she had neither insight nor methods
of coping with the forces driving her from within. She was under both the
physical strain of childcare and the emotional strain of adapting to Kayo's
regular absences, sometimes for as long as two weeks. These absences genuinely terrified her, and she could not conceal the terror from her disapproving family, who saw her as childish and spoiled. Her mother's move from a
nearby suburb to the North Shore after Linda's birth enhanced Anne's feelings of isolation. Moreover, Sexton seems to have vested newborn Joy with a
symbolism that invited catastrophe as Joy grew up: "This one's for *me*," she
told herself.

Thus, all the relatively minor random losses Sexton suffered, separations neither permanent nor unpredictable, must have sunk into an old pool
of unconscious fear and pain until it overflowed. The normal development of
Linda and Joy into little beings demanding to be let go may have broken the
meniscus that held the flood in place, overwhelming Sexton's never secure
confidence in her home base. These babies were supposed to be her "answer"; instead they made "demands on my emotions," they did not feed her
hunger for acceptance but demanded her response to their separateness. As
an adult Sexton was supposed to be able to participate intuitively in this
dyad, as intuitively as did her children. But the side of her called into play by
their demands *was* a child—the child not sufficiently nourished when she
needed it, tormented with fear of rejection, able to seek satisfaction only
through unconscious behavior—depression—and the hidden rage she en-
acted by quietly taking an overdose of sleeping medication two times within
seven months of each other: in November 1956, then again in May 1957.

An exclusively psychological interpretation of Sexton's suicidal depression omits to notice, though, how widespread among women of the white
middle class was this illness. The problem of meaninglessness Sexton's notes
articulate was an outcome for many women of coming to adulthood in the
evolving consumer economy of postwar America. Relatively affluent women
with no expectation of competing with men in the professions or the world of
business were subjected to continual propaganda encouraging them to ideal-
ize the housewife's role. After her "boy-crazy" girlhood culminating in early
marriage, and especially after the birth of two children, Sexton was a kind of
caricature of the ideals promoted in the movies, and at women's college

commencements, and overwhelmingly in national advertising. One of the magazines Sexton may have been reading as she twirled her hair into snarls that day in January was her copy of *Life*—the magazine's "special issue on women" (December 1956), with its glowing reports on the "completely fulfilling" moments of a woman's life: the first prom, the first kiss, the first baby. Depression was a very common response of women in this cultural environment, so trivializing of women's values and expectations. Moreover, glorifying the housewife's role denied most women's experience of the reality of doing boring, repetitive work in the isolation of a suburban home. Nor did it give women insight into the emotions of rage and guilt inspired in them by the behavior of small children: women were supposed to be naturally good at childcare.

Anne Sexton rejected, largely by getting depressed, a line of work for which she had little instruction, no confidence and only satisfactory models. Fortunately, the "Dr. Martin" of her early poem encouraged her to try writing as a form of therapy; once she discovered her talent, she was a changed woman. She claimed, often, that poetry had saved her life. It did not cure her illness: no form of therapy ever successfully liberated her from the anguish of the many psychological disorders to which she was prey. But writing offered a way of making use of illness, and the use was transformative to Sexton's sense of self. A poem such as "The Double Image," written in 1959 and addressed to her daughter Joy, illustrates the paradoxical incarnation of strong poet in suffering mental patient:

> All that summer I learned life
> back into my own
> seven rooms, visited the swan boats,
> the market, answered the phone,
> served cocktails as a wife
> should, made love among my petticoats
>
> and August tan. And you came each
> weekend. But I lie.
> You seldom came. I just pretended
> you, small piglet, butterfly
> girl with jelly bean cheeks,
> disobedient three, my splendid
>
> stranger. And I had to learn
> why I would rather
> die than love, how your innocence
> would hurt and how I gather
> guilt like a young intern
> his symptoms, his certain evidence.

Illness and eloquence were to be Sexton's principal routes of liberation from confinement in a housewife's role. Because she did, with the help of

"Dr. Martin," free herself for other work, the eloquent last sentences of the notes she made in 1957 vault free of the unique moment of their writing to express a female dilemma so widely shared that it became the base of a political movement in years to come. ("My feeling for my children does not surpass my desire to be free of their demands upon my emotions . . . . What have I got? Who would want to live feeling that way?") Sexton did not take much interest in the politics of liberation, but her intelligence and her gift for expression make this wisp of writing seem in retrospect like a tell-tale in a strong wind, or the hair in the barometer that registers a shift in air pressure, signaling change.

Notes

1. Anne Sexton's journal has been placed in a restricted file in the Anne Sexton Archive at the Humanities Research Center, the University of Texas, Austin. I am grateful to Linda Sexton for permission to quote from this journal and from other unpublished material quoted in this essay.

2. I am grateful to Linda Sexton, Alice Ryerson, and the Radcliffe College Archives for permission to quote from this interview.

3. I am indebted to Dr. Ellen Bassuk for pointing out the significance of this timetable. Succeeding paragraphs on attachment and separation are indebted to John Bowlby, "The Making and Breaking of Affectional Bonds," *British Journal of Psychiatry* 130 (1977): 201–10.

INDEX